# PAINT & BODY
# HANDBOOK

REVISED & UPDATED

## by Don Taylor & Larry Hofer

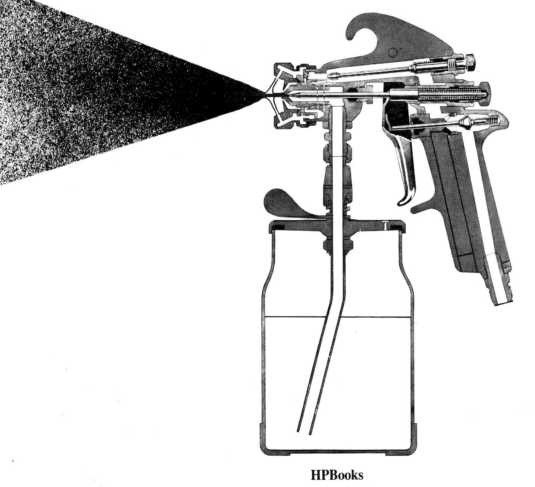

**HPBooks**
are published by
The Berkley Publishing Group
A division of Penguin Putnam Inc.
375 Hudson Street
New York, New York 10014

ISBN: 1-55788-082-4

Library of Congress Catalog Number: 93-48885

10 9 8 7

# CONTENTS

1  The Basics . . . . . . . . . . . . . . . . . . . . . . . . . . . . . . . . . . . . . . . . . . . . . . . . . . . . . . . . . . 3
2  Disassembly . . . . . . . . . . . . . . . . . . . . . . . . . . . . . . . . . . . . . . . . . . . . . . . . . . . . . . . . . 7
3  Welding . . . . . . . . . . . . . . . . . . . . . . . . . . . . . . . . . . . . . . . . . . . . . . . . . . . . . . . . . . . . 28
4  Shaping Sheet Metal . . . . . . . . . . . . . . . . . . . . . . . . . . . . . . . . . . . . . . . . . . . . . . . . . 44
5  Sectioning & Rust Removal . . . . . . . . . . . . . . . . . . . . . . . . . . . . . . . . . . . . . . . . . . 58
6  Perfect Panel . . . . . . . . . . . . . . . . . . . . . . . . . . . . . . . . . . . . . . . . . . . . . . . . . . . . . . . 68
7  Aluminum & Fiberglass Repair . . . . . . . . . . . . . . . . . . . . . . . . . . . . . . . . . . . . . . 80
8  Paints & Painting Products . . . . . . . . . . . . . . . . . . . . . . . . . . . . . . . . . . . . . . . . . . 90
9  Painting Equipment & Techniques . . . . . . . . . . . . . . . . . . . . . . . . . . . . . . . . . . 103
10  Spot Repairs, Color Matching & Custom Finishes . . . . . . . . . . . . . . . . . . . 123
    Troubleshooting . . . . . . . . . . . . . . . . . . . . . . . . . . . . . . . . . . . . . . . . . . . . . . . . . . 137
    Glossary . . . . . . . . . . . . . . . . . . . . . . . . . . . . . . . . . . . . . . . . . . . . . . . . . . . . . . . . . 142
    Index . . . . . . . . . . . . . . . . . . . . . . . . . . . . . . . . . . . . . . . . . . . . . . . . . . . . . . . . . . . 143

# ACKNOWLEDGMENTS

Although **Don Taylor** and **Larry Hofer** appear as authors of this book, many individuals came forward to contribute their talents, products and time to make this a comprehensive book on paint and bodywork. We thank them for their help.

Among those who helped are Scott Schaffer and Ray Cruz of Martin Senour Paints; they provided the painting supplies. Gordy Bown of R&M Paints provided enough research material for two books. Others who contributed information for the paint section are Wolfie and Mike Pores and their head painter, Rick Talamentes, of MAACO Auto Painting & Body Works. Further help came from Mike Jr. and Sr. of Pap's Paint. The section on painting flames was demonstrated by Ed Hopkins of Dave Meyer's Corvette Specialties. Thanks, Ed and Dave, for putting up with us for three days!

Mark McConnell of Luxury Lacquer helped us with the fiberglass section. Larry Storck and Dave Seward of Unique Metal Products helped with the aluminum section.

Ray Steck of Steck Industries, Bill Mitchell of Matco Tools and T.N. Cowen of Cowen Industries provided tools, time and equipment.

Don Foster and Jerry Olmsted of Hilltop Classics provided immeasurable help in the bodywork section. Bruce Mather from Oak Distributors helped with information on repairing high-strength steel.

About 1000 photographs were processed with the help of Bob and Damon Hill of the Photo Darkroom Limited and Greg Smith of Photographic Illustrations of San Diego. Thanks also to B&M Auto Parts for our Barracuda project car.

A special thanks goes to Grace Dinger, a long-time friend, who typed the manuscript and tried to correct our creative spelling and punctuation.

Finally, a book is only a manuscript until the editor puts it all together. Our editor, Tom Monroe, is the best in the business. Thanks, Tom, for all your help, input and patience.

# 1 THE BASICS

Duesenberg speedster exemplifies paint finishes of the '30s, the decade that ushered out nitrocellulose coatings and ushered in synthetic enamel. Photo courtesy of Roger Huntington.

Pride of craftsmanship: That's probably why you picked up this book. You'd like to be able to make that dented fender look like new without turning it over to a bodyman. Yet, short of banging it out with a claw hammer and rock, you probably have very little idea of how metal can be moved and returned to its original shape. Yes, there is a certain amount of finesse and skill involved, but even major repairs can be performed by the novice. It's simply a matter of moving along, step-by-step, with an understanding of how metal is worked and how the tools are used.

We'll demonstrate these step-by-step processes: how to use the tools, how metal is worked and how to achieve a flawless, factory finish.

Your pride of craftsmanship will be rewarded when people see your work and say nothing—because they'll never know bodywork was performed on that body panel!

## BODY TYPES

Two principal types of auto-body construction are unitized and body/frame.

**Unitized bodies** consist of individual metal parts welded together to make up the body assembly and total vehicle structure—there is no separate frame.

Engine, driveline and suspension systems are mounted on submembers and/or reinforcements in the underbody area. These reinforcements and submembers provide additional strength to the body, eliminating the need for a separate frame making for a lighter, stronger vehicle.

**Body/frame** construction is as the name implies—a body that is bolted to a separate frame. This was the basis of all automotive construction until the late '50s and early '60s, when the unitized body came into vogue.

Today's average passenger-car body consists mainly of steel, aluminum, fiberglass or a combination of these. Of the three, steel is the strongest and least expensive. Its strength-to-weight ratio and relative low cost make it the most popular material in automotive use. Aluminum is lightweight and strong, although not as strong as steel.

The third material, fiberglass, is the

Damage to left front of Olds Cutlass involves several materials: fiberglass-reinforced-plastic (FRP) front piece, sheet-metal fender and flexible-plastic bumper filler panel.

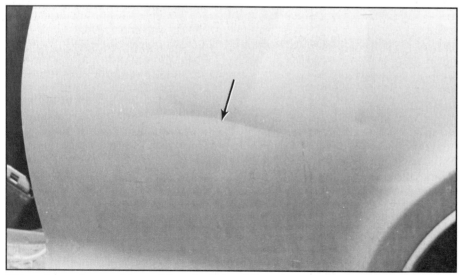

Crease in quarter panel (arrow) is a simple bend. It can be repaired using spot-repair techniques discussed in Chapter 10.

least used. Its strength-to-weight ratio is about the same as aluminum, but fiberglass is not as stable. It is favored for trim pieces, decoration, body add-ons and, of course, as the prime material in the Corvette body. Each material has its place, considering weight, strength and cost. Therefore, we find them all used in today's automobiles.

This book demonstrates how to repair each of these materials. Because steel is the predominate material, it will be given the most attention. However, aluminum and fiberglass are also discussed in detail.

## ASSESSING DAMAGE

When determining the kind of repair procedures, you must determine the construction of the damaged panel; angle of impact; speed of the impact object; and size, rigidity and weight of the impact object. You must be able to visualize how the metal folded during impact.

The impact angle will be a direct or glancing blow with a resulting effect on all the other areas of the car. In fact, a large frontal impact can cause misalignment at the rear of the body. If the impact angle is glancing, much of the impact force will be absorbed by the panel. If the angle is large, some of the energy may be diverted, creating only minor damage. A sharp object will drive some of the metal in front of it, pushing the metal forward and stretching it in the rear. This often happens in the typical sideswipe-type impact.

Body damage can be separated into five types: simple bends, displaced areas, rolled buckles, stretches and upsets.

**Simple bends** are as the name implies. They are bends in the metal, such as minor dings and bumps, and damage in which high stress was not a factor.

**Displaced areas** are metal sections that have been moved but not otherwise damaged. This is best illustrated by what is called an *oil-can dent*. This often occurs when a door panel is struck. Although the panel may be buckled inward, pushing it from the backside will pop it out, restoring its original shape. Often there is no damage at all. If there is any, it will be around the edge of the displaced area.

Displaced sections will often hold a dented area out of place. When a displaced section is defined and relieved, the section may be restored to its original shape. Then, only the small, buckled area will need repair.

**Rolled buckles,** or S-shaped bends, are pronounced displaced areas with the metal folded or tucked under itself. This is sometimes found in front- or rear-end collisions and in severe impacts. Rolled buckles require a considerable amount of metalwork, starting with pulling or pushing the panel back into some semblance of its original shape. Final reshaping of the buckled area is then done with hand tools.

**Stretches** are caused by tension rather than compression. For example, a gouge results from stretching. This can be seen where a bumper rakes down the side of a car and penetrates the metal at the end of the crease. Welding, shrinking and filling are required for this type of repair.

**Upsets** happen when opposing forces push against an area, causing it to yield. Caused by compression rather than tension, this is sometimes called an *accordion pleat.* The metal surface area is reduced and thickness increased. Sometimes, an upset can only be found as you feel for ripples by running your hand over the surface.

You must diagnose each type of damage much as a doctor diagnoses a medical disorder. For both the bodyman and the doctor, it's only through diagnosis that the remedy can be determined.

Throughout the book, we diagnose the problem and apply the remedy.

## UNDERSTANDING METAL

You should be familiar with three properties of sheet metal to do quality bodywork: plasticity, work hardening and elasticity. An understanding of these properties will help you move metal, maintain or restore its strength and produce a smooth panel.

**Plasticity** is the property that allows metal to be reshaped when enough force is applied to it. This is the same property that allowed it to be stamped into a fender, hood or door. When the flat sheet is modified by the dies in the press, it undergoes *plastic deformation.* How much deformation is possible without breaking or tearing is relative to metal hardness.

Obviously, the harder the metal, the less deformation possible.

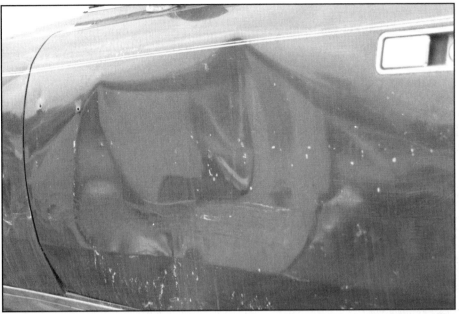

Infamous "oil-can dent" can be largely corrected by pushing out from inside door or pulling out with suction cup, photo page 54. A little hammer-and-dolly work at perimeter of dent will restore sheet metal to original shape.

Rolled and buckled damage to front corner of fender will require considerable metal forming to restore it to original shape.

Conversely, the softer the metal, the greater deformation. This is why such radical bends can be made without failure in soft aluminum.

**Work hardening,** or cold-working, occurs when metal is bent, stretched, shaped or moved. How much a piece of metal can be cold-worked has a limit, after which, it will break. As the metal is worked toward this limit, it becomes harder and harder. With this increase in hardness, there is an increase in strength and stiffness as a result of *work hardening.*

A good example of work hardening can be demonstrated by bending a piece of wire back and forth until it breaks. After the first bend and return, the wire cannot be straightened at the point of the bend.

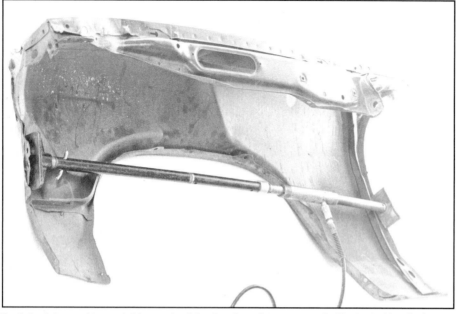

Body jack is used to assist in repair of fender. Complete process is illustrated beginning on page 45.

Car is rolled out of paint booth after painting. This is what paint-and-body work is all about: restoring body to as-new or better condition, or making your vehicle stand out from the crowd with custom paint. This book tells how to do it all.

Eventually, the wire becomes so hard—and fatigued—it breaks.

**Elasticity** is the property of metal that allows it to regain its original shape after being deflected. For example, you've pushed against a fender or door and felt it give, then spring back when you released it. Of course, the harder the metal, the greater the elasticity—elasticity increases with hardness. The elastic limit is reached or surpassed when metal no longer springs back to its original shape—it has reached its *yield point.*

In the following chapters you'll see how the properties of metal can be used to make body repairs. We show how to use different tools to assist in making these repairs. For now, you need only to understand the properties of plasticity, work hardening and elasticity.

## BASIC SECTIONS OF BODY REPAIR

Bodywork is a step-by-step process. We use simple steps to perform major straightening and body-panel realignment. Then, we demonstrate how a panel or a body area is made smooth. With this completed, we turn our attention to preparing the damaged area or entire body for paint. Finally, we show you how to do a show-quality paint job in your driveway or back yard!

Read this book all the way through for an overview of the entire body-repair-and-paint process. Then go back and read each section before you begin a project. Finally, keep the book handy as you work and refer to it often. Follow this plan and your job should be entirely satisfactory and your pride of craftsmanship will be rewarded by a job well done.

# 2 DISASSEMBLY

Disassembly for bodywork or painting ranges from removing small trim parts to removing welded-on body panels. Cutting C-pillar is one step in removing a roof, page 26.

At first, disassembling a car body may seem like an overwhelming proposition. Initially, the car is seen as a complex whole. In fact, it is simply a series of small components. When you understand each component and undertake disassembly one at a time, the process is much less threatening.

Consider engine disassembly: As a unit, it's overwhelming. But disassembly begins with removing the carburetor. Then, each piece is removed in turn until only component pieces remain. This is our approach to body disassembly—to separate each section into its basic components.

About ninety-five percent of a car can be disassembled with common mechanic's tools. You can disassemble the remaining parts with inexpensive specialty tools readily available at local auto-parts stores. These include such tools as Ford and GM inside-door-handle-clip pliers, chrome-trim-clip removers and tools for windshield and rear-window removal. We show photographs of the tools and illustrate or detail their use. In addition to the tools, you'll need boxes, cans and paper bags to store the parts you remove.

It's remarkably easy to forget how a component went together, so make

photographs for future reference. A helpful device is the Polaroid camera. Photograph complex installations *before disassembly*. Mark every piece and its location, tag all the wires that aren't color coded, and keep written notes. This will make reassembly a pleasure rather than a headache.

It's highly unlikely that you will ever disassemble a car to the extent we show. However, this will give you a good idea about how body parts and those fastened to them interrelate. Where we have omitted a step required for your job, it may be covered in another chapter.

Before digging in, you'll need to

know that we made a few arbitrary decisions. *Early-model* cars refer to autos of the mid-'50s and into the late '60s or early '70s. *Late model* refers to cars of the '70s to the present. Obviously, there is a great deal of overlap, but we have classified them in this manner for simplification.

We also lump cars under the classification of *foreign* or *domestic*. Those engineered in North America are domestic. Those engineered outside of North America are foreign. On today's highways, it may seem that a Toyota or Nissan is as common as "mom and apple pie," but familiarity aside, their engineering is still foreign, even though they may have been assembled in North America. Where needed, we will refer to specific car models. Otherwise, they are called *domestic* or *foreign*.

## INTERIOR DISASSEMBLY, DOMESTIC & FOREIGN

**Manual Front-Seat Removal**—Most General Motors, Chrysler and European car seats unbolt from above the floor. Look under the seat and find four bolts. Two on each side secure the track to the car floorpan. Remove these bolts and lift out the seat and tracks.

It's much easier to remove the tracks from the floorpan than to remove the seat from the tracks. Accessibility between seat and tracks is almost impossible with the seat in the car.

If you leave the seat back attached to the cushion, the seat will fall backward when the front seat-track bolts or nuts are removed. Be careful at this point—have a friend help.

Unlike GM and Chrysler, Ford seat-track nuts remove from underneath the car. Jack up the car, supporting it firmly on jack stands. Crawl or roll under the car and search for the rubber body plugs, or caps, in the floorpan. These plugs seal the seat-mounting-bolt access holes. Carefully remove two on each side with a bench seat and four per side with bucket seats. Don't damage them. You will reinstall them afterwards to seal the floorpan so water, dirt and exhaust fumes won't enter the passenger compartment.

With a deep socket, remove the nuts holding the track to the floor. Repeat this on the other side and remove the seats.

**Power-Seat Removal**—For power seats, you have to disconnect the wires that run to the motor or switch

**Body plugs must be removed to expose seat-attaching bolts or nuts. Rear plugs have been removed.**

before removing the seat. In late-model cars, do this by disconnecting a single male/female socket. In earlier model cars, color-coded wires are connected individually. Disconnect each one, then lift out the seat.

## REAR-SEAT REMOVAL

Most rear-seat cushions are held in place by tension brackets. To release them, push in on the lower edge of the seat—don't push on the upper edge wire of the seat. The lower edge of the seat frame must be pushed back about 1 to 2 inches to clear the retaining hooks. It may be necessary to push with your feet to get it all the way back and out from under the retaining hooks. Push in until you feel the cushion release, then lift up and remove it.

With the seat cushion out of the way, look under the bottom edge of the rear-seat back. You should find two or three braces secured by sheet-metal screws or straps. Remove the screws or bend the tabs up to release the bottom edge of the seat back. The top edge is retained by hooks mounted to the package tray. Rotate the seat up from the bottom and out of these retaining hooks. Remove the seat back.

If the rear-seat back incorporates a center armrest, it may come out as a unit. If not, you'll now have access to its mounting bolts. Remove the bolts and armrest.

---

### PARTS INSTALLATION

Beginning from about age five, you were probably able to "tear apart" anything. However, putting it back together was a problem. This certainly holds true with the installation of automotive parts. It's relatively easy to remove parts. However, doing this without damaging them or being able to reinstall them satisfactorily is another matter.

We tell you how to disassemble parts and assemblies so they won't be damaged and so they can be reassembled properly. In many instances, it's more difficult to remove a part—such as a door trim panel—than it is to replace it. Then there are the parts or assemblies that are easier to remove than to replace. A headliner is such a beast. In this instance, it pays to take your car to a professional trimmer—auto upholsterer—and let him do the job. Even at his hourly rate, you will be money and sanity ahead. He will get the headliner in place, tear- and wrinkle-free. This also applies to a vinyl top.

If you remove a vinyl top, you'll

never get it back on. This must be done by a pro. However, if you can make a repair by lifting a small section of the vinyl, do it. Make the repair and glue the vinyl back in place. You'll need a good contact adhesive for this. Buy it at your paint-supply store. Coat both the vinyl and the body with adhesive, then pull the top down carefully and push out the air bubbles as you go.

When removing a part, whether or not you will be reinstalling it, keep the part and its fasteners organized so you'll know exactly how everything goes back together. For instance, put screws and bolts back in the holes from which they came. Hold these fasteners in place with masking tape. The same thing goes for shims, such as those used to align fenders or doors. Tape them in place. What seems obvious now will be a total mystery when assembly time comes. So organize removed parts like you won't be reinstalling them for 10 years. You'll think it's been 10 years if you don't, even though it may be weeks.

Push base of back-seat cushion rearward and lift up to free it from retainers.

Hooks at top hold back cushion in place.

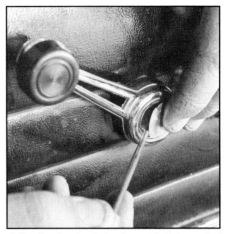

Adhesive-backed aluminum plate is peeled off to reveal Phillips-head retaining screw on Ford window crank. Plate is thin and easily damaged, so care must be taken when removing it. Handle will pull off once screw is removed.

## CENTER CONSOLE

A center console may incorporate the floor shift. If so, remove as much exterior hardware as possible: ashtray, map holder, courtesy light, and so on. Next, remove the sheet-metal screws along the bottom edge of the console. Then, check for sheet-metal screws or bolts attaching the console to the dash or separate brackets, and remove them.

If the console is not free at this point, check behind the ashtray and courtesy light for other mountings. *Don't force the console until you've removed all the fasteners.* Remove any additional screws. Lift up on the console, being careful not to damage any wires inside. If there are wires to the console, label and disconnect them, then remove the console.

## DOOR PANELS

**Early-Model Cars**—Begin door-panel removal by removing the window crank, door handle and armrest. Where applicable, remove the remote-control side-view-mirror actuator.

To remove the armrest, find the holes underneath it. Inside these holes will be Phillips-head or small hex-head screws. Remove these screws to free the armrest.

If door handles and window cranks are retained by *horseshoe clips,* you'll need a *door-handle-clip remover.* This tool is similar to a pair of pliers with thin steel jaws. These pliers are designed to fit behind and remove the horseshoe clip that retains the door or window-crank handle. Another tool, which is one-piece, also slips behind

the handle or crank to remove the clip. Door-handle-clip removers, such as K-D's, are available at most auto-parts stores.

To remove these clips with the pliers tool, depress the door panel, insert the tool, locking the nose around the edge of the clip, and rotate it clockwise or counterclockwise. The clip should pop out of its groove, allowing the door handle to slide off. Be careful not to scratch or mar the upholstery. If there are nylon washers behind the door handle or window crank, don't lose them. Store the washers with the clips.

Some door handles and window cranks are secured by a hex-, Phillips- or Allen-head screw. Ford went one further in the late '60s and through most of the '70s by hiding the screws behind adhesive-backed discs. Peel off these decorative discs to reveal the screw heads. Use a Phillips screwdriver or Allen wrench to remove the screws. Pull off the door handle and window crank.

Early GM cars used a drift pin to secure door handles and window cranks. Select a 3/32-inch pin punch and drive out the pin. This will release the door handle or window crank.

These are the more common methods of crank and handle retention. If your car uses something different, you can bet there's a removal tool. Check with your tool supplier for the correct tool.

Now, remove the door-lock knob at the top of the door and any garnish or reveal moldings holding the door

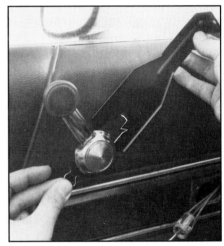

To remove horseshoe clip for door handle or window crank with one-piece tool, slip tool between door panel and handle. Push against open end of clip. Photo by Ron Sessions.

panel to the door. Generally, these moldings are held on with sheet-metal screws. You should now be ready to remove the door-trim panel.

The door-trim panel is fastened to the door by a series of wire springs or plastic clips. They are pushed into holes in the backside of the door. Using a flat-blade screwdriver, pull out the door panel until you see a clip. To remove the spring-type clips, slide the screwdriver directly under the clip and pry gently. Don't pry between clips. This may break the Masonite or fiberboard substrate at the clips.

On door-trim panels using plastic clips, you'll need — guess what? —

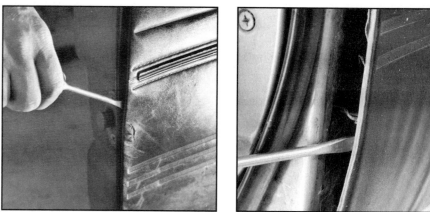

**Holes in base of armrest hide mounting screws. Sheet-metal screws pass through door-trim panel and thread into door-inner panel.**

**Pry out edge of door-trim panel to find clips. With screwdriver behind clip between trim panel and door, pry each clip from its hole. Check for sheet-metal screws or remaining clips if panel refuses to come off easily.**

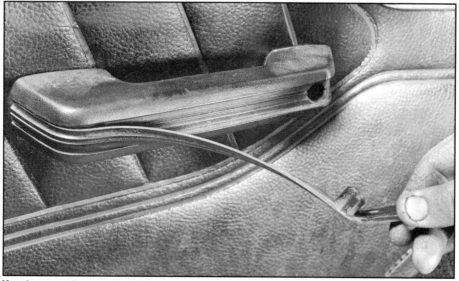

**Here's a sneaky one. Until trim strip was removed, we had no idea where armrest screws were.**

another tool. This means another trip to your tool supplier. If you don't use the correct tool for removing a panel retained with plastic clips, you'll break the clips.

When all clips are out, the trim panel should be free. Don't force it if there's any resistance. Look further. You may find sheet-metal screws at the corners of the door panel. Remove them, then pull the panel away from the door.

Disconnect any electrical leads for power seats or windows. Wrap each wire with a masking-tape flag and mark its location on the switch. Or, place masking tape on the back of the door panel above the switch and indicate the color coding of each wire to the assembly. This will prevent confusion when it's time to replace the door panel.

**Late-Model Cars**—On late-model cars, you're into a whole new ball game. Generally, the door handle is bolted to the frame of the door and hidden behind the armrest. And in more cases than not, the car will be equipped with power windows.

Again, begin with the removal of the armrest—unless the armrest is an integral part of the door panel. Next, remove the door-lock knob and any garnish molding around the window that retains the door panel. On many late-model cars there is no garnish molding—the door panel itself serves that purpose. The door-trim panel extends to the top of the door and wraps over the edge, serving as a door-glass seal.

As in early-model door panels, use a flat-bladed screwdriver to search for the trim-panel retaining clips. Pop

those clips free from the door-inner panel. With some upward coaxing, the trim panel should come loose at the top where it meets the window glass.

Again, disconnect and mark any wires for seats, windows, *wind-wings* (vent windows), radio speakers and any power locks that may be incorporated into the door panel. It may also be necessary to partially disassemble the door panel to remove the door handle if it is of the late-model *tuck-away* style. Generally, this is removed by slipping a drift pin, retained by a clip, from the top or bottom. When you remove the clip and drift pin, the door handle will come off.

**Foreign Cars**—Removal of a door panel from a foreign car is basically the same as that of a domestic car. However, access to the window crank, door handle and armrest have a few basic differences. To gain access to the door-handle and window-crank retainers on most foreign cars, pull back on the plastic that covers the door handle. You will find a sheet-metal screw or a small bolt. When you remove the screw or bolt, the door handle or window crank comes off.

If you can't find screws or bolts in the area of the armrests, check for a thin, plastic snap-on garnish. Pull this back, and you'll find the access holes. Using a Phillips-head screwdriver, remove the sheet-metal screws holding the armrest to the door panel; the armrest will come off.

As in domestic cars, door-trim panels are held on with spring clips. Often, these clips are plastic rather than metal. Either way, insert a flat-blade screwdriver under the clip and

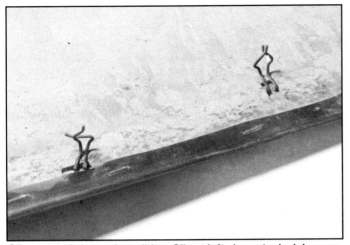

Clip at right is in good condition. Clip at left shows typical damage from incorrect installation. Try straightening clip with needle-nose pliers. If it breaks, replace clip.

Moisture shield is revealed once trim panel is removed. This one is treated paper; some are plastic. Take care that you don't tear shield as you peel it off.

pry it from the door. Finally, at the top of the panel, there may be a rubber seal that acts both as a weather seal and trim-panel retainer. An ingenious molding of this rubber allows it to lock the door panel to the door frame. To remove it, grasp one end and pull it out of its channel, thereby releasing the rubber, channel and trim panel in one stroke. Rotate the door panel up and away from the inner door panel. Remove the wires from any switches or radio speakers and mark them accordingly. With the door panels removed, turn your attention to the rear quarter panels.

**Moisture Shield**—If there's a *moisture shield*—waterproof paper or plastic—on the door-inner panel, peel it off. It may have come off with the trim panel; or it may be stuck on with body sealer.

## REAR-QUARTER TRIM

Some Japanese cars, such as the Datsun Z cars, had a special clip to hold plastic panels to the body. You will see the head of these clips protruding above the surface of the panel. They're about the size of a crowned dime. In the center of this clip is a spot about 1/8-in. in diameter. Essentially, this is a plastic pop-rivet. To remove it, use a long, thin, center punch or strong piece of wire to push on this spot. You'll push out a match-stem sized plunger from the body of the rivet. The clip (rivet) may then be removed from the panel. It will not be reusable so be prepared to purchase new ones. Typically, it will be necessary to remove the rear-seat cushion and back before the rear quarter-trim panels will come off.

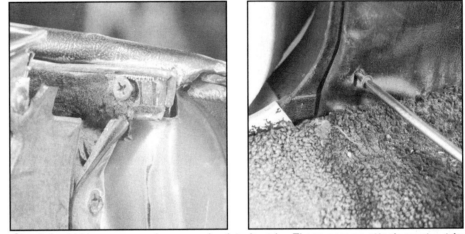

Check for hidden screws when removing interior trim. These screws attach quarter-trim panel. Screw shown in photo at left secures trim panel at top of C-pillar; screw at right is at bottom of panel.

With the cushion and back out, removal of the quarter-trim panels is similar to that of the door-trim panels.

After taking off the armrest, window crank (if applicable) and any other accessories such as cigarette lighter or courtesy light, remove any sheet-metal screws holding the trim panel to the body inner panel. Whatever garnish trim was used on the doors, a similar garnish will probably be used on the quarter trim. Remove this and any associated weatherstrip.

If the quarter-trim panel binds after removing all of the retainers, search for hidden screws along the door post and seat frame. The quarter panel should separate easily now. If the quarter and door panels are to be reused, and some time will pass before they can be installed, wrap them in *Visqueen* (plastic sheet), craft paper, plastic trash bags or old bed sheets. This will keep the trim panels clean while in storage.

Another mystery: How does window crank come off?

With the door panels and quarter panels safely tucked away, you can turn your attention to the kick panels.

## KICK PANELS

Kick panels, as their name implies, are panels that are kicked with great frequency. They are located between the door-hinge pillar and the fire wall, directly between the instrument panel and the floor.

Generally, kick panels are retained

Pull back plastic cover and voila! Small bolt holding crank is exposed. Remove bolt to free crank.

Remove wind-lace by pulling it off door-opening weld flange.

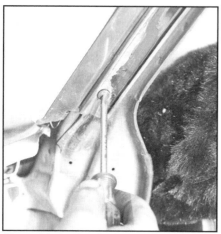

Channel is held to body with Phillips-head sheet-metal screws or rivets. Drill out rivets.

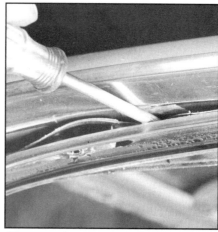

After removing screws or rivets, gently pry channel from body. Channel is sealed with body putty, so go easy. Force applied too fast will bend channel.

Sheet-metal screw fastening each end must come out before weatherstrip can be removed.

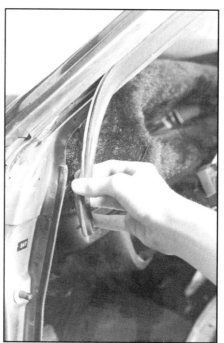

Once screws are out, pull weatherstrip from its channel.

with sheet-metal screws only at the rear and top. In some instances, as in '60- and '70-era Fords, the panel also serves as a seal along the front edge of the door opening.

Begin by removing any appliances fastened to the panel, such as emergency-brake pedal or handle, vent handles and courtesy lights. Many models also incorporated air-vent ducts that must be removed before the kick panel. In most instances, all of this hardware is fastened with sheet-metal screws to the sheet-metal inner panel through the kick panel. Remove these screws to free the kick panel from the body. Remove the panel. If courtesy lights are incorporated into the kick panel, disconnect the wire and tape its end.

## HEADLINER REMOVAL

The next major interior-trim piece to come out is the headliner. Removing the headliner starts with the removal of the garnish moldings that cover the edges of the headliner.

**Garnish Molding**—Although we've already referred to *garnish moldings,* here's a definition of the term. When a Thanksgiving turkey is baked, it may be decorated with sprigs of parsley, perhaps paper-frilled booties on the ends of the legs, some sliced fruit or some other trimmings to make the turkey prettier. The parsley, frills and sliced fruit are all *garnish.* The same holds true for automotive-trim garnish: It adds a finishing touch.

In the case of a vehicle interior, garnish moldings consist of those pieces that finish the transitions between the windshield, windows, between the headliner and body, around the rear window, and in any area where up-holstery trim is *finished off.* If the garnish is retained by sheet-metal screws, remove the screws to remove the garnish. However, if it is the plastic variety that snaps on, removing the moldings requires a little finesse.

Pull the molding away from the material and determine the fastening method. If plastic spring clips are used, depress them with a screwdriver and remove the molding. If it won't come off after removing the clips, check the molding ends to see how they are retained. Often, a plastic cap covers a sheet-metal screw at each end. Pull off the cap, remove the sheet-metal screws, and then remove the molding.

**Weatherstrip**—In many cases garnish molding incorporates a *weatherstrip.* Weatherstrip is the rubber piece that seals the periphery of the door or window from the elements: wind, rain and dirt. To remove the weatherstrip and its associated trim, open the door. Look in the area of the weatherstrip, directly above the instrument panel. Find the one or two sheet-metal screws that fasten the end of the weatherstrip. Remove these screws and gently pull the weatherstrip from the stainless-steel channel or garnish molding.

If the weatherstrip does not pull easily from its channel, peel back the interior edge of the weatherstrip and look for more screws; remove any before you continue. When the weatherstrip is almost off, remove the sheet-metal screw(s) at the other end. Mark the weatherstrip so you'll know where it goes at installation time; set it aside.

You can now remove the stainless-steel molding or garnish molding. In most cases, the molding is secured with additional sheet-metal screws. Typically, the screws that hold the weatherstrip also retain the molding. The final trim piece to be considered before the removal of the headliner is the snap-on *wind-lace.*

The term *wind-lace* comes from the horse-and-buggy days when the doors were literally laced so they wouldn't open from the force of the wind. Today, however, rubber or plastic seals take the place of *lacing,* but retain the name. In addition to sealing the door to the body opening, the wind-lace also covers the pinch-weld flange where the inner and outer body panels are joined at the door opening.

To remove the wind-lace, remove the scuff panel covering the door *sill,* or the area between the floorpan and top of the rocker panel. This stainless-steel, plastic or aluminum plate normally finishes off the edge of the carpet. Remove the screws that retain the scuff plate to the floorpan and set aside. The ends of the wind-lace are now accessible. Gently peel it back, working all around the door frame to the other end. Label the wind-lace and set it aside.

**Early Headliners**—If your car is a pre-'60 model, the edges of the headliner may be retained by tacks or staples. These are driven into wood or fiberboard *tacking strips* fastened to

Phillips-head screws retaining rear-window garnish molding are removed.

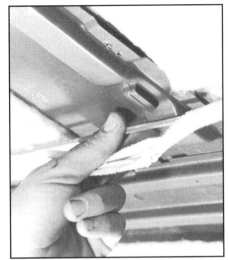

Tab on roof reinforcement supports bow at center. To remove bow from clip, simply push it out.

Reference arrow made with felt-tip marker ensures that headliner bow gets returned to correct hole.

Headliner bow is spring-loaded into holes. To remove, simply pull out end of bow at one side.

the car body by sheet-metal screws or nails. Carefully remove each staple or tack; age is a factor. If you aren't careful, the fiberboard or wood strip will crumble and have to be replaced. With care, you should be able to remove the tacks or staples without damaging this material. Don't damage the headliner itself if you expect to reuse it.

**Late Headliners**—By the mid-'60s, most auto manufacturers dropped the tacking-strip method in favor of glue, creating a new problem. To remove a glued headliner, you may have to remove the windshield, rear window, and their seals. Here's a shortcut, however. Peel back the rubber seal around the windshield or rear window. At the same time, use a razor

blade or X-acto knife to cut away the headliner as close to the rubber as possible. Gently pull the headliner away from the metal.

If you're doing anything more than a minor repair in the roof area, remove the windshield and rear window. This process is covered beginning on page 17.

After the full perimeter of the headliner is loose, it can be removed from the roof. It is retained by a series of three to seven bows that pass through *muslin* channels, called listings, sewn to the backside of the headliner. Lift the edge of the headliner and note the locations of the bows. In most vehicles, there are one to three holes directly in line with one another. This is the

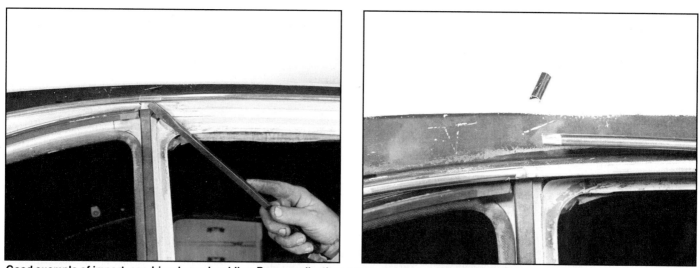

Good example of import-car drip-channel molding. Remove clip, then rotate stainless-steel trim off drip rail.

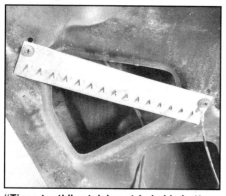

"Tiger-tooth" retaining strip holds bottom, rear edge of headliner at C-pillar. C-pillar trim panel extends from quarter-trim panel and over retaining strip.

result of the roof-inner panel being used in more than one body style. Mark the holes in which each bow is inserted.

Beginning at the front or back, gently pull down on the front or rear edge of the headliner, reach in and push down on the center of the first bow. Some cars have a sheet-metal clip retaining the bow to the roof at the center. This keeps the headliner from sagging. If clips are used, push the bow out of its clip, then push down. The bow can now be rotated backward or forward to pull it from its hole. Use care—muslin tears easily.

Leave the bow in the headliner for now. In a similar fashion, remove the remaining bows. If you plan to reuse

the headliner, wrap it, bows and all, and store it in a clean, dry place. However, if you're installing a new headliner, remove the bows one at a time, marking them front to rear 1, 2, 3, 4 .... Also mark the corresponding holes 1, 2, 3, 4 .... Then you'll be in good shape when it's time to install the new headliner.

As Detroit, Japan and Europe pushed harder and harder to reduce manufacturing costs, the bowed headliner has gone the way of the horse. It has been replaced by the one- or two-piece molded headliner. All of the previous directions, up to bow removal, are basically the same to remove this style of headliner.

In most instances, if you are dealing with a one-piece headliner, the garnish molding around the windows, windshield and sides of the roof line supports the headliner. When these and the courtesy light, rear-view mirror and hooks are removed, the headliner should simply fall down. This is the easy part.

There's a problem with many one-piece molded headliners: They can't be removed without first removing the windshield! This is because the headliner will be damaged if you fold it enough to get it out through a door. If you have such a headliner, it must come out through the windshield opening. Therefore, you'll first have to remove the windshield, page 17.

In the case of a two-piece headliner, you will find a center molding running the length of or across the car. In most cases, this is attached with sheet-metal

screws. If screws are not used, the molding is probably retained with plastic retaining snaps. Gently pull down on the edge of the molding, find the first snap, insert a screwdriver, and disengage it. When the molding is fully released, the headliner halves will come down. The only thing you may want to mark, in the case of a molded headliner, is FRONT and REAR, or RIGHT and LEFT. By now the interior of your car should be looking very sparse; you can turn your attention to the last detail of the interior—the carpets.

### REMOVE CARPETS

**Early Carpets**—In early-model cars the carpet was an afterthought. Carpet installation was saved for last. By removing the carpet, pad and appropriate access panel, the mechanic could gain access to many working parts of the car through the floorpan. So, if you are working with an early car, removing the carpet only requires removing the scuff plates and possibly the kick panels.

Check to see if drive nails or sheet-metal screws were used to hold down the edges of the carpet; if so, remove them. Remove the front of the carpet from the fire wall. You may have to disconnect the throttle pedal from the throttle linkage. Completely remove the carpet and pad.

**Late Carpets**—Detroit made other changes in car construction. It was no longer necessary to gain access to parts through the floorpan, so they made more-permanent carpet

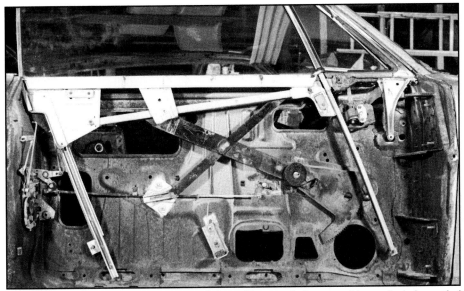

Looking from the outside-in, absence of door skin reveals inner workings of window, wind wing, and door-latch and -lock mechanisms.

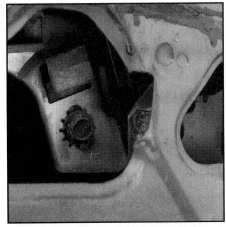

Bolt holds upper window stop to window frame. Stop must be removed before window can be pulled from top of door.

Two bolts retain and adjust front window-guide channel.

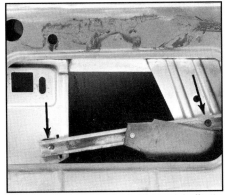

Arrows at each end of channel indicate screws that must be removed to allow removal of regulator from window-mechanism scissors.

installations. Aesthetics were also improved. Hence, we come to the *molded,* or formed, carpet.

Unlike its forerunner, the molded carpet has no seams. It is molded from one piece of carpet just as a fender is stamped from a single piece of sheet metal. If you haven't removed the seats from the car, it will be necessary to do so before the carpet can come out. Likewise, the kick panels and scuff plates must also be removed.

You'll find the carpet is glued to the pad and the pad to the floorpan. Run a large scraper or putty knife underneath the pad to separate it and the carpet from the floorpan. Do this gently because the pad is very delicate. When all the glued areas have been separated, lift out the carpet and pad. Because of the molded configuration of the carpet, it is best to store the carpet in a place where its shape will not be affected. Don't wad it up and throw it in a corner. Lay the carpet out upside down; don't stack things on it.

# GLASS REMOVAL

## DOOR GLASS

Four basic components are associated with removing door-window glass: the *regulator* moves the glass up and down; the *stop* stops the glass at its upper and lower travel limits; the *adjustments* adjust the angle of the glass; and the front and rear *channels* guide the glass as it travels up and down.

Early-model cars and most large pickups may also have a wind-wing, or *vent window* or *controlled-ventilation* (CV) window, as it's sometimes called. The wind-wing has two assemblies, the *supporting frame* and the *drive assembly.* The supporting frame, as the name implies, supports the wind-wing; the drive assembly moves it in and out.

**Remove Door Window**—To remove the window, first take out the access panel in the center of the inner-door panel—if there is an access panel. There may only be an access hole. Next, remove the upper and lower stops. Loosen and remove the front and rear channels if possible. Often it's not possible to remove these two channels until the window itself has been removed. In this case, loosen the bolts holding these channels and allow them to hang freely until the window is removed.

Lower the window until the *scissor assembly,* or *regulator,* is visible through the access hole. Disconnect this scissor assembly from the lower window frame. Some Fords have a horseshoe-style clip behind the stud. Remove this clip and slide the stud out of the frame. There are two clips and studs—one each at the front and rear of the window. With everything disconnected, you should be able to coax the window up and out through the top of the door.

It may be necessary to tilt the window forward and bring the rear of the window out first, passing it beyond the door-window frame and out toward the back edge of the

An extra pair of hands can come in handy. Don holds window while Larry removes scissor assembly.

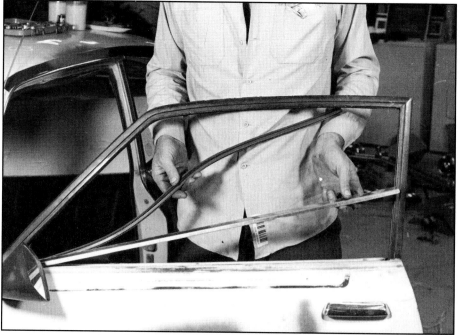

Imports have a number of unique innovations. Weatherstrip retains chrome trim to top edge of door. Remove weatherstrip and you also remove chrome trim.

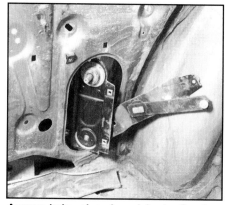

Access-hole size is minimal. Quarter-window-scissor assembly is slipped through access hole in bottom of quarter-inner panel.

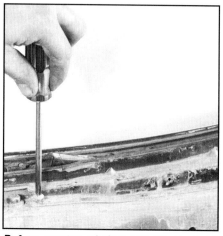

Before quarter window can be removed, weatherstrip and hardware must first come off.

door—if it's a sedan (above) rather than a hardtop. If the window jams while trying to remove it, don't force it. Push it back down into the door and start over. Be careful. Glass withstands little force if applied to a small area. Spread over a large area, the window will take a great deal of force.

For example, if a screwdriver is used for prying, the point where the screwdriver meets the window will likely crack or chip. Avoid using prying tools. Likewise, avoid using side pressure. The window will come out, but a lot of patience and a little jiggling are required. If you must pry, use a plastic or wood *trim stick*—a letter-opener-shaped tool.

**Remove Wind-Wing**—Usually the wind-wing frame doubles as the front door-window channel. So, after the window has been removed, it is usually a simple matter to remove the bolts associated with the front channel/wind-wing. Lift the wind-wing out of the door as one unit. In other instances you may have to remove the cranking mechanism or regulator first. If so, it is removed the same way the scissor mechanism is removed from the window. If this is the case, remove any parts that prevent removing the wind-wing and its channel frame.

**Remove Power Window**—For now, we'll leave the door-latch mechanism

and the rest of the window regulator inside the door. Let's consider removal of power windows. The basic components of a power window are the same as those of a manually operated window, but include the electric motor. Note: Early General Motors power windows used hydraulics rather than electric motors. If your car is so equipped, bleed the hydraulic line prior to removing each window. This will prevent spilling hydraulic fluid inside the door.

Carefully disconnect the hydraulic line and drain the fluid into a small container.

Removal of a power window is much the same as removal of a manual window, but includes some special considerations. Unlike a manual window, you won't be able to raise and lower the window once the motor is disconnected. You must move the window to the lowest position where it is still accessible. Remove the upper and lower limiting stops. Then remove the motor drive. This will allow you to raise and lower the window by hand. However, don't try to remove the window with the scissor mechanism still attached. It won't pass through the opening at the top of the door. Power wind-wings are removed the same as manual wind-wings, except the motor must be removed first.

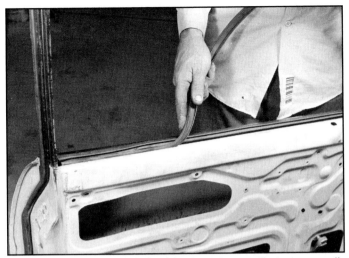

To remove door glass from some import cars, first remove all weatherstrip from around window opening from both sides of door.

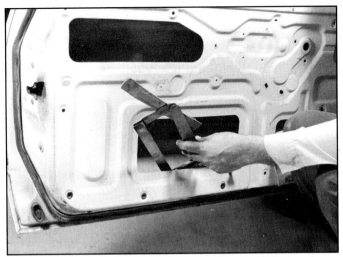

Scissor is removed through access hole in door inner.

After removing scissor assembly from bottom of glass, simply rotate glass forward and lift out.

Wipers must be removed before windshield molding or windshield. Mazda has bolt-on windshield-wiper arms.

**CAUTION:** Some power-window regulators are spring-assisted. If this is the case, there should be a hole in the regulator arms for pinning the regulator in position. Insert a pin through the holes or clamp the arms with Vise-Grip pliers to prevent them from moving. Failure to secure the regulator arms before removing the motor can result in injury to a hand or arm.

**Windshield-Wiper Arms**—Basically, there are three varieties of windshield-wiper-arm attachments: one is the bolt-on, used mostly on imports; another is a serrated force-fit that fits over the wiper-motor drive shaft; and the other is secured with a retaining clip.

Select the correct wrench for the bolt-on style and remove the bolt. The windshield-wiper arm will then slip off the wiper drive. To remove the force-fit style, insert a screwdriver between the wiper arm and the drive, and gently pry up. If the arm is retained with a clip, bend the wiper arm back to its farthest point, then slide the arm off the drive. Bending the arm all the way back disconnects the retaining clip, allowing it to pass over the drive shaft.

## WINDSHIELD

**Early Domestic & Some Foreign**—Early automotive windshields were retained with a rubber gasket that was first installed over the edge of the windshield. The window glass and rubber gasket were set into the frame and the outer rubber-gasket lip was brought over the metal flange of the windshield frame to seal and hold the glass in place.

To complete the installation, chrome trim was used on the outside of the gasket and garnish molding on the inside. This locked the rubber in place, which in turn held the windshield in place—a secure and satisfactory method of windshield retention.

To remove the windshield, start by removing the windshield wipers, then the exterior chrome trim and interior garnish molding. In most cases, the interior molding is retained with screws while the exterior molding is secured to the rubber gasket by a metal lip on the chrome trim. Sometimes, the exterior trim is retained by clips. Read on to see how this type of trim is removed.

The chrome trim on the windshield pillars may be retained with sheet-metal screws. Remove any such screws. Also, remove any clips that join the window-trim pieces. *Do not attempt to pull the trim loose from the rubber gasket.* The result will be bent trim or its retaining lip.

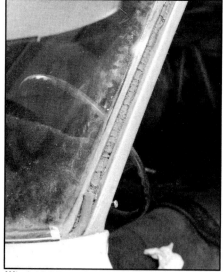

Windshield seal is exposed after windshield side molding is removed. This glue sealer retains and seals windshield.

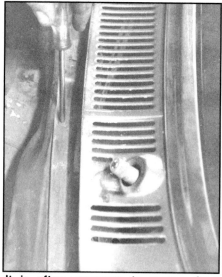

It is often necessary to remove front cowl—if possible—to gain access to bottom windshield molding.

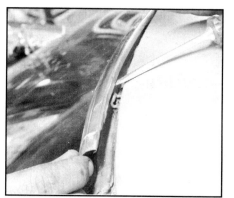

Top windshield molding is carefully pried loose from retaining clips. Note clip underneath.

To remove the windshield, use a razor blade to cut off the lip from the inside edge of the windshield gasket. Cut the entire lip away, flush with the window-frame flange. Now, with a helper ready to catch the window as it comes out, *gently* push the window from the top outward. Although it may not fall forward, it is wise to have someone there to catch the glass, just in case.

**Late-Model**—It's a much simpler operation to remove an old-style windshield than a later style. The reason for this is simple. Late-model windshields are glued in place with butyl-type seals, or *tape strips*. Regardless, the interior garnish molding must be removed. Next, the exterior trim must be removed.

Here, removal is more difficult because of the way the exterior trim is retained. Small metal or plastic retaining clips, spaced around the perimeter of the windshield, are fastened to the car body. The stainless-steel trim is then pushed into these clips. The pressure of the clip pushing the trim against the window frame holds it in place.

To remove trim retained with clips, it is necessary to pry it off with a screwdriver or trim stick. Available at your local auto-parts store, many of these tools are manufactured by K-D, and others. Tell the salesperson the make, body type and year of car you're removing the windshield from. He should then be able to provide you with the correct tool.

As stated earlier, exterior windshield molding can usually be removed with a screwdriver by simply prying it off. However this can cause two problems: More often than not, you will scratch the body paint. Worse yet, you may crack the windshield. So, don't use a screwdriver if you're not experienced with removing moldings. Use a trim stick. Be very careful as you work around the trim. To reduce the possibility of paint damage, apply a strip of masking tape over the paint, adjacent to the trim.

Now, gently use the screwdriver or trim stick to pry up the chrome strip and look for a clip. Move the tool so it is directly in line with the clip. Insert it under the stainless-steel molding and pop it loose from the clip. Work your way around the window in this fashion until all the exterior windshield trim is loose.

If you purchased the special trim-removing tool, insert the half-moon-shaped bit between the glass and trim. Disconnect the clip by rotating the handle away from the clip. This pulls the clip away from the trim. Before releasing the clip, lift the trim up with your free hand so it will not re-engage the clip. In the same fashion, work your way around the window until all the trim is loose.

If you break a clip—and more than likely you will—you should be able to find a replacement at an auto-glass shop. Bring a sample. Replacement cost is minimal. Don't worry about

the clips—concentrate on not cracking the windshield.

Once you have the interior and exterior moldings off, you can turn your attention to the difficult part, removing the windshield. One way to break the seal between the glass and the butyl seal is with a sharp putty knife. Force the putty knife between the glass and the seal. When the seal is completely penetrated, wiggle the putty knife around to guarantee complete separation. Then, withdraw the putty knife, move over the width of the blade, push it between glass and seal, and give it a wiggle. Repeat this process all the way around the window.

If you have trouble getting between the glass and seal along the lower edge because of the instrument panel, stop. You will break the windshield if you force the putty knife. To solve the problem, get a 1/4-inch-wide, double-edge knife made just for this purpose. It fits between the instrument panel and glass so you can cut the seal. This knife costs considerably less than a new windshield.

This method of removing a glued-in window is slow and tedious, but is the best way to replace the window without having to remove the butyl seal.

If you want to remove the butyl seal with the windshield, use solvent and a putty knife, or the special tool to separate the windshield from the seal.

Solvents for separating butyl from glass are available from glass shops. Describe what you want to do. They

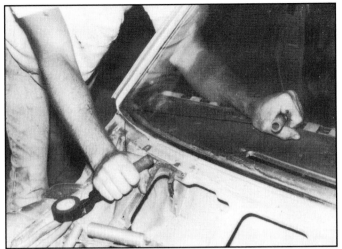

Using wire to cut butyl seal. Although one person can start, it takes two to do this job. Photo by Ron Sessions.

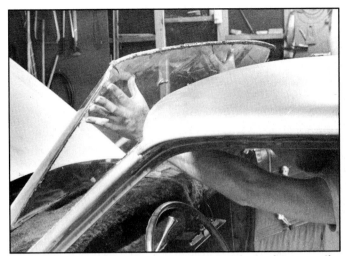

With seal broken between windshield and body, Larry gently pushes out windshield at top from inside car. Have a helper in front to catch windshield as it comes out.

should be able to supply you with the correct solvent.

To use solvent, saturate the area around the windshield where it bonds to the butyl. Do this on the outside and inside of the glass. This will soften the butyl. Now, using a putty knife, work the solvent between the seal and the glass. The putty knife should slide along. When glass and glue are fully separated, push the windshield forward, out of its frame. As with early-type windshields, it's wise to have a helper on the other side to catch the glass as you push it out.

The second method we prefer uses windshield-removal-kit 21400 by Steck Manufacturing. The kit consists of a wire, two handles and a "needle." The thin piano wire is passed through the butyl seal with the giant needle. A handle is then attached to each end of the wire. With you on one end of the wire and your helper on the other, pull the wire through the seal around the periphery of the windshield. It works great. Once separated, push the windshield out as previously described.

## REAR WINDOW

Whether your car is late- or early-model, the windshield and rear window, or *backlite,* are removed similarly. *Take special care not to scratch the heating grid on heated glass.* If scratched, it will not heat. If damaged, the grid line can be repaired with silver-oxide paint.

Now that the glass is out, care must be taken that it doesn't get broken. Be extremely careful while handling or storing glass. Never lay the glass face down—especially the windshield. The combination of weight and curvature can cause it to crack without any additional weight. Store glass in an upright position. If it will be out of the car for an extended period, it might be a good idea to build a small frame to set the glass in. Short of that, someone in a glass shop might give you a glass rack or glass-shipping carton.

## BODY TRIM

**Side Moldings**—Along with removing side trim, or moldings, let's also consider logos, decorations and distinctive markings. Most side trim, whether early, late or on an import, is attached in one or more ways. Trim can be held on with metal or plastic clips that are *Pop riveted* to the body, or with small bolts welded to the trim and retained with nuts. *Hollow-core rivets* are commonly known as *Pop rivets.* The third type of fastening is with pressure-sensitive glue.

**Glued-On Trim**—This is found primarily in the aftermarket. Hard-plastic strips glued to the side of the car to guard against parking-lot dings are a good example.

Working backward, glued-on molding, or side trim, is removed by gently pulling it loose from the body. Sometimes, if the trim has been on for a long time, you may lift the paint as you pull off the trim. To prevent this, use 3-M's *General Purpose Adhesive Remover,* part 08984. Saturating the area around the trim with this stuff loosens the glue, allowing you to pull off the trim—usually without damaging the paint. If this doesn't work, use a 750-watt heat gun to soften the cement. Be careful not to blister the paint.

**Clipped-On Trim**—Most aluminum or stainless-steel side trim is attached by clips. These clips are plastic or metal, depending on the particular vehicle, and are usually riveted to the car. The worst thing you can do to *attempt* to remove this trim is to pry between the body and trim with a screwdriver. This will result in scratched paint, bent trim, and trim that's still attached to the body.

You'll need a special tool to remove trim retained with clips. This means a trip to the auto-parts store. Generally, this tool slides between the body and trim to disengage the trim from the clips. As with the clips that retain the exterior windshield molding, these clips are replaced easily if damaged. Contact a dealer who handles the vehicle make and model you're working on.

If you can't find the correct clip locally, Au-ve-co carries every imaginable fastener. To locate the Au-ve-co distributor nearest you, look in the yellow pages under FASTENERS. Call them and ask for a catalog. Or, contact Au-ve-co directly at P.O. Box 17350, Covington, KY 41017. (606) 341-6450. You will find the fasteners you need somewhere in the Au-ve-co catalog.

Exterior door lock is removed by first disconnecting actuating rod at arm or by removing arm from lock. Clip (arrow) is pulled off lock, allowing lock to be removed. Rod at left runs from exterior door handle down to door latch. Disconnect rod at handle and fasteners to remove door handle.

**Fender Trim**—If your automobile has stainless-steel, aluminum, or chrome trim around the inside edges of the fender, it probably is held in place with sheet-metal screws. Remove these screws to remove the molding. In some cases this trim was fastened with Pop rivets. To remove a Pop rivet, simply drill out the head from the stem. This can usually be accomplished with a 1/8-in. or #30 drill bit. If the center indent appears to be much larger than this, select a correspondingly larger drill bit. This will separate the trim molding from the fender.

**Door Handles & Locks**—Although exterior door handles are considered necessary rather than decoration, they still fall into the category of exterior-trim removal. If you haven't already done so, the door-trim panel must be removed so you'll have access to the exterior door handle.

To remove a door handle and locking mechanism, begin by disconnecting the actuator rod from the inside door handle to the door-latching mechanism. Store and tag loose retaining clips so you'll have them come assembly time. You should then be able to reach through the access hole in the door-inner panel and remove the bolts or screws that hold the exterior door handle to the door.

The door handle is normally retained with two or three screws. If the door lock is part of the door handle, disconnect the cam from the door latch. If the door lock is not an integral part of the door handle, it will be retained by a spring clip. Reach through the door inner panel and grasp the bent end of the clip with a pair of pliers. Pull the clip out of the groove to release the lock.

Finally, disconnect the lock-actuator rod. Again, tag and store loose clips. Now, all that remains is the door latch. To remove this, use a large Phillips-head screwdriver or wrench and remove the three or four screws retaining the latch mechanism to the door jamb. Your door should be completely empty now, except for the scissor mechanism that raises and lowers the window.

If it's a power window, you still have the motor sitting in the bottom of the door. This is removed by lifting out the scissor mechanism. Remove any mounting bolts, disconnect the wires and lift out the motor through the access panel. You should now have a completely empty door. Mark on the parts RIGHT and LEFT, and UP and DOWN to avoid confusion when it is time to replace them.

We can now turn our attention to the major body-trim pieces such as grille and bumpers.

# MAJOR BODY TRIM

## GRILLE

**Early Models**—Early-model automobile grilles were bolted to the body. Then trim pieces were attached with sheet-metal screws or integral bolts and nuts. To remove this style of grille, remove the grille trim. If sheet-metal screws are visible, great. If not, open the hood and look underneath. Remove the screws or nuts, then remove the *edge* trim. After the edge trim is off, the fasteners retaining the grille to the body should be visible and readily accessible.

**Late Models**—The removal of a late-model grille is basically the same as an early-model one, but often more involved. These grilles frequently incorporate headlights and/or parking/directional lights and their bezels. Generally they are attached to the body with sheet-metal screws.

Find the screws, remove them, and remove the bezels from around the headlights. After the bezels are removed, you will find screws attaching the grille to the fender. Raise the hood; you should also find a series of screws in the top of the grille. Remove them. Find the screws holding the bottom of the grille behind the bumper, and remove them.

You should now be able to pull off the complete grille.

## BUMPERS

**Early Models**—Most early-model bumpers are mounted to separate brackets bolted to the frame. The easiest way to remove such a bumper is to unbolt the bumper brackets at the frame. Then remove bumper and its brackets as one unit.

Often, the bumper and bumper brackets on a car that has been in an accident will be damaged. This may make it impossible to remove the bumper or brackets with a wrench. Or, the bolts may be badly rusted. In either case, it will be necessary to use a *blue wrench* or *gas wrench*—nicknames for an oxyacetylene cutting torch—to cut off the bolts.

Bumper bolts are inexpensive and readily available. If you have a cutting torch, use it to remove the bumper and its brackets. The time spent "worrying" bolts off does not justify the money saved.

If you're working on a '50s- or '60s-vintage "Road Yacht," you will discover that the heavy bumpers often exceed 100 pounds. Therefore, take precautions. Support the bumper with a floor jack before removing the bolts. If possible, get a helper. This will reduce the possibility of an accident—or dropping the bumper and scratching the chrome.

**Late Models**—Beginning in the mid-'70s, passenger-car bumpers use *energy-absorbing units*—shock absorbers—to meet federally mandated bumper standards. These types of bumpers present different disassembly problems.

Shock absorbers add considerable weight, making bumper removal more difficult. Therefore, remove the bumper from the shock absorbers. Then, if necessary, remove the shock absorbers from the frame. The bumper will be considerably lighter and a lot easier to control.

**Today's Cars**—Styling changes have just about done away with bumpers on today's modern car. Only a urethane body panel remains. These are removed from under the car, under the hood and around the wheelwells. The quickest way to find out how your's is removed is to visit the dealership parts-department. They'll have a shop manual showing where the mounting points are.

Be very careful with a welding torch around these urethane panels. You won't just singe the paint, you'll melt the panel!

Best way to remove bumper from early-model domestic car is to unbolt bumper brackets at frame. You'll need a friend or jack to support bumper while you unbolt it. Store bumper and brackets together.

With bumper and grille removed, car front looks "naked."

## HEADLIGHTS

In most cases, a headlight assembly consists of three components: trim bezel, often called an *eyebrow;* retainer bracket with adjusters; and the bucket.

To remove a headlight, first remove its bezel. Usually the bezel is retained to the fender with a single sheet-metal screw at the bottom. When removed, the bezel can be rotated upward, disconnecting the top from a hook in the headlight bucket. If, as mentioned earlier, the headlight bezel is an integral part of the grille, several sheet-metal screws will retain the bezel. Remove these screws and, subsequently, the headlight bezel.

The headlight is retained to the headlight bucket with a combination of screws and springs. Beside each of these, two, three, or four screws holding the retainer ring to the headlight bucket, are two additional screws. Remove only those screws holding the retainer to the bucket. The other screws are for adjusting the headlight up and down, and right and left.

After removing the retainer-ring screws, unhook the tension springs with a pair of pliers. Let the springs hang. When doing this, be careful because both the retainer ring and headlight can fall out. Remove the retainer ring, pull the headlight forward and disconnect the 3-prong plug at the rear of the bulb.

Remove the screws holding the headlight bucket to the body. Withdraw bucket and wire as one unit. Note: If your car is equipped with four headlights, the inboard and outboard

Bottom screw holds headlight retaining ring. Top screw is one of two headlight-adjustment screws. Don't remove them.

lights are different. Outboard lights have high- and low-beam filaments; inboard lights only have high beam.

Before you lose track of where they go, mark the headlights **INBOARD** or **OUTBOARD**, and **RIGHT** or **LEFT**. This will prevent confusion later. If you should get them mixed up, the lights won't work correctly.

# MAJOR BODY-PART & PANEL REMOVAL

## HOOD

All hoods are removed in a similar manner: The hood is removed from

After removing headlight-ring retaining screw, remove retaining spring and ring; headlight can then be removed. Some headlight installations use screws only to retain ring.

its hinges. This is easier than removing the hinges from the inner fender skirt or fire wall.

If the hood is removed and replaced without any change in front-end configuration, use a grease pencil to trace around the hinges onto the hood inner panel before you remove the hood. This will allow you to reinstall the hood just as it was before you removed it.

Another way to assure the hood will realign is to drill a No. 30 or 1/8-inch hole through each hinge and hood inner panel. Be careful that you don't drill all the way through and out the top of the hood. Drill two holes through each hinge, one at each end.

Spring-loaded hinges support hood. To ensure proper hood fit when replaced, trace around hood hinges before loosening bolts.

Front hood-hinge bolts should come out first. Then loosen rear bolts. If you remove rear bolts first, hood will pivot on front bolts and fall forward, bending both hinges and hood.

Prop-supported hood: At center of photo is right-side hood hinge. At left is latch-type hood support. As on any hood—domestic, import, truck or whatever—trace around hinge before loosening bolts.

Weight and bulk of hood means you'll need a friend to help with removing it. Remove hood alone and you'll surely end up with a damaged hood, fenders and front cowl.

loosen them all and remove the front ones first. This will prevent the hood from falling forward. With all four bolts removed, lift off the hood. Like window glass, the hood should not be stored flat. It should be stored upright against a wall. To make sure it doesn't fall over, secure it with a wire stretched between two nails driven into the wall studs. If you're concerned about the hood's paint, place rags or pieces of cardboard between the wire and the hood. This will keep the wire from scratching the paint.

## TRUNK LID

A trunk lid is removed the same way as a hood. If the trunk lid will be replaced without any major work to it or the surrounding area, mark around the hinges with a grease pencil. Or, use the drill-and-screw method. Otherwise, remove the trunk lid without marking it. Follow a similar procedure for removing and storing the trunk lid.

## DOOR REMOVAL

Compared to the removal of interior door parts, removing a door is relatively simple.

Open the door and note how it is hinged. In most instances it will be easiest to remove the door from the hinges rather than the hinges from the door pillar. If they are welded at the body, you have no choice—unbolt them at the door.

Don't bother with marking the hinges for alignment. Once a door is removed it will have to be adjusted

When you return the hood to its hinges, these holes are aligned and No. 8 sheet-metal screws installed. This holds the hood in proper alignment while you install and tighten the hinge-to-hood bolts. Afterward, you remove the sheet-metal screws and close the hood, assured the hood will fit.

If major bodywork is to be done to the hood or inner fender, cowl, fire wall or grille areas, using reference marks or holes for realigning the hood becomes a moot point. The hood

must be readjusted to fit the new contours. Therefore, if work is to be done to the hood or inner fender, don't bother with reference marks.

Most hoods are extremely bulky and heavy. So, have a helper assist you with removing the hood. In the accompanying photograph, you can see that each member of the *team* is supporting the hood with a shoulder and one hand.

If a prop is used, remove it and support the hood with a broom handle. When removing the hood bolts,

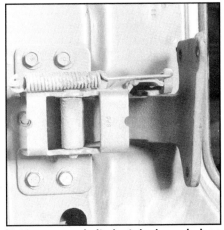

If hinges are bolted at body and door, remove bolts at door-side of hinge. You'll need someone to help support door while doing this. If hinges are welded to both body and door, you'll have to drive out hinge pin. This may require grinding off end of pin first.

Begin front-fender removal by loosening fender at bottom.

Work your way around inside edge of wheel opening, removing all bolts holding fender to wheelhouse.

when replaced. Unlike the hood or the trunk, a number of adjustments must be made together to make the door fit the opening.

With a floor jack and 2x4 or someone to help support the door, loosen the hinge-to-door bolts and remove them. Remove the door and store it upright, out of harm's way.

## FENDER REMOVAL

**Front Fenders**—Removing a fender may look like full-time occupation, but the job is greatly simplified if it's taken one step at a time. The first thing you know, the fender will be off.

Most fenders have three major mounting points: at the top rear; at the bottom rear; and at the front. Additionally, many unitized-body cars have a row of bolts in the fender flange, under the hood, that secures the top of the fender to the body structure. Most frame cars have screws in this area to secure the top of the fender apron to the fender.

Before you take off any fender-mounting bolts, remove any wires from the fender. Also check for and remove any fender braces. Frequently, braces are used to support the bottom of the fender, at the front or rear of the wheel well.

Remove all but two fender-mounting bolts. This will hold the fender on so it won't fall off. Rubber grommets and large body washers may be used with these bolts. Next, remove the sheet-metal screws along the bottom edge of the fender and in the wheel-well flange. If there's a

*valance,* or *modesty,* panel—the body panel that goes between the front fenders, under the front bumper—unbolt it from the fenders.

You should now be able to remove the fender. As with the hood, a fender is bulky and heavy, so get a helper. Lift the fender up to clear the wheel, and set it aside. To finish disassembling the front end, remove the opposite fender the same way. The assembly of body panels remaining on the frame forward of the fire wall and supporting the radiator, is called the *front clip.* If you're working with a fully unitized body, the front clip is an integral part of the body structure—it's not removable. Skip the following section and turn to the next page.

## FRONT CLIP

If you haven't already removed it, the front valance panel must be removed before you can remove the front clip. In most cases the front valance is attached to the front clip with a series of bolts and nuts. Remove these bolts, then the valance.

Additionally, there may be a *stone deflector*—a filler panel that installs between the front bumper and the radiator and front fenders. Remove its bolts and the panel.

Begin front-clip removal by removing the radiator. With the radiator out you will have access to the clip mounting bolts that are at the front. Generally, the radiator-mounting bracket—sometimes called the *radiator support* or *horsecollar*—is an integral part of the front clip. It bolts directly

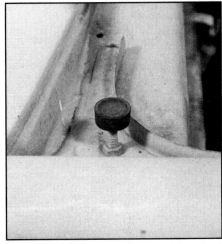

Rubber hood bumper fits over head of hood-adjusting bolt.

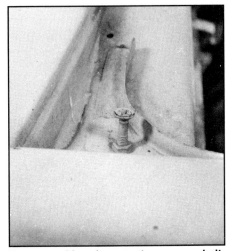

Remove rubber bumper to expose bolt head. Loosen jam nut and remove bolt.

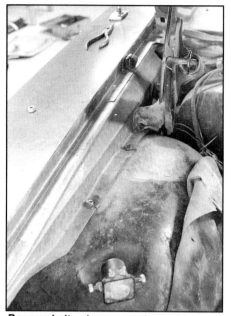

Remove bolts along upper fender flange to release top of fender. Two bolts on fender thread up through wheelhouse into J-nuts on fender flange (arrows); two thread into weldnuts on radiator support.

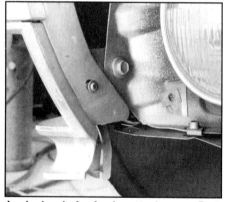

Look closely for fender attachments. Both screw and bolt must be removed to free fender.

With right front fender removed, front-clip supporting members are exposed.

Body mount on body/frame car supports front-clip at radiator support. Remove bolt at each mount to free front of front clip. After removing clip, replace bolts in frame with rubber mounts so they don't get lost.

Hood hinge comes off with fender. Note three holes for bolting fender to fire wall.

to the frame at the base of the mounting brackets. After removing the radiator, remove the bracket-mounting bolts from the frame. Remove the remaining front-clip mounting bolts at the rear.

At each side of the cowl of the example vehicle are two bolts with rubber caps. These are *hood stops*. The rubber caps protect the hood from the bolt heads. Each bolt is used to adjust the hood so it aligns with the upper cowl. If your vehicle is so equipped, remove the rubber caps, the bolts and their jam nuts. This bolt also holds the front clip to the cowl. When all the front-clip bolts are out, remove the front clip as one unit.

Lifting off a front clip requires three people—one at each inner-fender well, and one at the front. Together, and without twisting the clip, lift the entire unit over the tires and walk it away from the front of the car. A front clip weighs 150 to 200 pounds and is flimsy, so be extremely careful.

At this point everything from the front end of the car should be removed except the engine, front suspension, and related components. We can now move to the rear.

## REAR FENDERS & BACK PANEL

Most passenger cars built in the '50s and after have welded-on rear fenders; the seams are filled and the body finished. This gives the appearance of a seamless body at the rear. Such fenders are commonly called *quarter panels*. Earlier rear fenders are bolted on and use *welting* between the

fenders and the body. They are removed by simply removing the bolts.

A welded-on fender may be attached with a combination of spot-welds and gas or electric-arc seam welds. On the vehicle pictured, only *spot-welds* are used. They show up as slight circular depressions where two body panels are joined. Spot-welds join each quarter panel to the door-lock pillar, wheelhouse, trunk floor, and *lower back panel,* which fills the space between the trunk and trunk floor at the back. Additionally, spot-welds join the quarter to the *upper back panel,* or *rear cowl,* and to the *C-pillar*—rear roof pillar. Unfortunately, these joints—termed *coach joints*—are not visible as these *offset lap joints* are filled and finished smooth at the factory.

Removing a welded-on fender is considerably more difficult than one that's bolted on. You must first drill out the spot-welds.

Start with weld joints that have exposed spot-welds. Center punch each spot-weld, then drill through the first layer of metal using a 3/8-inch drill. It's not necessary to drill all the way through both thicknesses of metal. Drilling through one serves the purpose—to break the weld.

When the drill penetrates one thickness of metal, so the spot-weld is removed, proceed along the weld flange until each spot-weld has been drilled out. To check your progress, insert a screwdriver between the two panels and try to pry them apart. The weld flange should be flexible enough to move, providing the welds are

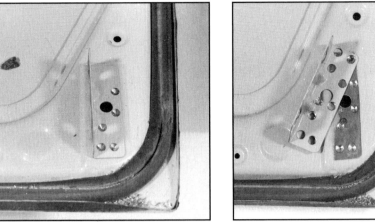

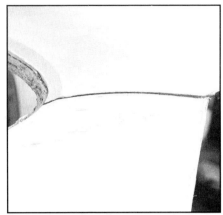

Neat cut results when proper tools are used.

To separate a spot-welded part, drill out the spot-welds. Spot-welds appear as small circular depressions in the weld flange. With a drill that's slightly larger than the spot-weld—about 3/8 inch—center the drill on each spot-weld and drill through the first thickness of metal. Drill out all spot-welds to free part.

broken. If not, check for missed spot-welds.

You'll have to use a different method to separate the quarter panel from other body panels joined by coach joints or seam welds.

A saber saw with a metal-cutting blade will do the job, as will a Skil saw or, as it is called in the woodworking trade, a *cut-off saw* with a masonry blade. Or, you could use an oxyacetylene cutting torch. Because of the danger of fire, do not use a cutting torch if the fender incorporates the fuel-tank filler neck. Also, a cutting torch will warp the edges of the metal, making it more difficult to install the new quarter and finish the joint. So, use a saw wherever possible.

Because a saw can cause sparks remove the gas tank from the car and immediate area before you do any cutting at the rear of the car. This will help to eliminate the possibility of a gas-tank-related fire or explosion.

There are inner panels between the rear window and quarter window that must also be cut. Because of the 1/2- to 3/4-inch separation between the inner and outer panels, a saber-saw blade probably will bind and break. For this reason, we recommend using a cut-off saw.

Regardless of your cutting tool, two cuts must be made. One cut is from the top edge of the door-lock pillar to the bottom of the backlite. The second proceeds from the end of the first cut, across the trunk drip rail. When these cuts have been made and the spot-welds drilled out, remove the quarter panel.

Masonry saw blade is used in circular saw to cut roof at C-pillar. Do as Larry is doing when cutting metal—wear eye protection.

**Plan Your Cuts**—Do not make random cuts when removing a body panel. Plan your cuts in advance and mark them clearly with a scriber or soapstone marker. If you have a new quarter panel, or are removing the replacement panel from a junked vehicle, let the *trim* of the replacement panel determine where you make your cuts.

Further, if you're cutting the replacement panel from another body, cut it *before* you cut the panel to be replaced. Then, you can make more accurate cuts. Another tip: Take measurements used to lay out the cuts from body areas that are undamaged. As you make your cut, be sure to allow for the width of the blade. This can be from 3/16 to 3/8 inch. If you are still uncertain about where a cut should be made, leave extra material so you can trim the panel to fit. It's considerably easier to trim away material than it is to add it.

Again, plan ahead and make measurements to ensure a proper fit.

No, this isn't how final C-pillar cut should look. We cut away outer panel to show how saw blade also cut roof-inner panel (arrow).

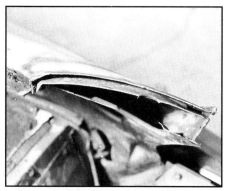

Bird's-eye view of finished C-pillar cut. In plain view are the three main C-pillar panels: outer, inner and C-pillar reinforcement.

A-pillar cut through with masonry saw shows inner and outer panels spot-welded together at windshield and door flanges. If your car is a hardtop, roof can be lifted off after A- and C-pillars are cut.

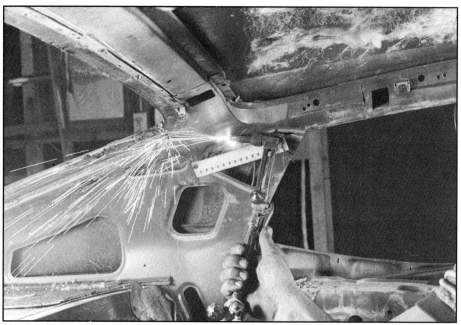

Using cutting torch to finish what masonry saw didn't cut. Be sure to leave 1/8 in. at section to allow for shrinkage when fitting new panel.

## ROOF

Unlike a quarter panel, drilling out spot-welds cannot be used to remove a roof panel. Cutting is the only method.

When cutting a roof panel, make the cuts as high on the pillars as you can. As you can see in the accompanying photos, we removed this top by cutting the top part of the front and middle, or *A-* and *B-pillars,* and the narrowest section between the quarter window and backlite, or *C-pillar.* If your car is a hardtop, it won't have a B-pillar.

After establishing cut lines, adjust the saw blade so it will cut through the outer panel at the C-pillar. At the A-pillar, adjust the blade so it cuts through both inner and outer panels.

After these first cuts have been made, the C-pillar inner panel is all that remains. The many lightening holes in large inner panels make using a saw difficult—see photo. Consequently, we used a cutting torch. It makes little difference on the inner panel whether or not the cut and resulting joint are clean and attractive because this will be covered by the headliner. Make this final cut on both sides and you can then remove the top.

Call out that poor, overworked helper to help lift off the roof.

For the most part, we have described the removal of all interior trim and exterior body panels. Because most body-repair jobs may require partial disassembly of the interior and/or exterior, use only the disassembly information needed to accomplish your job.

## SKINNING

Let's look at a trick of the trade called *skinning.*

Most body assemblies consist of two basic components: an inner panel and an outer panel. These include the hood, trunk, doors and roof. Many of these assemblies can be purchased new through a dealership. Like so many things today, they are expensive. It's not unusual for one of these assemblies to cost as much as half the value of the vehicle—if the part is available. That's the bad news. The good news is, factories stock many years and models of body-panel *skins.* Skins are the outer panel of the two-part component—the outside of the door, trunk, hood and so on.

A damaged outer panel, which in most cases is joined to an inner panel to make a body-component assembly, can be removed. A new skin can then be rejoined to the inner panel.

The skin extends past the inner-panel flange so its edges can be wrapped over the inner panel to join the two pieces. This wrap, which folds back on itself and the inner panel, is called a *hem flange.*

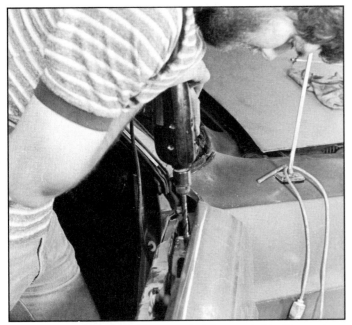

Door reskinning begins with removal of damaged skin. Door outer-to-inner spot-welds are drilled out at periphery of door. This job is easier if you remove door.

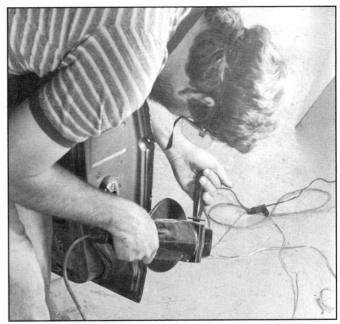

Larry uses body grinder to grind through edge of hem flange. Grind through only one layer of metal. Both ends and bottom of door must be ground.

Grinding bottom edge would be easier with door off car.

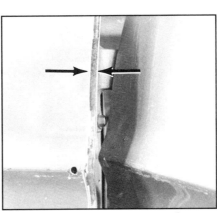

Outer panel is separated from inner panel (arrows).

After removing skin from door, remove hem-flange lip from inner panel. Door is now ready for new skin. To do this, new skin is fitted to door and edges are gradually bent over door-inner flange with hammer and dolly.

To separate the skin from the inner panel, grind through the hem-flange edge. Using the door skin as an example, note that Larry first drilled out the spot-welds along the top of the door. This completed, he used a No. 18-grit sanding disc on a body grinder to grind through the hem flange. After grinding the front, rear and bottom edges, he separated the skin from the inner panel. Then, with a pair of pliers, it was easy to peel away the remainder of the outer panel that was spot-welded to the inner panel.

Now, for about one quarter of the price of a new door assembly, we purchased a new skin and assembled it to the inner panel. This can also be done with a hood or trunk lid.

## CONCLUSION

Our demonstration car is now down to the bare bones. Everything that can be removed has been removed to show each body-disassembly process.

We've demonstrated a little of every operation involved in the removal of interior and exterior body parts. Of the thousands of models of domestic and import vehicles manufactured from the '50s to the '90s, it's impossible to detail each one. Therefore, you must proceed carefully and thoughtfully while disassembling the car.

Each piece is assembled in a logical sequence. To disassemble it, you must think out a logical disassembly sequence *beforehand*. If you run into something not covered or you don't

understand, stop. Don't throw up your hands in disgust. Think about what you are doing. Consider the alternatives, select the one you think will be most successful, then proceed with caution.

If you are still stumped, don't be afraid to ask for help. Most body shops will spend a few minutes discussing your problem with you. Many will even go to extraordinary lengths to help.

# 3 WELDING

**Complete gas-welding rig and extra tanks. Smaller tanks—sometimes called *cylinders or bottles*—are more practical for the home craftsman.**

Welding is a lot of fun. It's also a fast way to join two pieces of metal. Additionally, it's clean and efficient. And if you do it yourself, gas-welding is relatively inexpensive. For the home shop, the best types of welding techniques are *gas-welding* and *electric-arc-welding,* or simply *arc-welding.* If you must choose between the two, we suggest gas-welding. In the long run, gas-welding is more versatile. Of course, if you can afford an arc-welder, get one. If you get into body-work and plan on doing extensive repairs, an arc-welder will be needed to reweld such components as engine mounts, frame members and heavier-

gage steel used for chassis or running-gear parts. Although you can do some of this welding with a gas-welder, it's best suited to thinner-gage body sheet metal.

## GAS-WELDING
Two types of gases are normally associated with gas-welding: *oxygen* and *acetylene,* thus the term *oxyacetylene.* Acetylene is the fuel; it does the actual burning. Oxygen is required to support combustion, or burning, of acetylene for welding or cutting.

A gas-welding rig requires the following components: an oxygen tank and acetylene tank, or *bottles* or

*cylinders.* On top of each tank is a *pressure regulator.* Connected to the oxygen regulator is a green or black hose; a red hose connects to the acetylene regulator. The opposite end of each hose connects to the torch with a *welding* or *cutting tip* at its end. Let's back up and look at these components in detail.

**Tanks**—Oxygen tanks are larger than acetylene tanks—more oxygen than acetylene is used when welding and cutting, particularly cutting. At the top of each tank is a shut-off valve. Connected to the downstream-side of each valve is a pressure regulator.

**Regulator**—A regulator is required to

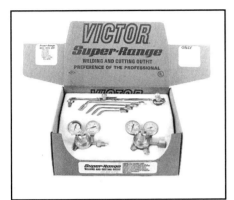

Oxyacetylene outfit includes gages and regulators, three welding tips, *rosette* tip for heating, cutting head and tip, and torch body.

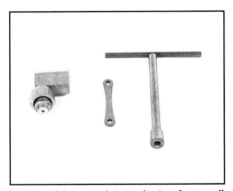

Left to right: regulator adapter for small tanks, acetylene on/off body for small tanks, and handle for larger tank. Oxygen tanks have water-faucet-style on/off handles.

reduce the high pressure from a tank and maintain, or regulate, it at the preset pressure while cutting or welding.

**Never** use unregulated high-pressure oxygen or acetylene.

In the regulator drawing on the following page, (1) is regulator inlet, (2) is pressure-adjusting screw, (3) is high-pressure gage, (4) is low-pressure gage, and (5) is regulator outlet. Familiarize yourself with these regulator parts and know how to use them—for safety sake.

Acetylene-regulator and -hose connections have left-hand threads; oxygen connections use right-hand threads. Nuts at the acetylene connections also have a V-groove around the center of the flats for further identification.

Attached to each regulator are two

## GAS-WELDING SAFETY

Improper use of gas-welding or cutting apparatus may be dangerous. It is necessary to understand and appreciate safe operating procedures. A thorough understanding of these procedures will minimize the hazards involved and add pleasure to your work. The following checklist provides safety information detailed throughout this chapter.

### WORK AREA

● The work area must have a fireproof floor. Concrete floors are recommended but wooden floors may be used if covered with sand or wet down with water prior to welding.
● Use heat-resistant asbestos shields, tin-roofing sheets or similar fireproof material to protect nearby walls or unprotected flooring from sparks or hot metal.
● Adequate ventilation is required to prevent the concentration of oxygen and toxic fumes. Although oxygen itself will not burn, the presence of pure oxygen accelerates combustion and causes materials to burn with great intensity. **Oil and grease in the presence of oxygen can ignite and burn violently.**
● Work benches or tables to be used for welding must have fireproof tops. Firebricks are commonly used for these surfaces and for supporting the work.
● Chain or otherwise secure gas-welding cylinders to a wall, bench, post, cylinder cart, or whatever, to prevent them from falling and keep them upright.

### PROTECTIVE APPAREL

● Protect yourself from sparks, slag and flame brilliance at all times. Select goggles with tempered lenses shaded 5 or darker to prevent eye injury and to provide good visibility.
● Wear gloves, long-sleeve shirt and pants, an apron and high-top shoes to protect skin and clothing from sparks and slag. **Keep all clothing and protective apparel absolutely free of oil and grease.**

### FIRE PREVENTION

Practice fire prevention when welding. A few simple precautions can prevent most fires and minimize damage in the event a fire does occur. Always practice the following rules and safety procedures:
● **Never** use oil or grease on or around any gas-welding device. Remember, even a trace of oil or grease can ignite and burn violently in the presence of oxygen.
● Keep flames and sparks away from cylinders and hoses.
● Move combustibles a safe distance from areas where gas-welding is to be done.
● Use fire-resistant shields to protect nearby walls, floors and ceilings.
● Have a fire extinguisher close by and check it regularly to ensure it is correctly working.
● Use gas-welding equipment only with the gases for which it was intended.
● Completely open an acetylene-cylinder valve. Keep the wrench, if one is required, on the cylinder valve so the valve can be closed quickly in an emergency.
● Never test for gas leaks with a flame. Use an approved leak-detector solution; soapy water works great.
● When working, frequently inspect the area for possible fires or smoldering material.

### NEVER USE OXYGEN:

● In pneumatic tools.
● In oil preheating burners.
● To start an engine.
● To blow out pipelines.
● To dust off clothing or work area.
● To create pressure.
● For ventilation.

Courtesy Victor Welding Company

gages. They are precision instruments and should be handled with care. The gage with the larger numbers is the *high-pressure gage;* it shows tank pressure in pounds per square inch (psi). The one with the smaller numbers is the *low-pressure gage,* also calibrated in psi. Although tank pressure drops as its contents are depleted, the pressure regulator maintains line pressure within tank-pressure limits. As tank pressure drops markedly, line pressure also drops. Line pressure then needs readjusting.

**Pressure-Adjusting Screw**—Regulator-adjusting screws control line pressure to the oxygen and acetylene hoses and torch. When turned clockwise, the regulator increases line pressure, and subsequently oxygen or

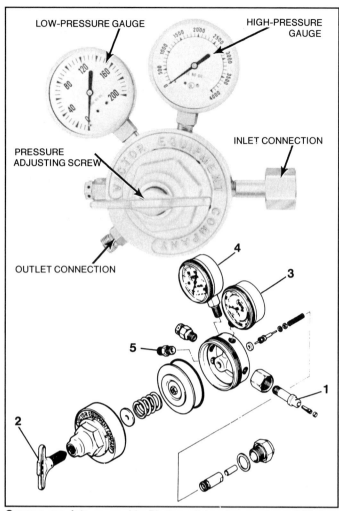

LOW-PRESSURE GAUGE

HIGH-PRESSURE GAUGE

PRESSURE ADJUSTING SCREW

INLET CONNECTION

OUTLET CONNECTION

4

3

5

1

2

**Oxygen-regulator assembly. Photo and drawing courtesy of Victor Welding.**

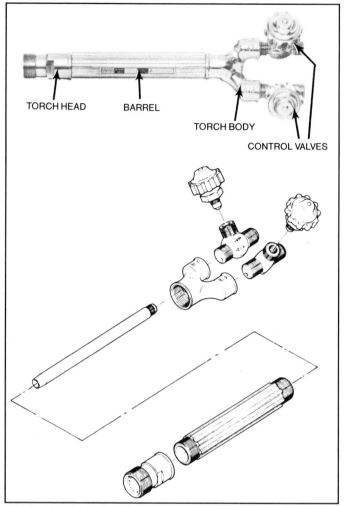

TORCH HEAD

BARREL

TORCH BODY

CONTROL VALVES

**Welding-torch body. Photo and drawing courtesy of Victor Welding.**

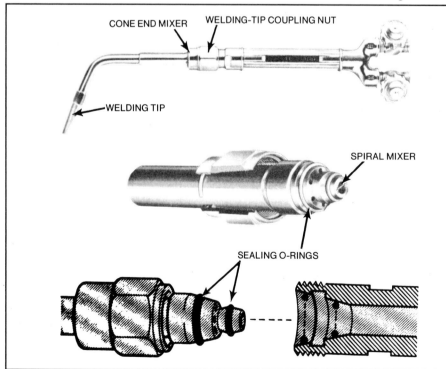

CONE END MIXER

WELDING-TIP COUPLING NUT

WELDING TIP

SPIRAL MIXER

SEALING O-RINGS

**Two O-rings seal welding tip to torch body. Small O-ring seals acetylene; large one seals oxygen. Photo and drawing courtesy of Victor Welding.**

acetylene flow, through the regulator to the hoses and to the torch. Of course, this assumes that the tank valve has been turned on, allowing gas to flow to the regulator.

**Outlet Connections**—Welding hoses attach to the regulator outlets. We like to use a *flame suppressor* between the regulator and hoses, to prevent the possibility of the flame backing up the hose to the tank and causing an explosion. Again, left-hand threads are used for acetylene connections and right-hand for oxygen. *Never lubricate regulator-outlet connections or any part of a gas-welder!* These connections should be kept clean at all times.

**Hoses**—The hoses route low-pressure gases from the regulators to the torch. They are bonded together for ease of handling.

As mentioned, welding hose is color coded: red for acetylene and green or black for oxygen. Gas-welding hoses are constructed of alternating rubber and fabric layers. The center is gum rubber, surrounded by

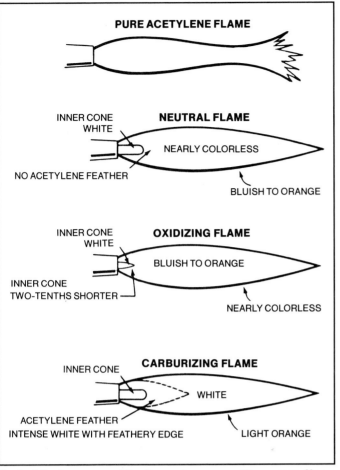

**PURE ACETYLENE FLAME**

**NEUTRAL FLAME**

INNER CONE WHITE

NEARLY COLORLESS

NO ACETYLENE FEATHER

BLUISH TO ORANGE

**OXIDIZING FLAME**

INNER CONE WHITE

BLUISH TO ORANGE

INNER CONE TWO-TENTHS SHORTER

NEARLY COLORLESS

**CARBURIZING FLAME**

INNER CONE

WHITE

ACETYLENE FEATHER INTENSE WHITE WITH FEATHERY EDGE

LIGHT ORANGE

Each of the four gas-welding flames have a specific purpose. Neutral flame is used the most; it's for welding. See color photos of flames on back cover. Photo courtesy of Victor Welding.

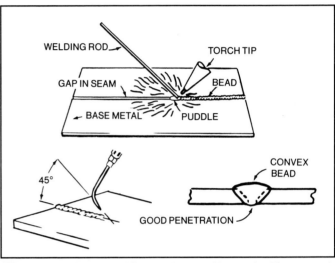

FOREHAND WELDING

DIRECTION OF WELDING

BACKHAND WELDING

DIRECTION OF WELDING

Forehand welding lays bead in the direction of flame; backhand welding moves in direction opposite flame direction. Use forehand technique when gas-welding thin material. Drawings courtesy of Victor Welding.

WELDING ROD

TORCH TIP

GAP IN SEAM

BEAD

BASE METAL

PUDDLE

45°

CONVEX BEAD

GOOD PENETRATION

When gas-welding, position torch and filler rod 45° to metal surface. A 90° angle will be between torch and rod. Move torch in and out to control heat. Dab rod in molten pool to add filler. Drawing courtesy of Victor Welding.

rubber-impregnated fiber, then covered with a vulcanized-rubber wear cover. All domestically fabricated approved hoses are flame *retardant.* They will burn, but will self-extinguish if the heat source is removed.

**Hose Care**—Welding hose can provide safe, efficient service for many months if cared for properly. Use these guidelines for hose care, maintenance and safe handling:

1. Blow out the preservative talcum powder from a new hose before using it for welding or cutting.

2. Keep welding hose away from open flames, falling slag and sparks.

3. Never walk or roll equipment over a hose.

4. Replace cut, crushed or charred sections of hose with the correct size and type of splicer and ferrule.

5. Never use an oxygen hose to splice an acetylene hose and vice versa.

6. Replace a welding hose if it contains multiple splices, or if it is severely cracked or worn.

**Welding-Torch Body**—The welding torch is essentially a pair of tubes with control valves. One valve-and-tube assembly controls the acetylene supply and the other controls the oxygen. The welding-torch body is not designed to mix the gases. This is done by the welding or cutting *tip,* which is attached to the body. The body functions only as a handle and a means to control the gas supply to the tip. See drawing on facing page.

**Control Valves**—The torch body has two control valves at the outlet end of the hose, one for acetylene and the other for oxygen. Occasionally, the packing nuts may require slight tightening, but *never lubricate them.* Remove dirt or dust with a clean cloth.

**Barrel**—The torch-body barrel is simply a *manifold* that separately routes the oxygen and acetylene to the tip. Oxygen is routed through a tube at the center of the barrel; acetylene goes through a number of orifices placed concentrically around the center tube.

**Tip**—The welding or cutting tip, or *head,* is threaded onto the barrel. Oxygen from the barrel is directed through a center oxygen port in the tip; acetylene passes into orifices around the oxygen port. A tapered surface inside the head mates with an O-ring to create a gas-tight seal. This external thread and internal taper may also be reconditioned if damaged. Remove dirt or dust with a clean cloth.

**Light Torch**—Let's assume that you've elected to weld 1/32-inch-thick sheet metal. The manual that came with your welding set recommends that a 0 tip be used with 3-psi oxygen and acetylene line pressure.

Start by opening the tank valves, but with the torch valves closed. Adjust regulator pressure to about 5 psi. When you decide to change tip size in the middle of a job, you must also readjust line pressures.

Now you're ready to light the torch. Begin, as always, by putting on your welding goggles. Open the torch

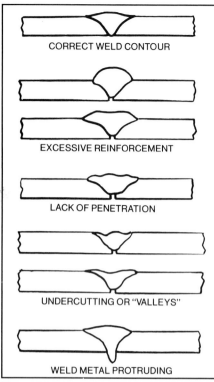

CORRECT WELD CONTOUR

EXCESSIVE REINFORCEMENT

LACK OF PENETRATION

UNDERCUTTING OR "VALLEYS"

WELD METAL PROTRUDING

There are many kinds of butt welds; one correct and many incorrect. Correct butt weld is at top. Drawing courtesy of Victor Welding.

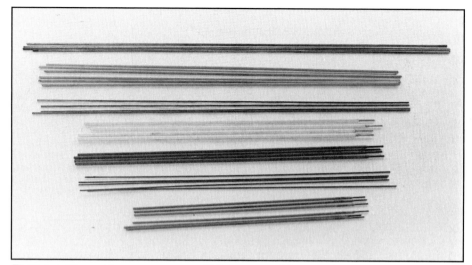

There is a filler rod for every purpose. Talk to your welding-supply dealer. He'll recommend the correct rod for your welding job.

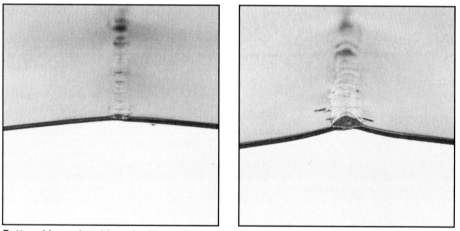

Butt welds made with and without filler rod: Weld at left was made without rod, as evidenced by smaller weld bead. Less heat and minimal warpage results when no filler is used. Welding without filler rod requires a no-gap fit between pieces being welded.

acetylene valve approximately 1/2 turn, and the oxygen valve about 1/4 turn. With a *torch lighter,* or *striker,* light the torch. *Don't use a match, cigarette lighter, or any open flame.* Point the torch away from people, animals, and the oxygen or acetylene cylinders. Open the oxygen valve until there is no black smoke or soot. Now, adjust the regulators to recommended pressure—3 psi in this case.

Once the line pressure is changed, readjust the torch so the flame is *neutral.* See page 31 for illustrations of different flames. Adjust the torch valves until a bright, light-blue inner cone appears in the flame. When the feathery edges of the flame disappear except at the very tip, a sharp inner cone is visible, and there is no hissing sound, the torch is adjusted correctly.

Adjust the flame until you are sure you have a *neutral flame.* If too much oxygen is flowing, you'll have an *oxidizing flame.* A loud hissing sound accompanies this type of flame. Instead of melting metal, an oxidizing flame will burn it.

A flame that is acetylene-rich is a *carburizing flame,* distinguished by a long, orange, coarse-feathered end. A carburizing flame introduces excess carbon into the metal. Instead, the flame should be pale blue, with the clearly defined bright-blue inner cone. With a good neutral flame, you are ready to begin welding.

## WELDING STYLES

Two styles are used in oxyacetylene welding: *forehand* and *backhand.*

The forehand method is for welding steel under 1/8-inch thick. This is the type you'll use in bodywork. The reason for using the forehand-type weld is to heat the metal ahead of the weld, but not to overheat the puddle, resulting in a *blowout,* or hole.

**Forehand welding** is when the torch points down at a 45° angle to the work and in the direction you will *lay* the bead; the welding rod goes ahead of the torch, as does the molten puddle. The torch tip is moved with a circular or oscillating crescent motion as it's moved along the weld seam, or joint. The filler rod is moved with even in/out dabs in the puddle. This distributes the heat and puddle to make a uniform and attractive weld bead.

**Backhand welding** is basically the same as forehand welding except for the direction of the weld. The torch is moved ahead of the puddle and rod as the bead is made. The flame points back toward the molten puddle, keeping it and the *parent,* or *base, metal*—material of the pieces being joined—hot. This is necessary for good weld *penetration* when gas-welding heavy-gage steel. Penetration is the complete melting together, or *fusion,* of the *parent metal* and the rod, or *filler material,* at the weld. Otherwise, the weld joint may fail.

Good penetration is one of many factors that make a quality weld. A weld that has poor penetration can look good, but is weak. On the other

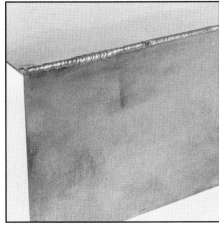
Outside corner weld was made without filler rod. Bead is from base metal.

Flux cleans metal being brazed, allowing filler material to flow and bond to base metal. V-groove weld seam is being filled with filler rod.

hand, a sloppy weld with good penetration will be strong. A good weld starts with a good joint. Therefore, be especially attentive when fitting the pieces to be joined. There should be no gaps.

To ensure that gaps don't occur as you weld, *tack-weld* the pieces together. Tack-welding is a series of short welds or spots. Not only does a tack-weld hold the pieces together, it preheats the metal for a smoother, more accurate final weld.

Like any other skill, welding requires a great deal of practice. Throughout this chapter are illustrations showing good welds and bad welds. As you practice, try to make your weld beads look like the good ones. All it takes is practice, practice, practice. Practice doing lap joints, T-joints, open outside welds and closed outside welds. When you think your welds are a thing of beauty and a joy forever, you're ready to begin welding on a car body.

**Brazing**—Now that you think you are a certified welder—you can weld upside down, inside out and wrong-side forward—you can move into a much easier type of welding. This is braze welding, or brazing.

Brazing incorporates a filler rod unlike that used in *fusion welding*—it is dissimilar to the parent metal. Brass- or bronze-filler rod is used.

In brazing, the filler rod fills a seam, such as a V-groove, to make a definite bead to join the parts. Brazing is similar to soldering. Molten filler flows into a tight-fitted joint through *capillary action.* The thin film of filler

Section of a lap joint.

Coat brazing rod with flux by heating it and dipping rod into can.

material bonds the two parts through *diffusion,* creating an extremely strong joint.

Diffusion is to brazing what penetration is to fusion welding. The filler and parent metals diffuse, or intermix at their mating surfaces, bonding them together. The resulting *alloy*—mixture of metals—is sometimes stronger than the parent metal, especially with high-strength brazing rods.

Brazing can be used in place of conventional gas-welding. It even has some advantages over fusion welding. For instance, it can be used to weld two dissimilar metals together, such as steel to copper; or two different kinds of steel. Additionally, brazing is done at a much lower temperature than fusion welding—just over 800F vs. about 2300F—resulting in less

warpage. This is an important consideration in bodywork. The lower temperature is also an advantage with heat-treated steel. The heat treatment is not affected when brazed.

Now that you know about the advantages of brazing, you should also know there are areas where these welding methods *should not* be used. Specifically, don't use either method for joining pieces that are highly stressed, such as suspension components, frame members, structural body panels and drive-line parts. For welding these parts, use electric-welding, page 38.

One thing is critical with brazing: The joint surfaces must be absolutely clean and free from contamination. Otherwise, the filler and parent metals will not diffuse. Clean the

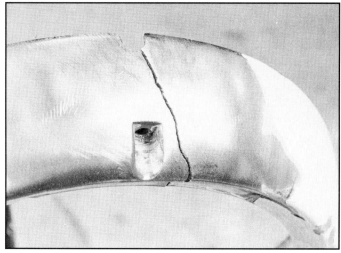

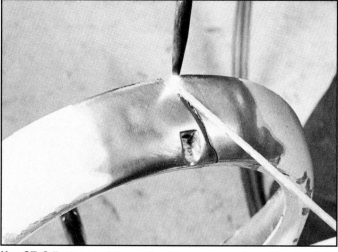

Valuable '56 Thunderbird *pot-metal* headlight eyebrow can be saved by welding.

Use ST-8 fluxless welding rod and low pressure to weld pot metal. Excess pressure will blow away weld bead.

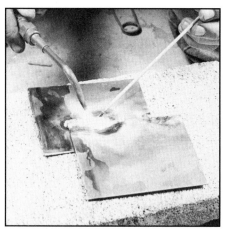

Making a lap-weld joint with flux-coated brazing rod. Brazing, like soldering, works by capillary action. Rather than depending on penetration at the joint, it bonds similar to glue.

parent metal by grinding, scraping, sanding or wire brushing.

An easier way to clean metal for brazing is to use a strong *flux,* or borax-based cleaning agent. However, this can create an additional problem. Flux may leave a difficult-to-remove residue. To minimize residue buildup, use a combination of the two: cleaning the joint, then a *low-residue* flux.

Flux can be found in three basic forms: powder, paste or as a coating on brazing rods. With powdered or paste flux you must heat the brazing rod 2- or 3-inches back from the end, then plunge it into the flux. This coats the rod with flux. This must be repeated as the 2 or 3 inches of rod is used. Coated brazing rods are available, but they are more expensive than plain

rods and separate flux. Still, they are much handier.

A good brazed joint should be smooth and bright, with edges that feather, or blend into the parent metal. A pitted or blistery surface or an edge that seems to stand on top of the parent metal, like water on a freshly waxed car, means an unsatisfactory job. A common brazing mistake is to overheat the surface. This shows up as a fine, white, powdery material on both sides of the joint.

Now, let's look at gas-welding other metals commonly used in autobody components.

## GAS-WELDING POT METAL

Yes, you can do a good job of gas-welding *pot metal,* or *white metal.* This is a zinc-based alloy used for cast parts, such as fender extensions, or caps. To gas-weld pot metal, you need a fluxless rod, such as ST-8 welding rod available from H. C. Fastener Company, Route 2, #27, Alvarado, TX 76009. You can order as few as five rods at about one dollar each.

The melting temperature of pot metal is about 730F, the same for ST-8 welding rod. Neither ST-8 rod nor pot metal melts immediately from a solid to a liquid. Instead, both have a *pasty* transition stage in a narrow temperature range. Auto-body solder, or lead, reacts similarly, but the temperature range for pot metal is much narrower. The correct temperature range for welding is in this pasty range—between the point where the metal begins to soften and the liquid stage. There is little latitude; tempera-

ture control is the key.

**Clean Part**—As with practicing any type of welding, practice on scrap pot-metal parts. If the part is cracked, file or grind a V-groove to the bottom of the crack. If the part is broken, bevel the broken edges. Make sure that all edges to be welded are clean so the metal is *bright and shiny.* Even the rod must be cleaned.

In addition, remove all chrome from the area to be welded by grinding or sanding, or have a plater strip the part. Having a plater remove it works best. You must have the part re-chromed after welding anyway.

Because of the porosity of pot metal, check for moisture in the area of the crack. To ensure it is dry, bake the part in the kitchen oven for an hour or so. Begin at 200F and gradually raise the temperature to around 400F. Don't heat the part too fast or the surface of the part may blister and pop.

**Support Part**—The part must be supported, or backed up, in the area to be welded. Otherwise, when heated to the correct welding temperature, the heated area will sag. To prevent this, rig a support. Any material that will not melt, burn or explode when heated to 730F will do for a support. A firebrick works best because it meets these qualifications and doesn't absorb much heat.

**Control Heat**—Adjust the torch to the smallest possible flame. Adjust the flame until it takes about 10 seconds at a distance of about 2 inches for the metal to begin to soften. A hotter flame is too difficult to control.

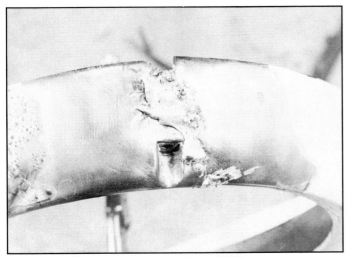

Although weld is not pretty, penetration is 100%.

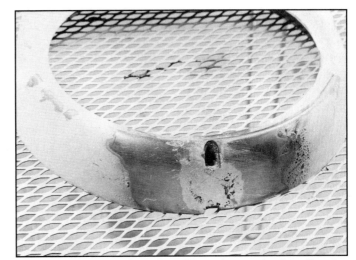

Weld bead is ground flush. Spot filler, primer and paint will make Thunderbird headlight eyebrow appear as good as new.

You must heat the rod and base metal at the same time. Put the tip of the rod directly on the area you are welding. Apply the flame to both the area to be repaired and the rod. While heating the two, tap the rod on the surface of the base metal so you'll know when the rod is beginning to soften and is near the correct working temperature.

The surface of the base metal will show small blisters or a slight sag or bulge when it's near the correct welding temperature. As soon as you see this, you should be able to push the now-softened end of the rod into the repair area as the two fuse together. Keep the torch close to the work. The instant the rod and base metal begin to fuse, you must pull the torch straight back—leave the flame pointed directly at the work.

If the torch is too close, the metal will overheat and you'll end up with a puddle of pot metal. Do not direct the flame away from the work and then bring it back. This will only cause the repair area to go from too hot to too cold. By pulling the flame straight back and leaving it pointed at the work, you can control the heat more consistently. When you get both metals to the pasty stage, keep adding more rod until a slight excess of filler material has built up.

After you've finished welding the part, grind, file and sand it until the welded area is flush with the surrounding area. Finish up with 400-grit sandpaper. Now the part can be re-chromed or painted; it should look as good as a brand-new part.

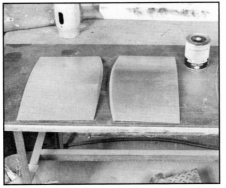

Aluminum pieces ready for gas-welding; flux and filler rod at right are cut from parent material.

Coat both material to be welded and rod with flux.

## GAS-WELDING ALUMINUM

Gas-welding aluminum is more difficult than welding steel or even pot metal because it requires a more delicate touch. Again, the only way to learn how to do it is by practicing.

Select pieces of scrap aluminum. Thoroughly clean the area to be welded with 400-grit sandpaper or 00 steel wool. Next, choose an aluminum-welding flux: Alcoa-22, Aladdin 73 or Union Carbide flux.

Mix the flux with water at a ratio of about three parts flux to one part water. Now, apply this to the area to be welded. It's best to apply it to both sides of the base-metal surface.

While the flux dries, cut 1/4-inch-wide, 8- to 10-inch-long strips from the same metal that you are going to weld. This is what you'll use as filler rod. Yes, you can buy filler rod at any welding-supply house, but by using the same material for welding rod as the base metal, you'll

be assured that both melt at the same temperature.

Turn your attention to adjusting the torch. Again, use a neutral flame. This is particularly important because aluminum oxidizes easily. Set line pressure low—about 2 psi to a maximum of 4 psi. With thinner material, the line pressure must be lower to prevent blowing holes through the base material.

Like pot metal, aluminum has a narrow welding-temperature range. The range is a little wider than pot metal, but a few practice passes will show you how easy it is to go beyond that range.

**Aluminum-Welding Lenses**—Unlike molten steel that is a bright cherry-red, molten aluminum and flux combine to give off an intense yellow glow. Because of this, the weld bead is difficult to see. Therefore, special welding lenses must be used for welding aluminum.

Start by tack-welding seam. This reduces warpage, which cause gaps, and preheats metal, making final weld easier.

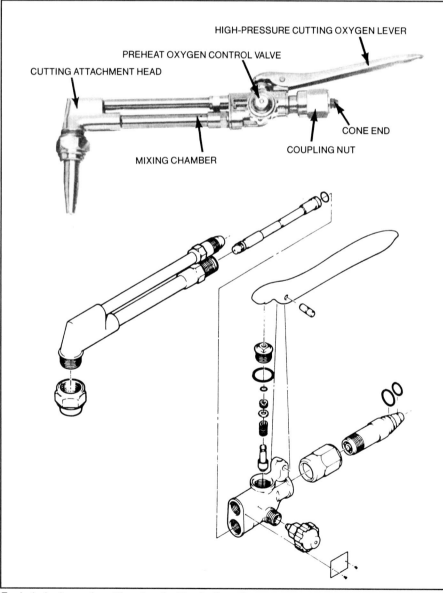

HIGH-PRESSURE CUTTING OXYGEN LEVER

PREHEAT OXYGEN CONTROL VALVE

CUTTING ATTACHMENT HEAD

CONE END

COUPLING NUT

MIXING CHAMBER

Exploded view of cutting torch. Torch threads onto main body in place of welding attachment. Photo and drawing courtesy of Victor Welding.

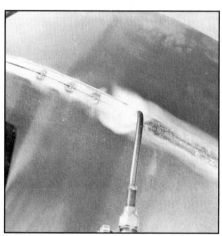
With extreme care and no gaps, aluminum-weld bead can be made without filler rod.

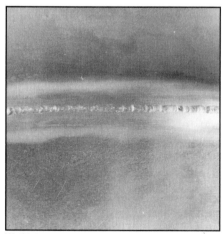
Weld bead after removing slag with wire brush or steel wool. If you had any doubts about whether or not aluminum can be gas-welded, you shouldn't now.

We strongly recommend the use of *cobalt blue* lenses for both eye protection and for better visibility. Cobalt-blue lenses are available at local welding houses. With cobalt-blue lenses, a handmade filler rod, a torch set with the 2- to 4-psi line pressure, the dried flux on the aluminum, you are ready to begin.

Use the same welding method as described for pot metal. But before you start welding, *preheat* the base metal. This is a good habit to get into when welding any type of metal—but particularly aluminum because of its *thermal conductivity* or, simply, its ability to rapidly absorb heat.

Heat the metal where you want to start the weld. Keep the metal pasty by moving the flame closer to or farther from the metal. Heat both parent metal and filler rod at the same time. Heating the base metal first will probably result in it dropping out before you get filler rod to the molten stage!

## FLAME CUTTING

Flame cutting is probably the fastest way to cut metal. The metal is heated to a molten stage with a gas torch, then it is blown away—*cut*—with a blast of oxygen.

Flame cutting is done with the same equipment used for gas-welding, except the welding tip is replaced with a *cutting attachment*. Remove the welding tip from the torch body and thread on the cutting attachment in its place. Some cutting torches have integral bodies. In this case, the hoses are disconnected from the welding-torch body and reconnected to the cutting torch.

Understanding the cutting attachment and the process of flame cutting will enable you to do a better job of flame cutting. Refer to the photo and drawing, page 36. Following are cutting-torch parts and their functions:

**1. Cone end and coupling nut** permit easy attachment to the welding-torch body—if the cutting attachment is non-integral. The tapered cone end is machined to mate with the torch body in place of the welding tip.

**2. Preheat oxygen-control valve** controls oxygen supply from regulator. To function correctly, oxygen valve on the torch body must be open completely—if cutting attachment and torch body are separate units. Preheat oxygen supply is increased or decreased by opening or closing cutting-attachment oxygen-control valve. Acetylene flow is controlled by acetylene valve on torch body.

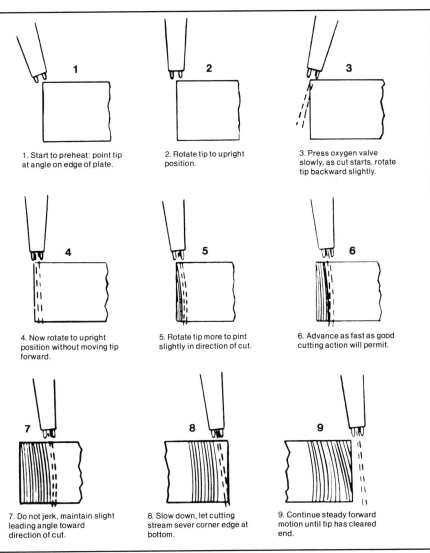

1. Start to preheat: point tip at angle on edge of plate.

2. Rotate tip to upright position.

3. Press oxygen valve slowly, as cut starts, rotate tip backward slightly.

4. Now rotate to upright position without moving tip forward.

5. Rotate tip more to pint slightly in direction of cut.

6. Advance as fast as good cutting action will permit.

7. Do not jerk, maintain slight leading angle toward direction of cut.

8. Slow down, let cutting stream sever corner edge at bottom.

9. Continue steady forward motion until tip has cleared end.

**As with welding, there is a proper cutting technique. Although material shown is obviously thicker than body sheet metal, principles are the same. Drawing courtesy of Victor Welding.**

**3. Mixing chamber**, located in forward portion of cutting attachment lower tube, mixes oxygen and acetylene to produce the desired preheating flame. Mixed gases flow through preheat orifices of the cutting attachment and into the preheat orifices of the cutting tip. These orifices—usually four or six—are spaced evenly around a central *oxygen orifice*.

**4. Oxygen lever** controls burst of oxygen from central oxygen orifice. When the metal is preheated to a molten stage, the oxygen lever is depressed, providing for a free flow of pure oxygen to molten work area. This burns and blows the molten metal away under high oxygen pressure.

**Practice Flame Cutting**—The first thing you'll need is some scrap metal to practice with. Start with a piece 1/4-inch thick or so. Lay out a cut line using *soapstone* chalk. Soapstone and holders are available at any welding- or machine-supply store. It works better than a grease or lead pencil because it is highly visible and won't burn away. Once you've established a cut line, turn your attention to the cutting equipment.

After rigging up the cutting torch, completely open the oxygen valve on the welding torch—if the cutting attachment is separate from the torch body. Next, open the preheat-oxygen control valve on the cutting attachment and adjust the oxygen regulator to about 25 psi. Close the preheat oxygen-control valve afterward.

In a similar manner, open the acetylene valve on the welding-torch body—cutting torch if it's the integral

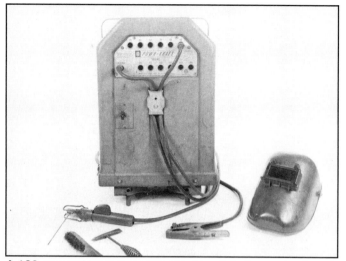

A 180-amp welder such as this should satisfy the needs of most home craftsmen. For arc-welding steel that's thicker than 1/2 inch, get a 225- to 230-amp welder.

Power cord is inserted in hole providing the *least* amount of amperage needed for sufficient penetration. Excess current gives too much heat and causes burn-through.

type—and adjust the acetylene pressure to about 1 psi. Close the acetylene-control valve on the torch handle.

As always, be sure you start by putting on your goggles. Even though the cutting flame may not seem as bright as a welding flame, there is still plenty of opportunity to damage your eyes. Momentarily depress the oxygen lever to purge the oxygen orifice. Open the oxygen-control valve slightly—less than 1/8 turn. Then, open the acetylene valve on the torch handle about 1/2 turn and ignite the acetylene. Increase the acetylene supply at the torch handle until the base of the flame clears the end of the tip about 1/8 inch. Reduce acetylene flow to return the flame to the tip. Now adjust for a neutral flame.

Do this by slowly opening the preheat-oxygen-control valve until the inner flame cone is sharp. This will give the desired neutral flame. Depress the oxygen lever. Note that the preheat flame changes slightly to a carburizing flame. Continue to depress the lever and open the preheat-oxygen valve until the preheat flame is neutral. You're now ready to begin cutting.

Support the cutting torch comfortably in one hand to stabilize the cutting tip. Leave the other hand free to operate the oxygen lever.

Now concentrate the preheat flame on the spot where the cut is to be started. Bring the base metal to a bright cherry-red. If the cut runs to the edge of metal, start there. When the red spot appears, depress the lever slowly.

When the cut starts, move the torch in the direction you wish to cut. Moving too slowly allows the cut to fuse together. Moving too fast prevents the metal from preheating sufficiently and the cut will be lost. You'll also get a shower of sparks back in your face and down your neck. Keep the oxygen lever depressed past the end of the cut line.

Reread this section a couple of times before you begin a cutting project. Like welding, practice is the key to doing a good job. Fire up the torch and start cutting on scrap metal first. The first cut will look like a fire-breathing dragon went after it; but soon you should be able to produce a clean smooth edge. Light filing or grinding should be all that's needed to remove any slag.

## ARC-WELDING

Although gas- and electric-welding may seem unrelated, the major difference between them is their heat source. Rather than burning gas, an electric arc is used in electric-welding to create and maintain the molten pool. So, if you've mastered gas-welding, you should have little trouble with electric-welding. All you need is different equipment.

There are many types of electric welders, but we recommend an a-c/d-c welder, or *buzz box,* in the 225- to 230-amp category. You can get by with 180 amp, or even one as low as 100 amp. However, a 225- to 230-amp welder is better, considering the relatively small price difference.

Although a welder may have a 235-amp capacity, it is unlikely that you would ever need this much amperage for your work. Half-inch-steel stock can be welded with 180 amps, 1/4-inch steel with 130—145 amps and 1/8-inch steel with as little as 75 amps. So the question is, "Why get a 225- to 230-amp welder?" For the same reason you like a car with a 300-HP engine—for the extra capacity. Even though you may not need it, the capability is there just in case—and the welder never has to strain.

Discuss your electric-welding needs at a welding-supply store. Outline to an *experienced* welding-supply salesperson what you plan to do and what your budget restrictions are. He will then recommend the welding equipment you should have. Remember, however, that the welder must satisfy your needs, not his.

The welder should come complete, ready to plug in. All you'll need is a 220-volt electrical service with a 50- to 60-amp fuse or circuit breaker to wire into. **Don't use the stove outlet.**

Although we don't recommend it, you can get a welder that's part of a kit. It comes with a welding hood, a *stinger,* or rod holder, and a ground clamp. It may even include a few welding rods, or *electrodes.*

We suggest that you discard the hood, clamp and stinger, and buy professional, heavy-duty ones. Hoods, stingers and clamps that come in kits usually don't last long because they are flimsy. If they seem suitable for your needs, however, try them. They

This state-of-the-art EQC helmet will set you back about three day's wages but you'll never get a flash in your eyes. The lens goes dark at the instant of the flash.

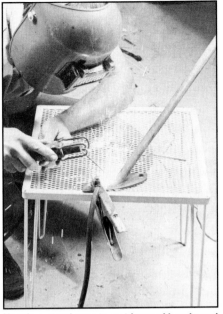

Here's a good way to get burned hands and arms from sparks and ultraviolet rays. Proper gear, including long-sleeve shirt and gloves, should be worn when arc-welding.

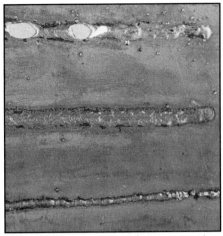

Weld beads from top to bottom: arc too hot, correct temperature and too cold. Too much heat results in burn-through and undercutting. Too little heat gives poor penetration and a weak weld.

will last for a while. You can always buy higher-quality equipment later.

**Electrodes**—Again, the electrode supports the electric arc. It also supplies the filler metal for the weld joint and flux for shielding the pool from contamination. Arc-welding rods are coated with flux. This melted coating, or *slag,* insulates the fresh weld, slowing the rate of cooling.

Arc-welding rod is sold by the pound. It is available in several types and sizes for welding steel. Don't buy more welding rod than you need. The coating on the rod deteriorates from moisture. Keep it dry! Consult your welding-supply salesperson about what type of rod you need.

## PRELIMINARIES

There's little about arc-welding that won't be revealed through practice, providing you select the correct electrode and set the welder at the right heat range for the type and gage metal you are going to weld. Refer to the instructions that accompanied your welder. As for how fast to move the electrode, how far to hold it from the work, and which angle is best, practice, practice, practice.

Before you plug the power cord into a 220-volt outlet, turn off the main switch at the meter box. Check that the receptacle ground wire will be connected to the welder ground wire. Also, be sure the fuse or circuit breaker on that circuit will handle the load—a 50- to 60-amp fuse should suffice. If the fuse or circuit breaker doesn't have sufficient capacity, the

fuse will blow or the breaker will open when you weld for any period of time. Conversely, if the fuse or breaker has excess capacity, you may set fire to the wiring.

Assuming that the above conditions are met, plug in your welder *to the special receptacle* and connect the ground clamp to the work or to the *steel* table the work is on. Make sure the ground connection is good or power will be wasted by heating the ground clamp.

In general, a bigger, thicker piece of metal requires a larger-diameter electrode with the welder set to higher amperage for more heat. Your welder should have instructions that give electrode-diameter and amperage information. But, because conditions vary so drastically from machine to machine, operator to operator and among power sources, no set rule will be correct for every application—particularly for amperage settings. Practice and experience will tell you if you are using the correct amperage.

Excess heat burns holes in light material, or the bead will be flat and porous. Also, the bead will likely *undercut* the work at its edges. Undercutting occurs when the base metal at the sides of the bead melts away, causing it to be lower than the normal surface of the base material.

Too little heat results in a bead that appears to lie on top of the work—penetration will be insufficient. The bead will be irregular and you'll have difficulty maintaining the arc. Finally, with amperage set too low, you'll have trouble striking an arc. The electrode will tend to stick or you'll have trouble maintaining the arc.

With the correct amperage, the arc will start with relative ease, laying the bead smoothly, without ragged edges. You'll have good penetration, but without undercutting or burning holes. With practice you'll learn to tell by the sound whether you are welding correctly. The sound of the arc should be similar to the crackle of steak over an open flame or bacon frying in a pan.

The speed at which you lay the weld bead can also affect penetration. Move too fast and penetration will be poor. Instead, the arc should be moved slowly, using a weave or motion described in the following pages to ensure good penetration and sufficient bead deposit.

**Helmet—You must have a protective helmet on before striking an arc.** A welding helmet not only protects your eyes from intense glare, it will protect you from radiation, flying sparks, molten metal and fumes.

The minimum *density,* or darkness, of a helmet lens for arc-welding is #9; #10 is ideal for most arc-welding. The darkest lens you should use is #14. A lens that flips up from the helmet is handy for starting welds and

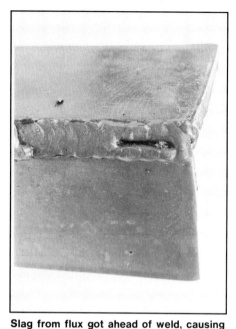

Slag from flux got ahead of weld, causing void at right. Not only is weld ugly, it's as good as no weld at all where slag displaced weld bead.

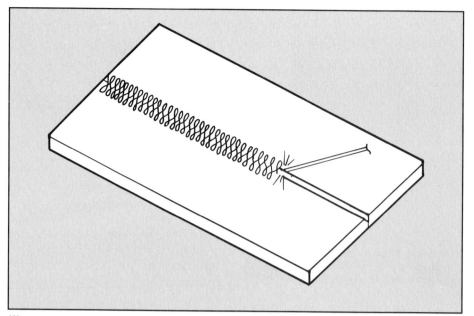

Weave bead is made by moving rod in a figure-8 or "Z" motion from side to side as you move along weld seam.

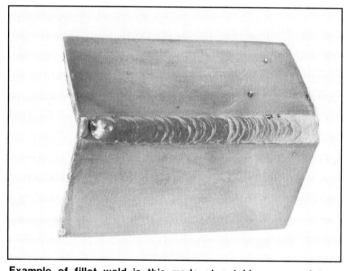

Example of fillet weld is this made at outside corner of two 3/8-inch-thick pieces of steel placed 90° to each other. Note tack-weld at left of seam.

Inside-fillet weld made on "L" shown at left.

Optimum butt weld: V-groove is filled with filler rod, there's good penetration, no undercutting and minimal bead buildup.

The Bilson-Vision helmet shows the lens in front of your eyes. Around the three sides you can peek out under normal light.

for protecting your face when chipping hot slag. In the photo on p. 39 you see the welder using the helmet just described. There are a couple of others available that can do a remarkable job. The Electronic Quick Change (EQC) helmet is one of the best examples. The wearer is able to see through the lens under normal lighting conditions. When an arc is struck the flash causes the lens to go dark instantly, preventing the wearer from getting a flash. There is no need to flip a lens up or down, it's all done automatically.

Between the hoses and pressure gauge body is the flame suppressor. The two hoses serve two torch bodies: one for welding and one for cutting. The operator can perform both of these operations without stopping to change bodies.

Another, less expensive model is the Bilson-Vision helmet shown nearby. This helmet has a dark (#9 to #14) lens in front of the eyes with a shade around three sides. This shade allows the wearer to see to either side and bottom under normal illumination. By holding your head up a fraction of an inch you can see the work piece. As the arc is being struck you need only move your head back that fraction of an inch to bring the protective lens in front of your field of vision. Both of these helmets are a bit expensive but if you plan to do a lot of arc welding it would be worth the investment.

**Clothing**—Gloves protect hands from burns. A heavy, long-sleeved shirt protects your arms. Welding with bare arms for a couple of hours will get you a "sunburn" equivalent to lying on the beach all afternoon on a clear summer day. Cuffless, long-legged pants are also a necessity. Cuffs are great spark catchers. There's nothing like a flaming pant-leg to make life interesting. Similarly, you should wear high-top shoes. A molten glob of steel in the shoe can make for some spontaneous dancing.

## STRIKING THE ARC & LAYING A BEAD

Now that you have an idea of what goes into making a good arc-weld, here's how you actually make the weld.

**Start Welding**—With helmet, protective clothing and gloves on, place the electrode holder in your right hand if you're right-handed; in your left hand if you are left-handed.

Position the end of the electrode about 1 inch from where you want to start welding. With a mental picture of the weld joint and rod position, flip down your helmet or helmet lens. With a sweeping motion, bring the electrode down against the metal to strike an arc. Immediately raise the electrode about 1/8 inch from the work. If you don't, it will stick.

If the rod sticks, swing the electrode holder from side to side until the rod breaks loose. If the rod doesn't break loose after a couple of swings, release it from the holder. Let the rod cool *before you attempt to break it loose* because it'll be red hot. Don't grab it with a bare hand!

Practice striking an arc using different gages of metal and amperage settings. Do this until you can successfully strike an arc and keep it going. Now you're ready to lay a bead.

After striking the arc, hold it for a second before moving the electrode forward to allow the molten pool to form. Keep in mind the arc-welding electrode is *consumable*—it melts away as you move across the work. To keep the arc and bead going, you must move the rod toward the puddle as well as from side-to-side in a crescent motion. Keep your eye on the point where the rod meets the puddle, filling it and moving at the same time.

**Stringer Bead**—The easiest bead to lay is called a *stringer bead*. It's created by making one continuous pass over the work without any weaving or oscillating movement. Right-handed welders move from left to right; southpaws from right to left. In both cases, it is necessary to tip the electrode about 15°. The average bead from a 1/8-inch-diameter electrode is about 1/8-inch high and 1/4-inch wide. Practice making stringer beads until you are able to make a smooth weld of consistent width and height with uniformly spaced "ripples."

**Weave Bead**—Another commonly used bead is the *weave bead*. This type is used for filling a gap between two pieces of metal. It's accomplished by weaving the electrode from one edge of metal to the other as you move along the weld seam. A momentary hesitation at each side of the weave provides the same heat at the edges as at the middle of the bead.

These are the most common weld beads, but how about the types of welds? Here are the most common:

**Butt Weld**—When two pieces of metal are placed edge to edge and welded, this is a *butt weld*. If the metal is more than 3/16-inch thick, each edge must be beveled to ensure correct penetration. These beveled edges should be about 45°. If the material is thick, more than one pass may be needed to fill the V-groove formed by the beveled edge.

**Fillet Weld**—A weld in a corner formed by the way two pieces are positioned to each other is a *fillet weld*.

## CONCLUSION

Our explanation of the welding processes are basic. Entire books have been written on the subject. Two-year college classes are provided for the amateur and professional alike, while master's and doctor's degrees are issued to those who have made a lifetime study of welding.

Obviously, we cannot teach you to weld. We can only describe the process. To truly learn to weld, you must practice, read books and practice. It's not necessary to devote a lifetime to the study of welding, but you should understand that there's more to welding than "melting" rods. The information in this chapter will get you started and provide the fundamentals needed to become a good welder.

Other **HPBooks**, such as *Welder's Handbook* and *Metal Fabricator's Handbook*, will carry you further into such exotics as MIG and TIG welding. For now, select some scrap metal and go to work. Cut them in half with the cutting attachment, then weld them back together. Practice all the different types of welds we just discussed, until you get them right. You'll be hooked!

# REPAIRING HIGH-STRENGTH-STEEL PANELS

## WELDING HIGH-STRENGTH STEEL

In the late '70s and early '80s, auto manufacturers introduced a new type of material called *high-strength steel*. This steel, because of its higher strength-to-weight ratio, could be rolled much thinner than previous low-carbon, mild steel, or about 0.024 to 0.1010-inch thick. High-strength steel could also be used thinner and still retain the same absolute strength as thicker mild steel. The result was lighter vehicles with similar strength. Let's take a little closer look at some high-strength steels.

High-strength steel is divided into three separate categories: High Strength, Low Alloy (HSLA), Special Aging and an alloy-free product used by Chrysler Corporation in their front-wheel-drive cars, called *Martensitic* steel or *Ultra-High-Strength Steel* (UHSS). Martensitic steel has a tensile strength almost ten times that of mild steel!

According to the world's auto makers, we can look forward to more and greater use of high-strength steels. In the late '70s and early '80s, Ford and Chrysler limited the use of these materials to body structures, reinforcements, gussets, brackets and supports. Most exterior sheet-metal panels continued to be manufactured from mild steel. However, the Japanese, specifically Toyota, began to use it in body structures *and* for exterior panels.

So what is the problem? This is it: Because of the high carbon content, HSS cannot be welded using conventional methods, particularly gas-welding. Some can only be heated to 700F. Others require precautions to prevent warpage. And *Martensitic steel cannot be welded or heated.* The crystalline grain structure oxidizes and disintegrates under high heat. If used, such a panel may cause a dangerous failure.

Perhaps you have seen old bones that have been exposed to the elements for long periods of time. These bones, normally very dense and hard, have become porous and brittle. Step on one and it will crumble underfoot. This is the result of oxidation, ultraviolet rays and other problems. It is also illustrates what happens to HSS after subjection to heat. So what can be done to overcome this problem?

## REMOVE PANEL

To remove an HSS-steel panel or another panel from such a panel, drill out the spot-welds or cut seam welds with a grinder. *Don't cut with a gas-torch.* To reattach panel(s), clamp the new ones in place as you normally would, but *MIG-weld them together if possible.* Otherwise, arc-weld them.

## MIG WELDING HIGH-STRENGTH STEEL

The first solution is to use *metal inert-gas* (MIG) welding. MIG welding is also known as *gas metal arc-welding* (GMAW). For our purposes we'll call it *MIG welding*. MIG welding concentrates the heat in a very small, confined area. By using a series of *plug-welds*—similar to the original spot-weld—you can replace an HSS part without damaging its structural integrity. If MIG welding is completely impractical, regular arc-welding may be used provided you follow the directions given below. Again, gas-welding should not be used to weld HSS.

## MIG WELDING— THE PREFERRED METHOD

MIG Welding, also called *wire welding,* is similar to arc-welding. The distinguishing feature is the inert-gas *shield* that protects the molten metal from atmospheric contamination. An arc is struck and a molten puddle is formed. At the same time a flow of gas envelops the weld puddle. The usual gas is carbon dioxide. Often, other inert gases such as argon or helium are used. Not only does the gas shield the weld, it also helps stabilize the arc.

Instead of using a coated rod, the MIG welder uses a wire that is automatically fed to the weld bead at a preset rate. Although the MIG welder will accept a variety of wire sizes, 0.03- to 0.035-inch-diameter wire should be used for welding HSS. At right, we've listed a number of manufacturer's part numbers for recommended wire for HSS welding. If you use one of these you can be certain of weld integrity.

Some advantages of MIG welding are:

1. Welding is fast.
2. Distortion of thin-gage sheet metal is minimized by the low current used; 1/4-inch plate needs less than 20 volts.
3. MIG welding is easy to learn.
4. Gaps are easily filled by making multiple welds, one on top of the other.
5. Overhead or vertical welding is relatively easy.
6. Different-thickness metal may be welded with the same-diameter wire.
7. All types of metals may be welded with one common type of wire.

So, if you have access to a MIG welder, use it for welding high-strength steel.

## ARC-WELDING HIGH-STRENGTH STEEL

It is possible to arc-weld high-strength steel successfully if you follow these directions: Use only

3/32-inch rods that meet AWS-E-014 standards; AWS means *American Welding Society*. This rod is specifically designed for HSS welding. Be sure your supplier understands what you want and provides you with the correct rod.

Rather than using continuous-bead welds to join panels, use plug-welds. A plug-weld is much like a spot-weld. Where two panels are overlapped at the joint, 1/4-inch holes are drilled through one panel at the overlap every 1 or 2 inches. These holes are then filled, or "plugged," with weld. This prevents the heat from spreading along a continuous line, causing a weak seam in the high-strength-steel panel.

## HOT WORKING HIGH-STRENGTH STEEL

You may want to straighten a high-strength-steel panel. It is OK to apply heat to a mild-steel panel to facilitate straightening it. However, replace an HSS panel if heat must be used to straighten it. And, if it's a door-intrusion beam or bumper brace, don't repair it—*replace it!*

If an HSS piece must be heated to straighten it, follow these procedures *as an example only* as most HSS should not be worked.

1. Temperatures must not exceed 1400F. A temperature close to this must not be maintained more than three minutes.

To determine this heat range, use temperature-indicating crayons (temp-sticks). These crayons come in a wide range of temperature ratings. Select a temp-stick that is designed to give you a reading *less than 1400F*—1350F is a good choice. Make a mark with it in the area you're going to heat. When that temperature is reached, the crayon mark will melt and disappear. Then you know the temperature of the metal is approaching 1400F and you should cease heating the area.

If you can't find temperature-indicating crayons in your area,

write Tempil Division, Big Three Industries, Inc., Hamilton Blvd., South Plainfield, NJ 07080. Ask for a listing of their Tempilstik temperature-indicating crayons.

2. When cutting body panels with a torch, cut the metal structure at least 2-inches away from the desired cut line.

This will prevent damaging the area where you'll want to make the final cut. When the section has been cut away with the torch, make the final cut along the originally intended dimensional line with a grinding-wheel disc, air chisel or metal saw.

## RESTORE ANTI-CORROSION COATINGS

High-strength steel is highly susceptible to corrosion. Because of this it is often galvanized or heavily primed with zinc-chromate primer. After working HSS, it's very important to quickly replace any rust inhibitor that was removed. The best way to do this is to use a primer rich in zinc. All major paint manufacturers make zinc-rich primer, so it should be easy to find. Apply the primer in two coats.

**Caution:** Zinc is very poisonous. Wear a good respirator when spraying zinc primer.

While we are on the subject of safety, there are a few other precautions we should mention.

## SAFETY

When using the MIG welder, wear a full hood with a #12 lens. It is worth mentioning again that you should wear full body coverage: apron, long sleeves, long pants, leather gloves and high-top shoes. MIG welding produces ultraviolet radiation and can give you a severe "sunburn."

Just as zinc primers are poisonous, so are zinc fumes given off during welding. To avoid inhaling these fumes, work in a well-ventilated area. Go a step further and set up a small fan to blow away the fumes.

To summarize, be aware of the following when working with high-strength steel: Replace an HSS panel rather than repair it when possible. If welding is necessary, use a MIG welder. The second choice is arc-welding; use 3/32-inch rod meeting American Welding Society Standard E-7014. Plug-weld rather than bead-weld. And, finally, *never weld HSS with oxyacetylene.*

## MIG-WIRE SUPPLIERS

| | |
|---|---|
| Airco Welding Products | A-681 |
| American Chain and Cable | Page AS-28 or AS-18 |
| Chemetron Corp | Spool ARC-88 |
| National Standard Corp | NS-15 |
| Reid Avery Co | 70S-G |
| Union Carbide Corp | Linde-6 |

To determine whether a panel is made from high-strength steel, go to your local bodyshop. The bodyman should have a set of Autodata, Chilton, Mitchell or Motor cost-estimating manuals. Ask him to look up your car. Knowing its year, make and model, you'll be able to determine whether a panel is made of high-strength steel.

These manuals are available from:

Autodata Manuals
P.O. Box 2913
Castro Valley, CA 94546

Chilton Book Company
Chilton Way
Radnor, PA 19089

Mitchell Manuals, Inc.
P.O. Box 26260
San Diego, CA 92128

Motor's Publications
555 West 57th Street
New York, NY 10019

Note: For specific information on the type of steel used for a given panel and how to repair it, consult your car dealer.

# 4 SHAPING SHEET METAL

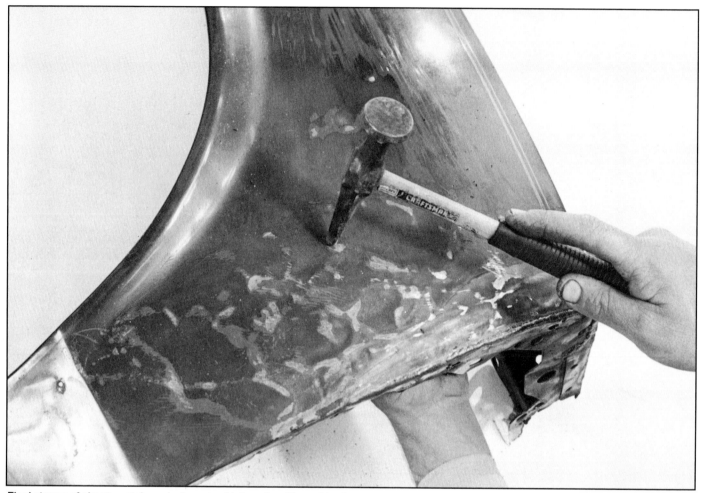

**Final stages of sheet-metal repair; lowering high spots with pecking hammer.**

Now we've reached the nuts and bolts of auto-body repair—shaping sheet metal. In this chapter, we discuss how to move metal—push, pull, hammer, heat—and, using a combination of these methods, return it to its original shape. Your goal should be to learn to use these techniques so you can do sheet-metal work that you'll be proud of.

Except for a frame straightener, all bodyworking tools and equipment are practical for the home craftsman. A body job that requires a frame straightener is probably a job that's beyond the capability of the home craftsman. This is not to say it's impossible, only extremely difficult. Therefore, we concentrate on work that you can do

at home. We also discuss how you can do heavy work using mechanical and hydraulic body jacks. Then we examine tools and techniques for lighter work. Finally, we show you some neat tricks, such as shrinking sheet metal and pulling dents out of a gas tank without drilling holes in it. No fair jumping ahead!

## ROUGH METAL SHAPING

Bodywork can be put into three basic steps: roughing the metal into shape; hammer-and-dolly work to achieve smooth contours; and grinding and filing to achieve a paint-ready body panel. If these steps are followed and correctly done, you will have little trouble doing bodywork.

Included in the step of roughing the metal is panel alignment. A collision in the right front quarter can affect the closing of the passenger door and hood. As the fender is roughed into shape, you must check alignments constantly. Do this by opening and closing the door, raising and lowering the hood, relieving a tension here, cutting and moving a member there. This is all part of doing rough bodywork. Roughing also means bringing the particular piece of sheet metal into general shape, including supporting members and reinforcements. These, too, must be pushed and pulled, heated and straightened so the *total* damage will be corrected.

The novice bodyman is always anx-

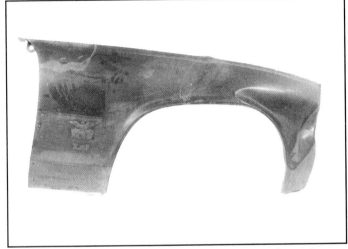

Although discarded in favor of a new one, a good metal man could've repaired this damaged fender in about three hours. We use it to demonstrate several aspects of body metalwork.

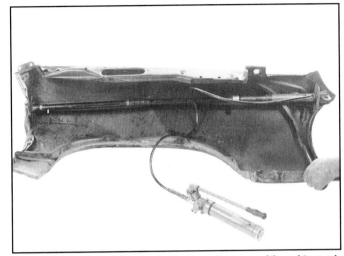

Jack, extensions and flat-end attachments are positioned to push front edge of fender forward.

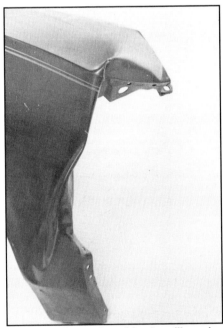

Damage at front edge of fender will require the most work.

stages will be successful are greatly improved. If the roughing stage is omitted or done improperly, all the hammer-and-dolly work, grinding and filing won't correct poor roughing work.

Once the rough shape is achieved and the panel looks more like an automobile part than the business section of a concertina, you can start the finer details of metalwork.

**Body Jacks—**When *body jack* is mentioned, the brand name *Porto-Power* likely comes to mind. The body jack is hydraulically powered. It consists of a separate jack, or *ram,* a hand-operated pump, and a hose in between. Because this device is relatively expensive, it is not practical for the part-time bodyman. A body jack can, however, be rented by the hour or by the day from local equipment-rental stores, and is one of the two handiest tools for heavy metal moving.

The Porto-Power body jack has attachments that allow you to perform many metal-moving tasks. By operating the pump, you can apply thousands of pounds of steady force to push or pull out the most stubborn dent into some semblance of the panel's original shape.

The body jack has no mind of its own. It pulls or pushes in opposite and

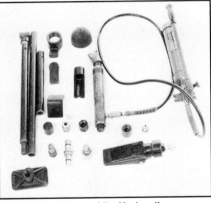

Basic Porto-Power kit: Hydraulic pressure supplied by pump at right activates jack. Assortment of extensions and attachments give needed flexibility for repairing various body panels.

equal directions at the same time. One end of the jack anchors to or against a heavy frame member or substantial body section. The other end goes to the damaged area, allowing the lighter metal to be pulled or pushed back into shape. This may sound simple, but it is easy to wind up pushing the supporting member instead of the damaged member. So plan ahead before you use a body jack.

When a dent is banged out with a hammer, there is a tendency to *upset* the metal—compress the molecules rather stretch them. This work hardens the metal. A similar situation can

ious to see what his finished product will look like. So he tends to move too quickly through the initial stages. Don't let this be your downfall. The roughing stage is very, very important, similar to laying the foundation of a house.

If the roughing stage is successful, the chance that the following two

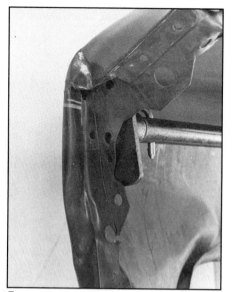

Front edge is rolled back on itself in a *fold*. Note position of jack end.

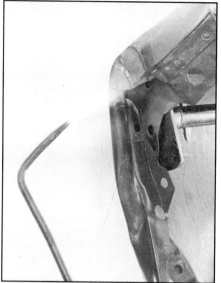

To prevent metal from tearing due to work hardening, area to be straightened is heated while force of jack is applied.

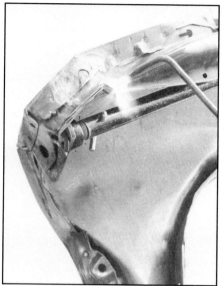

Heat is also used to assist with straightening buckled flange at front of fender.

All is fair in bodywork. Larry is using a 1x4-inch section of hardwood to reach a wrinkle from inside fender. Note that body jack is still in place. It will remain so until all pressure has been relieved.

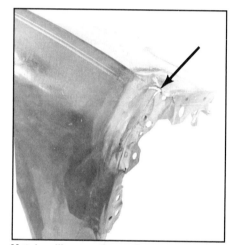

Metal will sometimes tear even when utmost care is used (arrow).

Larry welds tear and makes a few detailed repairs before moving on. Note clamps holding flanges tight against fender reinforcement.

occur when using extreme force to push a dent out with a hydraulic jack. Even though it may be easy to push a fender back into some semblance of its original shape, doing the final repair work can be difficult or impossible. The way to overcome this is by pulling instead of pushing.

Pulling is always the best method to use when moving body metal. This is particularly true with a large body-panel section that has a *low-crown,* such as a roof or quarter-panel side. Hammering or pushing concentrates the force in a small area. Pulling the metal reduces this tendency, resulting in less distortion and much less work hardening.

Determining the correct jack points for pulling a dent from sheet metal in-

volves several considerations: correct leverage angles, lift reaction, surface variations, and work hardening. Attach the jacks so the most leverage is applied directly to the bent area. As stated earlier, keep in mind that the jack applies the same force in opposite directions, so select a solid mounting point.

A wrinkle will have work-hardened areas due to the movement of the metal. When the metal is pulled back into shape with the body jack, the damaged area should be worked out with hand tools before the jack is released. Therefore, hold the metal under tension while working it back into shape with a body hammer and dolly. When the jack is released, the correct shape should be retained.

Jacks are fun to work with and serve a wonderful purpose in the body shop. But remember to move slowly. Don't try to rush. Move the metal a little bit, then stand back and look at it. Study it. Check to see if the mounting point is holding. Check other areas that were undamaged. Are they being moved? Are there any areas that are tearing? Easy does it.

In some cases of work hardening, the metal will become so hard that it will be impossible to pull or push a dent without tearing it. When this is the case, the gas torch can be brought into play. With tension on the metal, heat the damaged area to a *dull red.* A little additional force or some strategic blows with a body hammer should move the metal without tearing it.

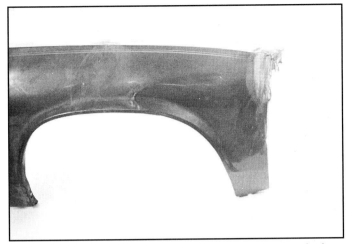

Fender begins to take shape. Areas that haven't been worked on directly regain contour, including wrinkle at peak line, directly above wheel opening. Hammer-and-dolly work and filler—talked about in later chapters—will get fender ready for priming and painting.

Fender is as good as new. Note: If you must leave metal bare for long—more than 24 hours—prime it to prevent rust. Primer or surfacer won't prevent rust for more than a few days because it absorbs moisture. So, install part and paint it as soon as possible.

Then recall our earlier words of wisdom: Go slowly!

**Morgan-Nokker**—A *Morgan-Nokker* is nothing more than an oversized slide hammer. It pulls rather than pushes large dents. It can't move metal as well as a body jack, but it has its place. It is best used in areas where body jacks are difficult or impossible to use.

Note the shaft with the heavy steel handle at the end in photos at right. A 10- to 15-lb weight slides forward or backward on the shaft to provide the hammer force. At the end opposite the handle is a 2-inch threaded section. This threaded section is for attachments: hooks, bars, chains or whatever is needed to get to the area to be pulled.

By attaching one of these fixtures to the slide-hammer end, hooking it to the metal, and sliding the weight so it slams against the rear handle, you can exert a considerable amount of pulling force. The speed at which you slide the weight determines the amount of hammering force.

Earlier we stated the problems of work hardening when using the Porto-Power. The same holds true when using the Morgan-Nokker. Unlike the Porto-Power, though, you cannot maintain tension with the Morgan-Nokker. It's necessary to be more liberal with the heat. Heat the area you wish to move, then make a few tentative raps with the slide. This will give you an idea of how much heat and how much force is needed. Then adjust the two accordingly.

The Porto-Power or Morgan-

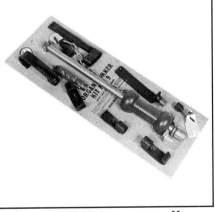

Heavy-duty slide hammer, or Morgan-Nokker, can be used for bumping out large dents. Kit includes all necessary attachments.

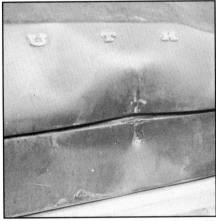

Mild rear-end "tag" is easily repaired with the Morgan-Nokker. Trunk and lower back panel was pushed in 1-1/2 inches.

As weight is slid back to bump back panel into shape, great care is used not to deform trunk-seal edge.

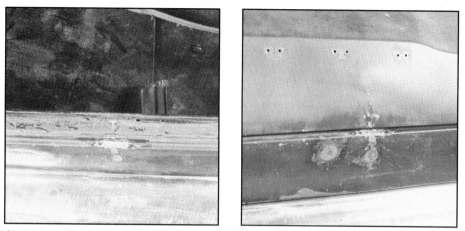

Six blows with Morgan-Nokker returns edge to original contour. Shrinking with a welding torch was required to restore panel to original shape. Trunk was also straightened with Morgan-Nokker, as shown at right.

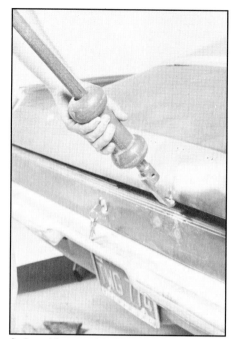

A few blows with Morgan-Nokker pulls bottom edge of trunk into shape.

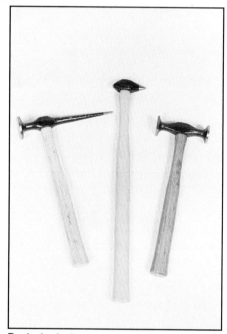

Basic body hammers used in every body shop, from left to right: long picking, short picking, and shrinking. Used in combination with the proper dolly, 90% of dents encountered can be straightened with one or a combination of these hammers.

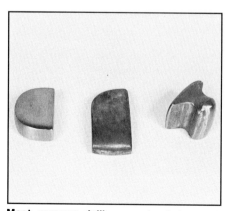

Most common dollies are: heel, toe, and general purpose.

Nokker can save hours of frustrating work. They can turn what would otherwise be an extraordinarily complex job into a relatively simple one. When the damaged panel or section has been worked back into its approximate shape, all major parts align, and doors, trunk or hood work correctly, you can begin the finer part of the repairs: hammer-and-dolly work.

## HAMMER-AND-DOLLY WORK

As the name implies, a hammer is a hammer—of the body variety, when used for bodywork. The next sentence should read: "And a dolly is a dolly." We'll forego that levity and explain that a dolly is a small, shaped, cast-iron, hand-held anvil.

**Body Hammers**—Compared to other hammer styles, body hammers are relatively light and must be treated with considerable care. There are many types and shapes of body hammers. Some have one head, but most have two heads, one with a large face and the other with a different-shaped large surface or a smaller and longer head. Which hammer you use is determined by the final contour of the sheet metal being worked.

**Dollies**—Dollies are no more than hand-held anvils. And, like hammers, dollies come in many shapes. Of the available dollies, the *heel, toe* and *egg* dollies are most common and useful. Which one you use is determined by the final shape of the metal being worked.

When used in conjunction with a body hammer, a dolly allows the metal to be formed to any conceivable contour. The question becomes,

"How are a hammer and dolly used together?"

First, the dolly is placed behind the metal to back it up. Then, the metal is struck with the hammer on the opposite side of the dolly in a specific spot. For the novice, accuracy in striking the dolly—sheet metal in between—in the right place is elusive. All it takes is practice.

In most cases, the dolly is hidden from view. Therefore, it becomes an educated guess as to where the dolly is in relation to the hammer head. As with any of the other techniques, it is best to practice on scrap metal. When you do zero in on the dolly with the hammer, the impact will be solid.

**Practice**—When practicing, the shape of the dolly or hammer makes little difference, simply that you have one of each. Place the dolly behind the sheet metal and attempt to hit it in the center with the hammer. Try moving the dolly around, hitting it with the hammer as you go. Move the dolly in circles, zig-zags or any other pattern while you strike the metal directly in the center of the dolly.

Once you are able to strike the center of the dolly from a blind position with each hammer blow, you're ready to try the *hammer-on technique*.

**Hammer-On Technique**—Hold the dolly firmly against the back of the sheet metal. With not much more than the weight of the hammer, strike the metal in the center of the dolly and let the hammer bounce back. The dolly will bounce a little, but do not let it move far from the metal.

Although you will be using light blows, avoid letting the hammer rebound and hit the metal again. Strike the metal sharply, allow the hammer to bounce back about twice as far as the dolly. Then strike the metal again.

This is the hammer-on technique. You are hammering on the dolly. The hammer-on technique is effective for raising a low point in the sheet metal. The opposite reaction of the dolly will begin to lift the metal even though the hammer is tending to push it down. If the dolly is held against the sheet metal with more force, there is an increasing tendency to raise the low spot.

Use this technique sparingly because it tends to stretch the metal. The term *stretch* is not entirely correct, according to body-shop terminology, but we'll use it for now. Proceed with caution. Too much hammer-on will cause "too much" metal where it's least needed.

**Hammer-Off Technique**—After mastering the hammer-on technique, try the *hammer-off technique*. Instead of striking the metal with the hammer in the center of the dolly, strike it adjacent to the dolly. This tends to push the metal in front of the hammer. The force of the hammer is, however, transferred to the dolly. As a result, the dolly tends to push the metal in a direction opposite to that of the hammer. If the metal was flat, it would force the metal into an S shape.

When using the hammer-off technique, hammer on the high metal adjacent to the low spot. Conversely, use the dolly to back up the low spot. Otherwise, don't use the hammer-off technique. It will simply distort the metal.

To find a high spot and a low spot, brush the palm of your hand across the metal surface. Closing your eyes may help. Even better, use a cloth glove or shop towel. You will soon develop the ability to "feel the metal." The hand can be so sensitive to surface irregularities in the metal that even the tiniest flaws can be felt. Use the hammer-off technique when you find a high spot adjacent to a low spot.

You must determine how far the

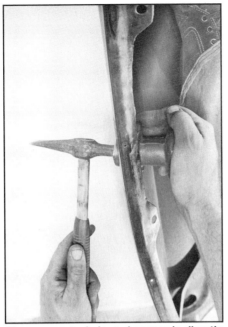

Hammer-on technique; hammer is directly opposite dolly. Go easy when using hammer-on technique so you don't stretch the metal.

Hammer-off technique moves metal quickly. Normally, hammer would be about 1/2 inch from dolly, but for clarity we show it farther away.

dolly should be from the hammer. Normally, the distance would be between 1/4 and 1/2 inch. However, large dents require drastic measures that may require the dolly and hammer to be 1- to 1-1/2-inches apart. Again, practice will show you what is required.

### SHAPING TOOLS
**Pick Hammer**—Let's examine the *pick hammer*. In general, a pick hammer is used without a dolly. Its primary purpose is to remove tiny dents in sheet metal, normally working from the back side of a panel.

The pick hammer has a standard face and a long, skinny pick, or head, that ranges from 2- to 6-inches long. If the pick is in the 6-inch category, it will have a gentle curve that matches the hammer swing. This makes the pick hammer easier to use. The pick end usually has a relatively sharp point. However, short picks are more blunted.

To use a pick hammer, first run your palm across the panel surface to find the low point. Then, using the pick end of the hammer, gently work the low area up so it's flush with the normal surface of the panel.

You can also work from the top of a panel to lower high spots. Generally,

however, the high spots are simply ground off with the body grinder. We're talking here about high spots that are in thousandths of inches!

The pick hammer is a finishing tool, such as grinders and files, but we've included it with the hammers because that's what it is—a hammer.

**Pecking Block**—A *pecking block* is used to back up sheet metal being worked with a pecking hammer, to show exactly where the metal was hit. How is this possible? The file-tooth pattern of the pecking block transfers directly to the opposite side of sheet metal where it was struck with the pecking hammer. After the low or high spots are corrected, the file marks are smoothed by filing or grinding.

Unfortunately, you cannot buy a pecking block. You have to make it. Use a 2-inch-wide *bastard*—coarse-tooth—file. Break it into two 4-inch-long sections. Sandwich the two pieces together or arrange them in a T-shaped configuration and braze them. Round the sharp corners with a grinder so the block will be more comfortable to handle.

**Spoon**—The third member of the hammer-and-dolly team is the *spoon*. Spoons are used primarily to flatten less-severe high spots to distribute

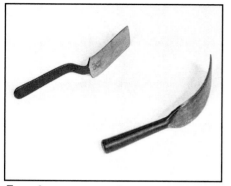

Two of many spoons that are available: at left is light dinging spoon; at right is inside medium-crown spoon. Spoon spreads force of hammer blow over large area.

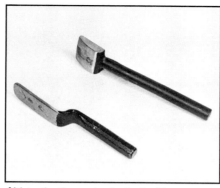

Although these tools look like spoons, their specific purpose is to reach into tight areas. They are struck with a hammer similar to a punch or chisel. Tool at right can also be used as a dolly in tight spots.

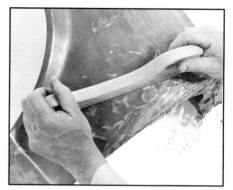

Body file quickly reveals high spots.

hammer blows over a wide area.

Spoons, like hammers and dollies, come in many shapes and sizes. Which one you use—*dinging spoon, surfacing spoon, medium-crown spoon,* etc.—depends on the surface contour of the panel being worked.

To use a spoon, center it directly *over*—not under—the area to be worked. Work outward from the center as far as there are signs of distortion. Avoid the mistake of using the spoon on too sharp a buckle. If you encounter such a buckle, go back and rough out the damaged area before you use a spoon.

Use a hammer other than a good body hammer. A ballpeen or claw hammer will be OK. This will help keep your body hammers in good shape for hammering directly on sheet metal. Remember that imperfections on a body hammer, dolly or spoon will transfer directly to the sheet metal being worked.

Grip the spoon lightly, holding it flat against the panel surface, but not so lightly that the hammer blow forces the edge of the spoon into the metal. This will leave a mark in the metal. After each hammer strike, move the spoon to another spot on the raised area until it is worked out.

**Prybar**—The *prybar* is the last of the major bodyworking handtools. It is a specialized tool. It was designed to reach into narrow areas to push or pry out dents—for example, at the bottom of a door, between a quarter panel and fender well, and in some cases, far back in the rear of a fender. Prybars come in 1- to 3-foot lengths. They incorporate many end contours. The ends can be center-punch-like, with a sharp-pointed cone, chisel-like

with a flat curve and a sharp edge, shoe-shaped with a sharp toe, or like a flat-bladed screwdriver. The most common prybar has a combination of the chisel- and center-punch-style ends.

Like the other body tools, use the prybar with care and go slowly! It's easy to raise a bump when you wanted only to lift a depression. With too much leverage, you can even puncture the metal. So be careful. Accepted prybar technique is to use a series of small pries rather than one large one. Pry carefully around the surface of the dent, working from the outer periphery toward the center of the dent, gradually pushing it out.

Use the prybar as a last resort. There are other options that we cover later. These may do a better job.

We have now looked at the first two phases of bodywork: roughing out, and hammer-and-dolly work. One section remains: finishing. Now that you've roughed out the panel and hammered it into shape, it's time to perform the finishing touches.

## FINISHING TOOLS

We must state one more time: Work slowly. Be absolutely certain you take each step as far as possible, and are totally satisfied with the condition of the metal *before you move to the next step.* This is important because you are at the stage where you'll begin to remove metal. If the panel is not basically smooth at this point, grinding and filing may go through the panel at the high spots.

Be absolutely sure you have brought the panel back to its correct contour, used the pick hammer to work out the low spots and are abso-

lutely ready to do final finishing. Keep in mind that most experienced bodymen can work a panel so well that there is little need to use lead or plastic filler to finish the job. They're able to *level*—or smooth—the metal with a few passes of a file or body grinder.

Some great bodymen can metal finish both sides of a panel without using *any* filler. Of course, these people are highly skilled, possibly with 20 to 30 years of experience. Don't expect to be able to achieve this level of perfection on your first job. Regardless, you should be able to finish a flat panel with a minimum amount of filler.

When you think the panel is in the smoothest possible condition, you're ready to use a *body file.*

**Files**—Although there are many files, we concentrate on the *body file,* see above photo. This file has the singular purpose of smoothing both sheet metal and lead.

When used correctly, the many cutting teeth across a body-file width remove minor surface irregularities that stand above the normal surface of the metal panel. When a file is drawn over a freshly straightened surface, the blade teeth cut the high or level spots and leave the low spots untouched.

The file should be moved along the flattest area of the crown, while being held at about 30° to the direction of travel. This produces a cutting swath of about 3 inches rather than the narrower width of a file. Also, it correctly applies the file-blade teeth to the metal surface. Your hands will "feel" the teeth cutting as you move the file across the panel. Likewise, you will feel it when the file is not cutting.

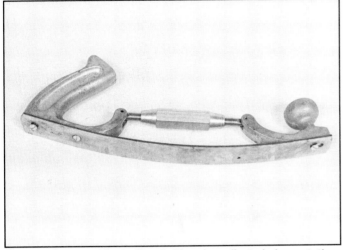

Curve of curved-body-file holder is adjusted by rotating turnbuckle. Use curved file for inside, or concave, curves.

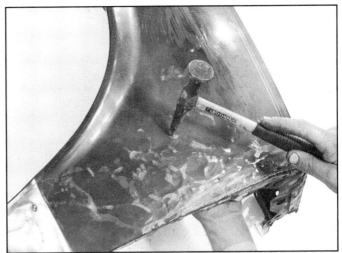

After file highlights high spots, pick hammer is used to bring them down level with surrounding metal.

As you pass the file back and forth over the metal, low spots gradually will appear. Use your pick hammer to lift these spots. Bring them up until they feel level with the normal surface. Then, make two or three passes with the file to remove any high spots brought up with the hammer. Recheck for remaining low spots and pick them up.

The body file will serve you well in this type of usage because it removes little metal. However, the next metal remover we talk about—the *body grinder*—will remove a lot of metal. Take care to avoid making the panel too thin.

**Body Grinders**—There are two types of disc grinders, or sanders, one of which we detail now. We talk about the second in following chapters. The first is the *body grinder*. The second is the *double-action (D.A.) disc sander*. The D.A. sander is used primarily on painted surfaces to remove paint or to smooth a surface. The body grinder grinds metal. This is the tool we're interested in at this point.

Like the file, the body grinder can be used to contrast low spots in the metal. Take great care to avoid removing too much metal. Also be careful to avoid running the edge of the disc into an adjacent piece. If this happens, a big slice will be ground out of an area you didn't want to touch. This is easy to do.

A body grinder seems to have a mind of its own. Spinning at several-hundred rpm with #34- or 36-grit

Both sides of metal may be worked with pick hammer. Here, high spots are raised.

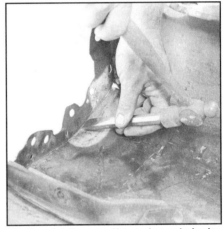

Don't restrict yourself to using only body-working tools. Chisel and ball-peen hammer are used to accentuate 90° bend.

sandpaper, it can "walk" right across a panel with no help from you at all. If you have never operated a body grinder, practice on a scrap body panel before you use it on a good one.

**Disc Size**—Disc size refers to disc diameter. Disc diameters vary from 7 to 9-1/8 inches, but the disc should not be larger than the backup pad by more than 1 inch. This will prevent strain on the grinder and the possibility of the disc disintegrating or coming apart.

**Grit**—Disc abrasive is designated by a grit number that ranges from very fine (#180 to #200) to very coarse (#16). As you can see, the smaller the number, the coarser the grit. Most bodymen prefer #34 to #36 grit for all but finish work. These discs are available in *closed-coated* or *open-coated* types.

Remember: Body grinder removes metal quickly. Use one sparingly and exercise all safety precautions.

**Closed-coated** discs have the abrasive grains completely covering the backing surface. Closed-coated discs are best used for metal removal.

**Open-coated** discs have spaces between the abrasive particles, leaving a portion of the backing exposed. This allows the open-coated disc more flexibility, with much less tendency to load up. Typically, open-coated discs are used for removing paint.

---

**SAFETY FIRST**
The body grinder is a very dangerous tool if not used correctly. Use every safety precaution, especially safety glasses, goggles or face shield. Even though particles are usually thrown off to the side, they can glance off other surfaces and end up in an eye, down your neck or on anyone nearby. There have been instances where discs disintegrated, injuring the operator or people standing nearby. Keep onlookers out of the work area while you're grinding.

Finally, think of the grinder as you would a circular saw. That rotating disc is just like a saw blade. If it drops or contacts your body, it can cause a serious injury. A welder friend of ours has a 10-inch scar across his chest where he was hit by a body grinder. So think safety first when using this or any similar tool.

---

**Practice**—The best area to practice on is the upper crown of a fender. Then you can stand up, work a flat surface from side to side, and a curved surface forward and backward.

Hold the body grinder with both hands, press the switch to start the disc rotating, then prepare to place the grinder on the metal. Holding the grinder so the abrasive disc is at a slight angle to the metal, set it down against the fender using only the weight of the grinder.

As it touches the fender, the grinder will move in a direction opposite of pad movement at the point of contact. When you have moved about 24 inches to your left or right— depending on whether you are right- or left-handed—angle the grinder in the opposite direction. The grinder should automatically move in the other direction. By tilting the grinder up and down, or right and left, you can control its direction.

Practice with the grinder until you

have a good feel for how it moves. Although great amounts of metal can be removed with the body grinder, small amounts can also be removed—if the tool is used correctly and with the correct abrasive.

Professional bodymen often use a disc grinder in place of a body file because of its speed. Don't attempt this unless you're proficient in the use of the body grinder. Here's how it's done.

Pass the grinder over the hammered area with one or two passes, right or left. As with a file, abrasive swirl marks highlight high spots and leave low spots untouched. Using the pick hammer, lift any low spots, then pass the body grinder back over the work area. *Do not grind the metal down to match the low spots.* This will thin the metal excessively and may buckle the panel due to the high heat generated by the grinder. Develop the lightest possible touch with the body grinder.

After you've finished hammering, filing and grinding, go back over the repair area with a file to pick up any remaining spots. There will be so many swirl marks from the grinder that the low spots will be difficult to see or feel. A final pass or two with the file will expose these spots.

When using a body grinder on a *reverse crown*—concave surface—it is often impossible to pass the grinder from left to right across the crown. In this case, the grinder must be worked lengthwise, from the area farthest from you to the area closest to you. Turn the grinder on the farthest edge of the disc against the metal and draw it toward you. Repeat this as necessary to cover the desired area.

Some bodymen cut the disc into a star-shaped pattern to prevent the edge of the disc from cutting into the metal. This star shape allows the edge of the disc to flop rather than cut. Obviously, the more severe the reverse crown, the more stars would have to be cut into the disc.

**METAL SHRINKING**
One of the most useful metalworking tricks is being able to shrink metal. As metal is worked—beaten, pushed, twisted and subjected to numerous tortures—it is thinned and stretched. The result is "more metal" in the repaired area than before the damage.

If a repaired area was originally flat,

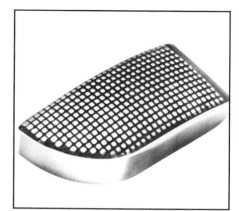

Waffle pattern on shrinking dolly is key to its shrinking ability. Shrinking hammer has same pattern. Each peak creates a small peak and valley, thereby decreasing effective surface area being worked.

it will now have a crown. If it had a crown, it will have more crown. No matter how much conventional hammer-and-dolly work you do, it will only make matters worse. To overcome this, the area must be shrunk, or *gathered*.

There are two ways to shrink sheet metal: *hot* and *cold*. Let's take a look at *cold shrinking* first:

**Cold shrinking** is done with a special hammer and dolly. Shrinking hammers and dollies have *waffle* faces. See above photo. Each has a pattern of raised squares covering its working surface.

You don't use a shrinking hammer and shrinking dolly together. You use one or the other with a conventional body hammer or dolly.

To cold shrink, first determine the size and shape of the stretched area. Backing up this area with a dolly of the same contour, strike the metal with the shrinking hammer using the hammer-on technique. Or use a shrinking dolly and strike it with a conventional body hammer. Strike the metal a little harder than when you straightened it.

After the first blow, look at the metal. Notice that the waffle pattern of the hammer head or dolly transferred to the metal. Small areas of the metal lowered while the others raised. This miniature lowering-and-raising effect gathers the metal, and can be demonstrated simply:

Crumple up an 8 X 10-inch sheet of paper—crumple and crumple and crumple, wrinkle it, push it, shove it. Compress it into a tight ball. Get lots of tiny wrinkles running throughout.

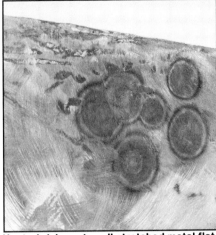

Heat-shrink spots pull stretched metal flat. Heat shrinking with a small-tip welding torch and a hammer and dolly is better than cold shrinking with a hammer and dolly.

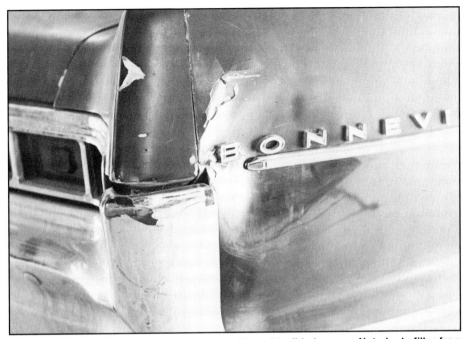

Parking-lot dent is a good candidate for repairing with slide hammer. Note body filler from previous repair.

After it has been crumpled and there are many tiny lines running every which way, flatten out the paper and lay it over a fresh piece of 8 X 10-inch paper. You will discover that the paper you crumpled is 1/8- to 1/4-inch smaller from top to bottom and side to side. This is because of all the minute "hills and valleys." Similarly, the shrinking hammer forms the metal, pulling it closer together.

Cold shrinking has its drawbacks. It requires more finish work before painting. And, an area larger than a coffee cup shrunken with a shrinking hammer or dolly is easily disrupted by body-grinder or hammer work in an adjacent area. Fortunately, there's another shrinking method.

**Heat shrinking** is quicker, faster and easier than cold shrinking. Larger areas can be covered and greater shrinking can be developed over the area of a panel. And once done, it stays.

Use a conventional body hammer and dolly in conjunction with gas-welding torch to do heat shrinking. We have found heat shrinking is best done by two people—one to apply the heat and the other to work the hammer and dolly.

To do heat shrinking, the center of the area to be shrunk is heated using a gas-welding torch with a neutral flame. Do this until an area the size of a penny turns cherry-red. Not only will it become cherry-red, it will lift dramatically in the shape of a cone as the heat causes the metal to expand.

The actual shrinking process starts now. Quickly place a dolly behind the red-hot spot and strike it three or four times around the spot with a body hammer. Direct a final blow toward the center of this spot.

As you are hammering the metal, you will actually see it shrink. What you can't see is that the same area also *thickens*.

There are precautions to observe when heat shrinking. Avoid the old axiom, "If a little bit is good, a whole lot is better." Do not try to heat a large section red-hot and try to shrink it all at one time. This simply makes things worse because it will buckle the panel. Keep the red-hot area about the size of a penny. Work three or four of these areas individually when shrinking large sections. Finally, do not try shortcuts. This results in the very best shrinking job.

One more step in the hot-shrinking process will shrink it even further. This is called *quenching*.

**Quenching**—Quenching is a process of rapidly cooling the heated area to "freeze" it in its shrunken state. By quenching the material, you can achieve up to 100% more shrinkage than with the heating, hammer-and-dolly work alone.

After shrinking an area with a hammer and dolly, quickly pass a wet cloth or sponge over the area. The longer the wet cloth or sponge is against that area, the greater the shrinking. Likewise, the longer it is held there, the harder the metal becomes due to a physical transformation in the steel. So you pay a price: Extreme quenching, hard metal; hard metal, the risk of cracks. Therefore, if you're planning more hammer-and-dolly work, use quenching in moderation.

Again, practice is your best teacher. We can describe the technique, but you must practice it to become proficient. We've seen bodymen burn holes right through a panel. This can present a bigger problem when you're trying to repair the dent. So, try heat shrinking first on something of little value. Practice until you are comfortable with the technique. Then apply it.

# QUICK & DIRTY METALWORK

"Quick-and-dirty" is a good description of some of the metalworking techniques commonly used in bodywork. These allow the bodyman to do a job quicker and easier. The problem is that speed and simplicity are a trade-off for what some would view as a lack of professionalism.

You must decide if these are techniques you wish to use. We present them for your consideration.

Oil-can-type dents can sometimes be pulled out with suction cup made specifically for this purpose. Suction cups work particularly well on large panels with oil-can dents.

Molding is removed by drilling out rivets. Trim letters push out from inside trunk. Fender extension must also come off. Paint and filler from previous repair will be ground off to get better view of dent contour.

Pulling one area and hammering another is similar to the hammer-and-dolly hammer-off technique. Note that pull holes are drilled on dent crease lines.

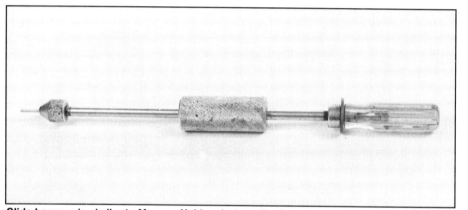

Slide hammer is similar to Morgan-Nokker, but smaller. Interchangeable sheet-metal screw threads into drilled hole. Slide weight is bumped against handle to pull out dent.

## PULLING METAL

**Slide Hammer**—These are intended to quickly pull dents from panels, such as doors and quarter panels that cannot be accessed from their backsides with a hammer and dolly.

The slide hammer is a smaller version of the Morgan-Nokker. It is so popular that you can find this tool in any parts house or most department stores. Here is an overview of the process.

Holes are drilled into the dented part of the panel. The slide hammer, equipped with a #8 or #10 sheet-metal screw at the end, is threaded into one of these holes. Then, using the impact of the slide against the handle, the metal is pulled out.

This process is continued until the dent has been pulled into some semblance of its original contour. Next, a body grinder is used to level the raised dimples made by the slide hammer. The whole area is then covered with plastic body filler, finished and painted. You can see how quickly this process would move along. But, heed this warning: The metal has been weakened by the holes. So, if the panel is damaged again, chances are it won't stand up to more bodywork.

Here's a more thorough look at the use of a slide hammer.

First study the contour of the dent. You should be able to find the point of impact. It will have lines radiating out to the undamaged area of the panel. To highlight the damage, draw over these lines with a felt-tip pen. Then draw around the full perimeter of the damaged area. Depending upon the gage of the metal, and the extent of the damage, select a #8, #10 or #12 sheet-metal screw for your slide hammer. Select a corresponding drill bit. The heavier the metal, the closer the drill-bit size must be to the screw size. Conversely, the lighter the metal, the smaller the drill bit can be. By making this judgment, you can thread the sheet-metal screw into the metal three or four times without pulling it out while using the slide hammer.

On the radius lines you drew, drill a series of holes spaced about 1/2- to 2-inches apart. As you get closer to the point of impact, the holes can get farther apart.

Now thread the screw into the outermost hole as if the slide hammer were a giant screwdriver. Tap the slide against the handle. You must judge the amount of impact needed to move the metal. If the first tap was insufficient, make the second one a little harder. Increase the impact until you can see the metal begin to move. Don't try to do it with one blow.

After the first bit of movement, remove the slide hammer and move it to the next hole on that line of impact. After working two or three holes, move to the next impact line. Start again with the outermost hole. Follow this pattern until you come back to the starting point. Work two or three more holes, lifting a little each time. Move around in a similar manner until you reach the center or the area of impact. If necessary, go back and repeat the process until the damaged area is back to its original shape.

After you've finished with the slide hammer, run the body grinder lightly over the damaged area. This should reveal any low areas. To bring up a low area, drill a hole in its center. Insert the slide hammer and bump it up to the level of the rest of the panel.

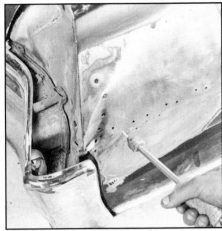

Working from front to back, dent is gradually pulled out. Slide allows a great deal of control by varying impact against handle.

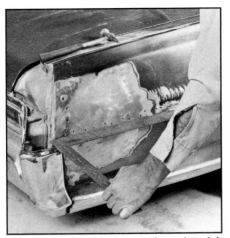

Carpenter's framing square shows how job is progressing. Always have a straightedge handy for checking work.

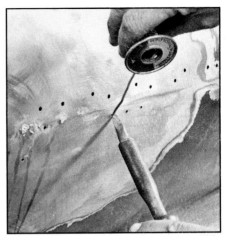

Filling holes with lead solder is preferable to using plastic body filler. Brazing creates excess heat, resulting in warpage. See completion of project on page 75.

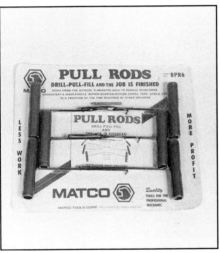

Pull-rod kits can be found at most auto-parts stores. This kit includes six pull rods and 9/64-inch drill. The bottom two are pick pulls—with fish-hook ends.

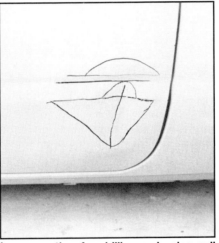

In preparation for drilling and using pull rods, dark marker was used to outline dent and indicate crease lines.

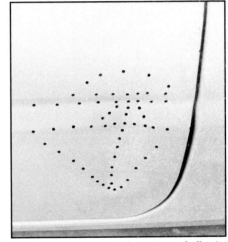

Drill holes for pull rods in pattern similar to what you would for slide hammer.

After you've pulled up the low spots, recheck the panel. Pass the body grinder back across the panel. If it checks out OK—the panel is straight and smooth—the only thing left to do is fill a number of holes. We'll discuss filling holes using both plastic and lead in the next chapter. For now, let's move on to the use of *pull rods.*

**Pull Rods**—Pull rods, or *hooks,* work similar to slide hammers, but with light sheet metal and/or where there is little crown. Examples are door panels, quarter panels and hoods.

Note that there are two styles of pull rods. One is a flat hook for pulling. The other, a more pointed hook, works like a pick hammer. Note also in the accompanying illustration

that you can pull with one or a number of rods. This, of course, depends on the damage and strength of the metal involved.

Pull rods are used in much the same manner as a slide hammer. Again, you must determine the point of impact, consider the radiating lines and drill holes. In this case, you don't have to make a determination for the size of hole. All pull rods are designed to use a 9/64-inch hole. In fact, in the pull-rod kit, you'll find a 9/64-inch drill bit. Working from the outer edge toward the area of impact, insert the rods and begin the pull.

On this page is a photo of a pull-rod kit. Each kit is provided with an illustration demonstrating the way a single rod or series of rods are used, and the

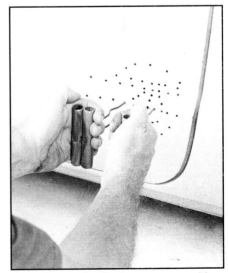

Using three pull rods at once; any combination that does job is acceptable.

55

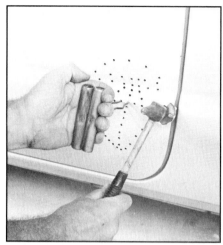

Another version of hammer-off technique, except pull rods are used instead of dolly.

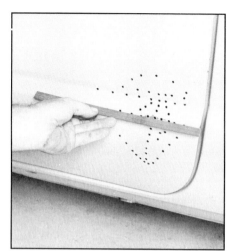

Check your work as you go. A 12-inch machinist's scale is used here.

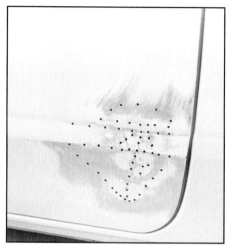

Low spots are readily visible after grinding. Soon panel will be ready for filling.

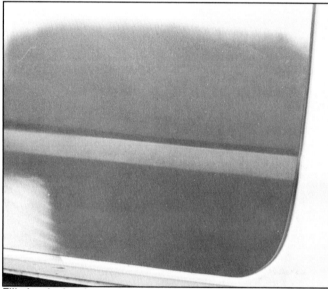

Filled and primed, complete job took less than 45 minutes.

Dented water tanks or receptacles are perfect for Uncle John's Penny Trick. However, do not use this technique on a gas tank or any tank that has stored flammable liquids.

manner in which the points are directed. On our demonstration Honda, the pull rods worked so well that the dent was pulled back into some semblance of alignment on the third pull.

Drill 9/64-inch holes along the dent crease lines. Insert the pull rod and pull out the dent. As shown, more than one pull rod can be used at one time. After raising the damaged area, go over it with a body file to highlight any low spots.

Notice that the pull rod with the point looks like a fish hook. This *pick pull* is used for doing the same job as a pick hammer—to raise small low spots.

Now, drill a hole in the low spot using a 9/64-inch drill bit. Insert the

pick pull and give it a few sharp tugs. This will raise the low spot without disrupting the surrounding metal. After all low spots are worked this way, pass over the area with a body file to check for remaining low spots. Work these in a similar manner. Finally, pass over the area with a body grinder, fill the area with lead or plastic and the job is finished.

These little rascals do a job and have their place in the bodyman's bag of tricks. Now we come to one of our favorites we call "Uncle John's Penny Trick."

**Uncle John's Penny Trick**—Uncle John has been a friend of the family since the '50s. A retired shop teacher, he spent most of his life figuring out the easiest, simplest and cheapest

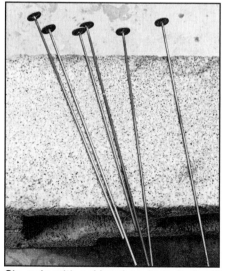

Six rods with soldered-on "pennies" will be more than sufficient to do job.

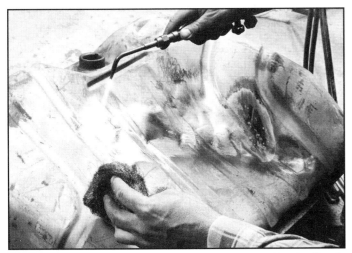

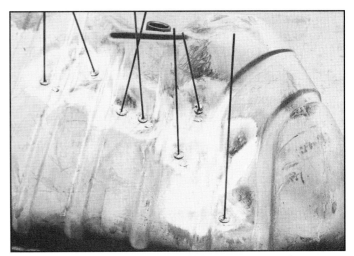

*Tinning* tank in preparation of soldering on "penny" rods. Small welding tip is used to apply solder to damaged area. Cleaning is done by wiping surface with steel wool.

Rods are soldered to deepest areas of dent.

ways of doing body-repair jobs. Rather than hoarding these methods, he passed them on to his students—and friends.

The penny trick allows you to pull up low areas the same way as with a pull rod or slide hammer, but without drilling holes in the metal. This works wonders on areas that are thin, or any area you wish to pull without drilling holes. Here's how it works.

The basic idea is to braze a piece of welding rod to a circular copper or brass disc the same size as a penny—a penny can't be used because it's illegal to deface or deform currency. Next, the "penny" is soldered to the clean, bare-metal surface of the dent. With a pair of Vise-Grip pliers clamped to the welding rod, the dented area is pulled out. The "penny" is then removed by heating the sheet metal locally. Then proceed with the filing or grinding. There are no holes to fill, though. Pretty nifty, huh?

Let's look at the penny trick more closely: Cut a 1/8-inch welding rod into pieces that correspond to the depth of the dent. Next braze these to "pennies" and allow them to cool. For the best contact, grind the opposite surface of the "penny" smooth. This will increase surface-area contact for a stronger solder joint.

Using a body grinder, remove any paint, dirt, corrosion or debris from the dented area. *Tin* the area completely, using a propane torch and very-coarse steel wool. Also, tin each "penny." Read about tinning in Chapter 6, pages 69 and 74.

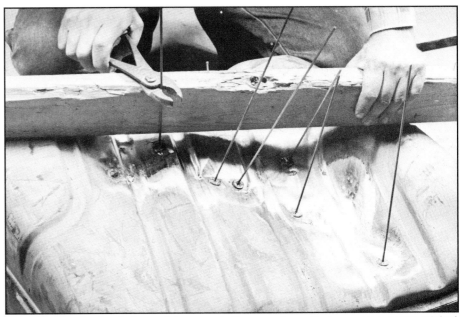

Pulling out dent using 2x4 as a fulcrum and pliers as a lever. Tank was restored to original volume and with no leaks.

With the sheet metal and "pennies" tinned, hold a "penny" against the surface of the panel. With a propane torch and solder, sweat the "penny" to the panel. You can also use an acetylene welding torch, but the tip must be small and you need a delicate touch. Quickly remove the heat and allow the solder to set. When you have the "pennies" placed along the lines of impact, pull the dent out using Vise-Grip pliers. Clamp on each welding rod, one at a time, and pull. If the dent is stubborn, lay a 2x4 on edge along the area of the damage. Then, bend the welding rod over with the Vise-Grips. Use the 2x4 as a

pivot. This will give you the force needed. When the dent has been pulled out to shape, heat each "penny" to remove it from the panel. Smooth the damaged area with a file and grinder.

## CONCLUSION

The only way to learn how to perform the techniques discussed in this chapter is to practice them. While doing them, you will discover new tricks and techniques. We have given you the basics. Remember to go slowly, be safety-conscious and strive for quality of craftsmanship *first;* then you can work on speed.

# 5 SECTIONING & RUST REMOVAL

Ouch! 1956 Thunderbird "bought it" at an intersection. Damaged sheet metal such as this can usually be straightened by a good bodyman. However, previous damage and rust has taken its toll. Note rust above wheel opening and body filler throughout—a prime candidate for sectioning.

## SECTIONING

Sectioning is the process of replacing the damaged portion of a body panel with an undamaged section of an equivalent panel. This applies to a fender, quarter panel, hood, trunk or any other part of a vehicle.

Sectioning is usually performed when a panel is too badly damaged to get it back into shape, or when the area has been repaired several times before. Previous repairs can leave the metal too thin to rework. When this happens, the damaged section is cut out and replaced with the corresponding section from another panel. This can save a lot of money, but not necessarily time.

Why would you sacrifice time for money when time itself is so expensive? In some cases, time is cheaper than the cost of replacing a panel. The severely damaged right front fender of a '56 Thunderbird is a good example. In this case, there is no such thing as buying a new fender from your Ford parts man. They are no longer available. However, you may find someone who has such a fender used. The problem is it probably would cost $1,000 to $1,500, and this isn't necessarily a complete, straight fender—just a fender.

After assessing the damage to the fender, the bodyman elected to replace, or section, the front half.

Here, he was able to purchase the front half of a '56 Thunderbird fender for considerably less than it would cost for the complete fender. This is because the seller can sell the rear half of the fender to someone else and come out ahead. That's how valuable these parts are.

The bodyman can, therefore, spend a lot of time on this fender and still stay under the cost of a replacement fender. As the photos show, the job can be just as good as a replacement fender.

Although rust removal is covered beginning on page 64, a tiny rusted area can be repaired by sectioning it. Again, this can be considerably less

Heavily damaged areas are marked and cut away. Note fender and nose panel are still welded together at lap joint. Seam will be separated later by drilling out spot-welds. For now it provides extra support for nose panel.

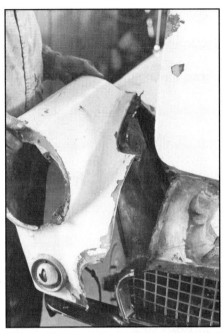

After cutting oversize from used, but good fender, replacement section is set into place for trial fit. Note that new grille and gravel shield are temporarily installed to ensure proper fit.

expensive than replacing a complete fender, quarter panel or door. Therefore, sectioning is a very important skill.

**A Quick Look**—Before we jump into a detailed explanation of sectioning, let's overview it. First, assess the full extent of the damage. Careful inspection will determine to what extent the panel is damaged. The panel will be cut just beyond this damage. If, however, the damage ends close to a seam, the cut will be made along the seam line. When the damaged section has been removed, a similar section is cut from the replacement part. Generally, this is cut a few inches larger so it can be trimmed for an exact fit.

Next, the new section is carefully fitted and aligned to the cutout area. It is then tack-welded in place and re-checked for fit. The new section is fully welded so it becomes an integral part of the body panel. Unfortunately, welding tends to warp and distort the metal. However, this can be corrected by *hammer-welding*.

Hammer-welding is a process of heating small areas of the weld seam with a gas-welding torch. A hammer and dolly is then used to work the red-hot area flush with the contour of the body panel. This heating and hammer-and-dolly work is repeated until the weld bead, warpage and distortion are smoothed and reshaped so they conform to the contours of the body panel. Hammer-welding is fully discussed on pages 62—64.

## SECTIONING BY THE NUMBERS
**Assess Damage**—Before sectioning a panel, assess the damage. Carefully define the damaged area so the sectioning can be kept small. If possible, make cuts along a factory seam. To find these, look on both sides of the panel for spot-welded lap joints. Such joints will be filled with lead on the exterior side of the panel.

Use a torch to remove the lead and expose the spot-welds. Drill out the spot-welds to free the panel at the factory joint. If this isn't possible, let the

damaged area determine the cut line. Check first to be sure you don't go through a support member or double-walled panel.

**Mark Cut Lines**—Mark cut lines clearly. Masking tape does the best job. If you don't like a line after you lay it out, peel up the tape and move it. Lay out cuts in this manner.

Now that you have them marked, stand back and assess your planned cuts. Double-check for support members, frame members, double-walled panels and above all, electrical wires. Be especially careful not to cut electrical wires, hoses or any part not associated with the panel you're sectioning. When you're sure everything is OK, begin your cut.

**Cut Metal**—*Never use a cutting torch to section a panel.* Several problems arise when you use a cutting torch. First, the heat warps and distorts the panel. Second, the resulting cut line will be ragged and covered with slag. Remember, you need a smooth edge to work with. And, if you're working with a mid-'80s or newer vehicle with

59

Contours must match and weld seams must be gapless.

Clamps and tack-welds hold section in place for accurate fitting and trimming. Time taken now avoids headaches later.

Trimming and fitting is done and redone until replacement section fits perfectly.

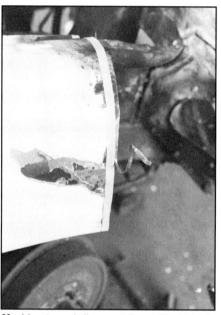

Masking tape defines cut lines. Final trim is made with aviation snips—oldtimers call them *Dutchman's.* Never use a cutting torch.

high-strength-steel body panels, the heat will harden the metal and cause the panel to crack and break.

If you have to make a repair that involves a high-strength-steel panel, farm the work out to an experienced bodyman. He should have the experience and equipment to make the repair correctly. Read about welding and repairing high-strength steel, page 42.

As we said before, avoid using a cutting torch to section a panel. Instead, use one of the following: Tinner's snips, aviation snips, hacksaw, sabre saw or hand or power nibblers. Any of these cutting tools will give you a satisfactory cut with the least amount of distortion and the cleanest cut. Using one or a combination of these tools, cut out the bad section following your masking-tape cut lines.

After the damaged area has been removed, clean up any burrs or ragged edges that may cut you or interfere with fitting the replacement section. Then use a hammer and dolly to smooth the metal along the cut line. Be very careful not to stretch the metal. Work carefully and gently. You're now ready to fit the new section.

**Fit New Section—**If it's not already done, cut out the new section just like the old section, leaving about 2 inches of extra stock all the way around. Again, don't use a cutting torch; use the same tools you used to cut out the damaged section.

Lay out the cut line of your new section. This will allow for any variations between the two cut lines. It's considerably easier to remove sheet metal than it is to add it. Note in the photo on page 59 how much larger the replacement section is than the section removed.

Bring the new section up to the body and clamp it in place. Use C-clamps, Vise-Grips or any other clamping device that will hold the section in place so you can align it. Adjust the new section until it fits perfectly. Check it against the panel on the opposite side of the car. Take several measurements from stationary points, then readjust the new section as needed. Check for alignment, centering and squareness. These steps are important. If the new section is welded in the wrong position, you'll have some serious problems. If you have to start all over again after trimming and welding, your sectioning job can turn into a real "monster." So, be absolutely certain everything aligns before you go further. Now, mark the new section for trimming.

**Trim Section—**With a sharp scribe, outline the contour edge of your cut on the new panel. Run the scribe back and forth until you have a bright, clean, easy-to-see line. Scribe all the areas you plan to cut. Then scribe *alignment marks*—marks across both panels and their trim lines. Make

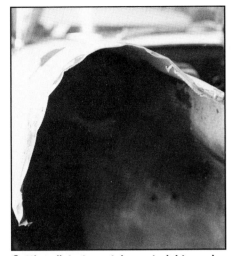

Cutting distorts metal, so straighten edge before welding.

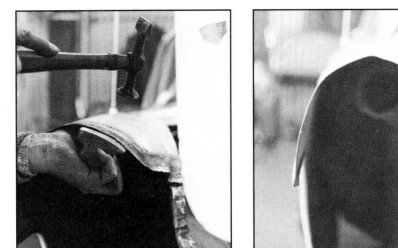

Hammer-and-dolly work straightens things right up. Note how close dolly fits fender contour. Compare fender contour before (far left) and after (right) hammer-and-dolly work.

alignment marks at the extreme ends of the section. Now, when the new section is removed and trimmed, it can be realigned quickly and accurately by matching the alignment marks with each other.

After you've scribed the cut lines and the alignment marks, remove the section. Trim along the scribe marks. Later, hammer and dolly the contours to shape. Reposition the trimmed section. Clamp it in place, being sure the edges butt together as close as possible—no gaps or overlapping. Check the gap carefully. It should not exceed 3/32 inch at any point. If it does, check for misalignment or burrs. If necessary, remove the section, and trim and file the trim line to get a better fit. Once you've achieved a perfect edge-to-edge alignment, you're ready to tack-weld.

**Tack-Weld Section**—If you have achieved a no-gap fit, you shouldn't need a filler rod to make the tack-welds. Tack-welding is best done by starting at one end or the other, not in the center of the seam. Then move to the other end of the seam and make another tack. Divide the distance between these tack-welds into imaginary quarters and tack-weld there. Divide those areas into halves and tack-weld again. This prevents overheating one area of the panel, and limits warpage of the weld seam.

As you weld, you may find the metal distorting on either side of the tack-welds. If so, you'll have to do some hammer-and-dolly work to even up the seam edges. Once the seam has been tack-welded every 2 to 4 inches, check the contour of the sec-

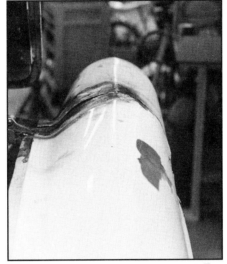

Crown and right side of fender fit well. The 3/8-inch gap to left of crown can be corrected with a hammer and dolly.

Final check of weld seam: File work on high spots will close gap. Paint and filler should be removed from top and undercoating and road grime from underneath about 2 inches back from seam before tack-welding.

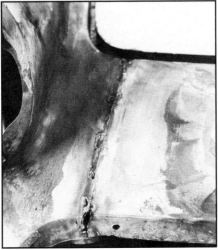

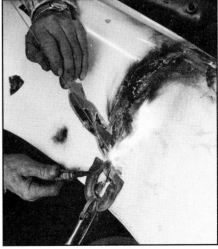

Tack-weld seams once everything is in perfect alignment. A *little* heat and a lot of wire brushing removed most of the lead at this joint. However, rewelding fender to nose piece was difficult because of lead contamination.

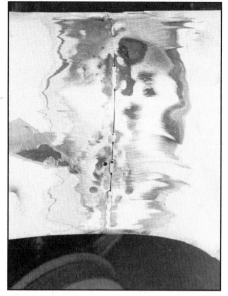

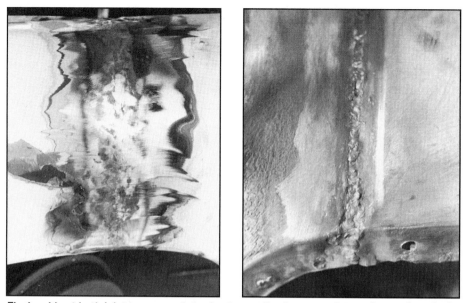

Tack-welded joint is ready for final welding. First, align seam with your hammer and dolly.

Final welds at both joints are complete; fender section is now an integral part of car body. Hammer-welding will flatten weld bead and straighten seam due to warpage from welding.

tioned area at the seam. Do this by comparing the contour of the area you are sectioning to the *symmetrically opposite* area—the same area on the other side of the car. If they aren't the same, figure out why. If necessary, cut one or more tack-welds and rework the metal. There's no easier time to change things than right now. So be doubly certain everything is correct. When you're satisfied, you can begin welding the seams.

**Gas-Weld Seam**—Although you could MIG-weld the seam—or if you're one of the lucky ones, *heliarc-weld* it—gas-welding is the standard body-shop approach.

A gas-welded joint generally leaves the metal in the area of the weld seam softer and with less warpage and distortion. This means less metal finishing.

Before you get set to do the final weld, make sure your hammer and dolly are within reach. The metal may move around as you weld. You can use the hammer and dolly to realign the weld seam as you're making the weld. And, use the smallest possible welding tip to prevent excess heat and the resulting warpage.

Weld the seams just as you did with the practice section. Avoid burning holes, oxidizing the metal or heating any one area excessively. When you finish welding, stand back and admire your work. Heat will have distorted the metal in the weld area, but hammer-welding should bring it back

Practice hammer-welding with scrap metal. Butt two pieces together and clamp them.

into shape. It's now time to get a helper for hammer-welding the seam.

## HAMMER-WELDING

Because of the high heat generated during gas-welding, the metal along the weld seam warps and distorts. To correct this, we use the hammer-welding technique. Refer to the demonstration photos on pages 62—63 as you read the following:

With the seam welded and the contour as close to perfect as possible, you're ready to hammer-weld. Hammer-welding can be done by one person, but it's easier with a helper.

Using a gas-welding torch, heat a 2- to 3-inch area on the weld-bead to a bright cherry-red. A 3-inch area is about all you can work without the

Tack-weld pieces together.

metal getting too cold. Then quickly, with a hammer and dolly, work the bead flat. Be sure the dolly matches the contour of the metal as closely as possible. Avoid sharp-edged dollies because metal in the red-hot stage can be punctured by a sharp corner.

Heat another 2- to 3-inch area adjacent to where you just hammer-welded and repeat the process. Keep your work area directly over the seam and don't try to heat-shrink while you're hammer-welding. This will come later if necessary.

You can now see that a partner is of great help when hammer-welding; one person heats the metal while the other does the hammering. If you don't have help, you'll need provi-

After tack-welding, align seam with hammer and dolly. Then, do your final welding.

Note how forward edge of metal is curled up and weld bead stands above metal surface. This will be straightened and leveled by hammer-welding.

Hammer-welding starts by heating a small area—1-inch diameter maximum—bright cherry red. Find a friend to handle the torch so you'll be free to do the hammer-and-dolly work.

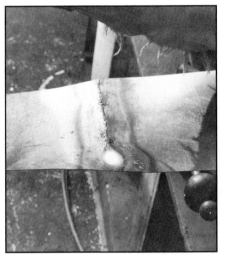

Before it cools, use hammer and dolly to flatten weld bead and form weld seam to desired shape—flat in this case. Repeat process until full length of weld bead is flat and seam has desired contour. Note: Some bodymen prefer combining welding and hammer-welding. Run a 1-inch bead, then hammer-weld it. Continue this process until seam is welded and hammer-welded.

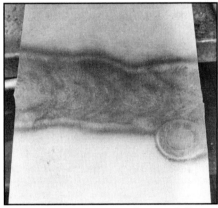

Hammer-welded seam is flush and distortion free. Note shrinking spot at lower right of weld seam.

sions for hanging the torch when you do the hammer-and-dolly work.

You must work the metal while it's red-hot. It'll be necessary to set the torch down quickly, pick up the hammer and dolly, and begin hammering quickly. Select something on which to place or hang the torch so it can't fall or twist and burn you or anything else. Make some dry runs with the torch before you begin working the metal. This will let you know if your torch "rack" is stable and correctly positioned.

After hammer-welding the full-length weld seam, recheck the panel contour.

Hammer-welding should, for the most part, bring the weld-seam area into contour with the rest of the

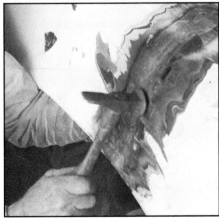

Hammer is a blur as bodyman *levels*—hammer-welds—weld seam. Out of view is helper with torch. Helper heats small area, then it is worked smooth with hammer and dolly. Process is repeated until entire weld seam is hammer-welded.

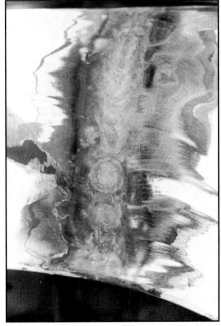

Hammer-welded seam: Weld is difficult to distinguish from parent metal.

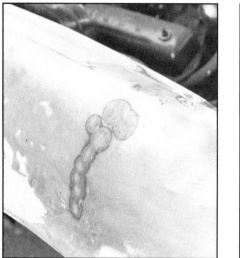

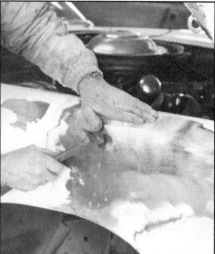

Final sectioning stages: Grinding, a little shrinking, some taps with a pick hammer, and job will be ready for filler. Note heat-shrinking spots at left.

Completed job, filled, primed, sealed, painted, assembled and ready to roll.

Who would have known fender was damaged? All that's left to do is undercoat bottom side to inhibit rust.

Once again, stand back and take a look at your work. You should not be able to tell where the seam is. The sectioned panel should look like it's one piece. Alignment and contours should be perfect and you should be ready for the final phases: filling, finishing and painting.

## RUST REMOVAL

**Cut Away Rust**—Rust removal follows the same procedure as sectioning. The only difference is that smaller areas are usually involved. Let's hope the rusted area you're about to repair is smaller than the sectioned area on our '56 Thunderbird fender.

You may want to use a replacement piece from another part or you may wish to make your own replacement piece. We demonstrate how to make a replacement piece later in this chapter. Regardless, you must clean up the rusted area.

With a body grinder or paint remover, clean the metal surrounding the rusted area. A body grinder is best because it'll reveal rust that's about to pop through. These thinned areas will turn red and then blue as the grinder is passed over them. Doing this will let you see exactly how far the rust has penetrated virgin metal.

Be extremely careful when using a body grinder around ragged edges. Don't let the grinding disc catch the edge. This will tear the disc or throw the grinder from your hands.

With a felt-tip marker, grease pencil or masking tape, lay out your cut line about 1/2 to 1 inch beyond the edge of the rust. Check the backside of the metal to be sure the rust doesn't go farther. When your cut line is made on perfectly clean, unrusted metal, remove the rusted section using tinner's snips, hacksaw, or any other cutting tool except a torch.

After you've pulled out the rusted section, use a file to remove burrs and smooth any ragged edges. Then straighten the edges with your hammer and dolly.

Don't throw the old piece away. Use it to determine cut lines for cutting the replacement section. Or, use the rusted section as a pattern for fabricating a replacement section from scratch.

**Form New Piece**—Some bodymen are left who can take a flat piece of sheet metal, then with a hammer,

panel. It is not the last step in the process to get a flawless panel, though. There is some detailed metalwork left. Not every area of the seam will be flush. Some additional hammer-and-dolly work along and around the area of the weld will be necessary. You may also have to do some heat shrinking to bring any stretched metal into place. This and the hammer-and-dolly work should give you a *near*-perfect panel.

The last step in the hammer-welding process is the same as that for other bodyworking processes. Drag out the files, body grinder, pick hammer and picking block: The detail bodywork begins. Work the entire panel to achieve that flawless contour.

For our rust-sectioning demonstration we selected a '56 Ford Victoria left front fender. Bottom of fender, behind wheel opening and forward of front door, is a rust-prone area for most cars.

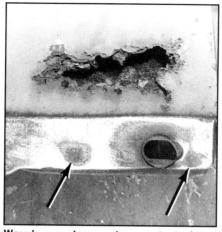

Worm's-eye closeup shows extent of rust damage. To find spot-welds (arrows), pass over suspect area with very coarse sandpaper. Because spot-welder makes depressions, normal surface is sanded to bright metal; paint on depressions made by spot-welder remain untouched.

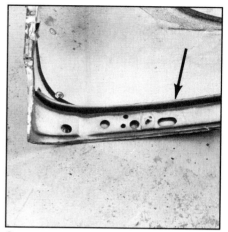

Spot-welds must be drilled out so fender reinforcement (arrow) can be pulled away from rust area.

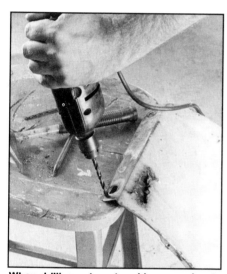

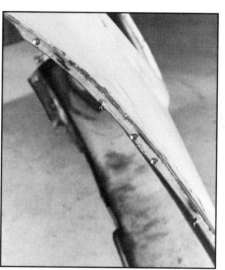

Reinforcement is pulled away to allow access to rusted area.

When drilling out spot-welds, remember to drill through one thickness of metal—not both. Pieces will come apart once all welds are drilled out. Holes from drilling can be used to *plug-weld* pieces back together. See drawing at bottom right.

dolly, *shotbag* or *sandbag, shrinker, stretcher* and *slapper,* shape a new fender. Fortunately, this metal-forming project is not as involved. We mention this only to point out that forming a flat piece of sheet metal with hand tools is not impossible.

In the old days of hand forming sheet metal, every bodyman had a leather bag packed with sand or lead shot. By placing a piece of sheet metal on the bag, and using a ball-peen hammer, wood mallet or a curved-faced body hammer, he could work that piece of sheet metal into almost any contour he desired. Sandbags or shotbags are hard to find today and are treasured by the bodymen who have them. Unless you have a dear friend with one, it's unlikely you'll be

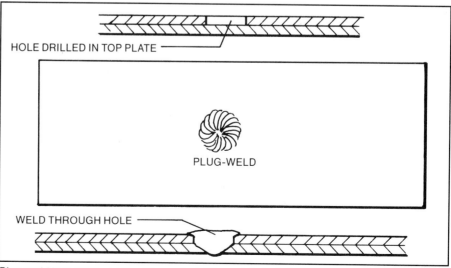

HOLE DRILLED IN TOP PLATE

PLUG-WELD

WELD THROUGH HOLE

Plug-weld is made by adding filler material through hole drilled in overlaying piece. Take advantage of holes you've already drilled—plug-welds simulate spot-welds in both strength and appearance. Drawing from HPBooks' *Metal Fabricator's Handbook.*

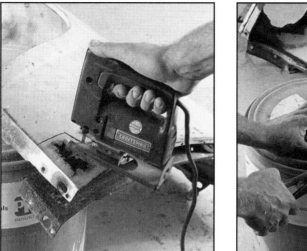

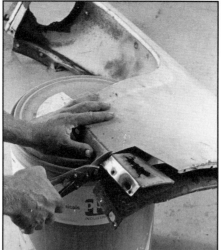

Saber saw is used in combination with aviation snips to cut out rusted area. Rusted section is used as pattern for making replacement section.

Blank for replacement section is cut to general shape of old one. Leave about 1-1/2 inches extra stock at periphery of blank. Final trim will be done after part is formed.

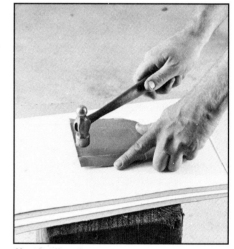

Our "shot bag" is this 1-ft-long 8x8 wood block and four pieces of cardboard. They will be used to form slight curve in new section to match rusted section.

Formed over edge of steel workbench with a wood block and hammer, 90° lip corresponds to fender lip at door edge. Larger 1-1/4-inch lip at bottom edge is formed later.

Hammerforming shape using ball-peen hammer over wood block and cardboard. Practice technique before you work on final project.

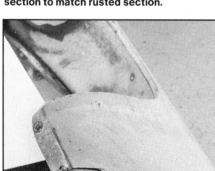

Clamped between two wood blocks in a vise, lower lip was bent to match fender. Fitted section is clamped in place so trim line can be scribed.

able to borrow one from the bodyman down the street. There is another way to achieve similar results, though.

At a lumber yard, buy the largest piece of scrap wood in excess of 4 X 4 X 8 inches you can find. The optimum piece measures 6 X 6 X 10 inches. Cut 3 or 4 pieces of cardboard from a cardboard box. Place these pieces on top of the wood block. Now, with the sheet metal on top of the cardboard, you can *hammerform* it into nearly any contour you wish.

Select a piece of sheet metal that's slightly heavier than the body sheet metal. For example, if the body panel is made from 16 gage (0.0598 inch), use 15-gage (0.0673 inch) sheet metal. Cut it 2 to 3 inches bigger than the section you wish to replace.

Start your hammerforming career by practicing. Using the hammer face of your ball-peen hammer or a slightly curved-faced body hammer, gently hammer in the center of the metal. Tap around in circles, moving from the center out. If you repeat this process over and over, you will eventually have a large bowl-shaped piece of metal. Unless you are making a headlight bucket, chances are this is not the contour you wish.

We'll assume that you do need a curved contour. The more you work the center of the metal, the deeper the contour will get. The more you work out from the center, the shallower it will be. Count on going through a few pieces of metal before you get the hang of this technique. But by doing

When fit is perfect, section is put in place for tack-welding. Inside edge of bottom flange needs to be trimmed before repair section is tack-welded.

Tack-weld section at opposite ends, then add tacks in between. Use hammer and dolly to align seam edges before final weld is made.

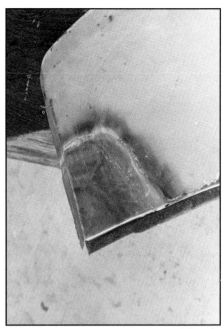

Final weld is made; hammer-welding is next step.

it, you should get the feel of it very quickly.

Once you are comfortable with hammerforming sheet metal, turn your attention to making the repair section. Work the metal atop the cardboard and block until you feel the contour is close to original. Trial-fit the piece in the cut-out area. Check its contour on the other side of the car, working and checking until you're satisfied with its shape. Then, clamp the section in place, scribe, cut, tack-weld and hammer-weld it, just as you would if you were sectioning a large piece of the panel.

This is the correct way to repair a rust-damaged area. You have seen other types of repairs ranging from a relatively good repair job with fiberglass, to a job where a ''professional bodyman'' filled a rusted area with a wadded T-shirt, spread plastic filler over it, ground it smooth, primed and painted it, and called it good! Obviously, we don't recommend this technique, so we won't demonstrate it.

If you choose the T-shirt-and-filler method, don't expect the repair job to last long. If you plan to keep the car and want to be proud of your work, use the method we described earlier. The repair will be just as strong as the original. There'll be much less chance of the paint cracking. And it should take considerably longer to rust out this time if you rustproof the backside of the panel with paint, undercoating or oil.

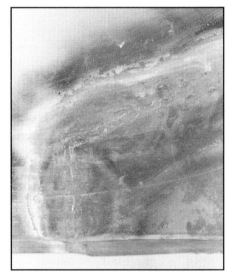

Finished hammer-weld job: Hammer-and-dolly work and grinding will complete sectioning job. Reinforcement will be rejoined to fender by plug-welding holes drilled in old spot-welds. Filler, primer and paint will complete rust repair.

# 6 PERFECT PANEL

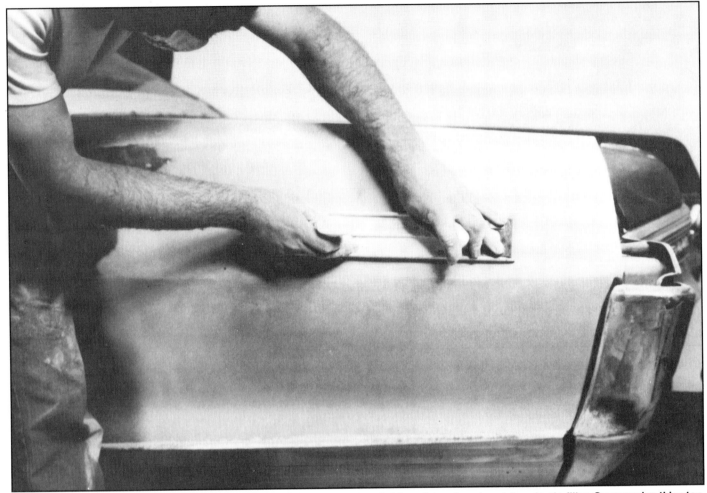

Final stages of achieving perfect panel: Leveling plastic filler after doing finish metalwork and applying plastic filler. Compromise this step and you compromise final paint.

Now that the panel is straight and rust-free, wouldn't it be nice if you could throw on the paint without doing more bodywork? The problem with this is that every flaw would show—nicks, scratches, hammer-dings or any other surface irregularities. No matter how thick you apply paint, it won't correct poor or unfinished bodywork. That's the stage we're at now—ready to do final bodywork finishing.

More than any other stage of bodywork, this one shows off the talents of the bodyman in the final paint. Is the panel finished well enough to support a black-lacquer job? Dark colors show flaws the most, and black

is the worst. If it's good enough for black, it's good for any color.

## THE PERFECT PANEL

Two methods are used to achieve the *perfect panel*—a panel that is ready for paint. The first method is called *finish metalwork*. Here, a pick hammer and file are used to work the metal until it is flawless. Every dip is raised, every high point lowered. Then the panel is filed. It is worked until it looks and feels smooth. The second method uses *body fillers*.

One problem encountered when doing finish metalwork is removing excess metal, possibly even going through the metal. And, because

finish bodywork is time-consuming, you must have patience to do a good job.

Body filler allows you to build up an area and file it without removing much metal. You don't have to raise every single low spot. Lead or plastic filler can be used to do the final smoothing. However, if you have the time and patience, by all means try finish metalwork. If you can do it, you'll have a tremendous sense of pride and accomplishment.

In this chapter we discuss fillers used in paint and body shops. We discuss tools for working fillers and demonstrate how they are used to achieve the perfect panel.

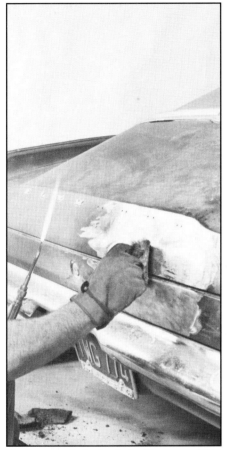

Tinning area to be leaded with gas-welding torch, steel wool and tinning compound. Read about leading on page 73.

## HEAVY BODY FILLERS

There are two types of *heavy body fillers:* lead and plastic. Although plastic has an undeserved bad reputation, it is more widely used than lead. The mystique, however, is in favor of lead. An antique, classic or special-interest car buff would roll over and die before he would allow a bodyman to use plastic filler on his pride and joy. Finish metalwork and lead are all that would be tolerated.

**Plastic Filler**—Plastic's bad reputation came from its overuse following its introduction in the early '50s.

Under the trade name *Black Magic,* plastic body filler fell into the hands of novice auto customizers and fast-buck bodymen. Why take the time and effort needed to straighten a dent? Mix it with *catalyst*—curing or hardening agent—fill the dent, let the filler harden, sand, prime and paint it and call it good! So what if all 10 pounds of filler falls out the following month? The job is out the door and the money is in the pocket.

Eventually, Black Magic gave way to another plastic filler called *Bondo.* Now, Bondo has become synonymous with plastic filler. Unfortunately, it has also assumed the bad reputation.

Be aware that plastic body filler is an excellent body material when used correctly. It adheres well and works quickly and easily, is economical and, *when applied in layers less than 1/8-inch thick,* endures as well as or better than lead! This has been plastic's nemesis since its introduction—not adhering to a panel. More often than not, it was used to replace metal, such as rust holes, rather than for its primary function—as a filler.

**Lead Filler**—Like plastic filler, lead also has its place and its bad reputation. Similar to plastic, lead was used often in place of metalwork. And, when used improperly, it fell out too. The reason you seldom hear of lead falling out nowadays is because it is rarely used. When lead is used, it's done with discretion because of its cost. No one can afford to overuse lead the way they do plastic.

Lead has one great advantage over plastic: When used sparingly, additional hammer-and-dolly work can be performed over the lead. It won't crack, chip or break loose. The disadvantages of using lead are numerous: It's slow, expensive and wasteful—unless you are willing to sweep up the shavings, remelt them and use the lead over. The real attribute of lead, however, is that it is fun to work with. And, in spite of its shortcomings, its mystique still serves it well. You'll feel like you've accomplished something after completing your first leading job.

"Yes, Virginia," there really is a thing called *Bondo!* So many manufacturers have plastic body filler that we tend to view them all as Bondo—one manufacturer's trade name. Accompanying gallon of body filler is hardener (catalyst), plastic spreaders, a Surform file and a body-filler file manufactured by Bondo.

### LEAD POISONING

You've probably heard about the dangers of lead poisoning. These are true! And, you can get lead poisoning from using lead body solder. Here's how to avoid the problem.

Don't smoke, eat or drink while handling lead. Wash your hands and face with soap and water immediately after handling lead.

Don't breathe fumes from overheated-lead solder. Lead heated to over 1000F will generate fumes that poison. Keep the temperature between 250 and 900F and there's almost no danger. So how will you know what the temperature of the lead is? You won't. Fumes will be minimal if you only heat the lead enough to make it pasty; just enough so it flows—no more.

Harmful effects of absorbing lead into the human body are largely cumulative. If exposure is for an extended period of time—years—lead can accumulate in the body and cause various nervous disorders and anemia. Paralysis and death can occur in extreme cases. Regardless, if you experience colic, muscular cramps or constipation when using lead, stop immediately and consult a physician.

**Plastic vs. Lead**—If you have to add more lead to an area you've just leaded, say goodbye to the lead that lies within an 8-inch radius. Because heat is needed to apply lead, it melts when you reapply heat. Plastic does not suffer from this shortcoming, so you can add new plastic filler, which bonds readily to the old. In fact, with plastic filler, you can build up and cut down as many times as needed until you've achieved the correct shape.

Plastic is flexible. It will stand a lot of stress without breaking or cracking. But, it will not withstand sharp blows. Other disadvantages are its tendency to pit, adhere poorly, and crack when incorrectly applied. These disadvantages are overcome by its relative low cost, its ease of use and wide availability. So use it in good conscience and follow the directions provided—it should serve you well.

## LIGHT BODY FILLERS

**Light body fillers** are those materials sprayed or spread on a body surface to fill the tiniest imperfections. Typically, light body fillers contain solids in a liquid carrier. The ratio of solid to liquid determines what they are called and how they are used. Of these materials, paint primer has the least solids-to-carrier ratio.

**Primer & Primer/Surfacer**—Not only do small imperfections show when paint is applied directly to bare metal, it can also shrink and fall off. Paint needs something to cling to.

Our main interest is with primer/surfacer. Primer is used as a bonding agent between metal and paint. With a 20/80 solids-to-carrier ratio, primer has little ability to fill voids in the surface beneath it. Primer/surfacer has a 60/40 solids-to-carrier ratio. We prefer using primer/surfacer because it serves both needs: that of a metal primer and surface filler.

Primer/surfacer may be obtained in both lacquer-base, enamel-base and water-base carriers. When thinned with the proper reducer, it can be sprayed on metal, lead or plastic.

**Glazing Putty**—Designed to fill larger voids and some pinholes, *glazing putty* contains 80% solids. Consequently, it cannot be sprayed. Instead, glazing putty is applied with a spreader. Its cousin, *spot putty,* has the largest percentage of solids.

There are many types of sandpaper, each for a particular bodyworking application. Sandpaper is expensive, so use it wisely—but time is even more expensive. Trying to make a worn-out sheet of sandpaper last forever is false economy. When it quits cutting, don't waste time. Get a new sheet.

**Spot Putty**—*Spot putty* is similar to plastic filler in viscosity. With 90% solids, spot putty can be used to fill 1/16-inch-deep voids. Like glazing putty, spot putty is applied with a spreader.

**Polyester Filler**—A relatively new product, polyester filler is a combination of surfacer and plastic filler. *Featherfill*—the most common brand—polyester filler opened up a whole new vista to the bodyman. To understand the advantage of polyester filler, let's take a look at the greatest shortcoming of conventional light filler—shrinkage.

The tendency of filler to shrink is caused by evaporation of its carrier and reducer. Here's what typically happens: The bodyman applies the light filler, allows it to dry for 30 minutes and levels the surface. He returns the next day and discovers that the surface scratches beneath the filler show through.

Continued evaporation and the resulting shrinkage caused this. Usually, the problem can be corrected with additional sanding. The real problem arises when it is necessary to paint the area within a few hours of applying the light filler. The carrier and reducer evaporate under the paint, causing the filler to shrink into the sanding scratches and other surface imperfections. This shrinking draws the paint with it. Polyester filler helps overcome this problem.

Similar to plastic body filler, polyester filler is also mixed with a catalyst. As soon as it is mixed, the filler should be applied by spraying directly from the can—according to manufacturer's recommendations. Instead of drying by evaporation, it dries—cures—by chemical reaction. Although manufacturers suggest shrinkage will be no greater than 5%, several of our bodymen friends swear polyester filler expands. Manufacturers make no claim to this observation.

The lack of shrinkage, the ease with which it works, and the amount of void it can fill makes polyester filler one of the best body-related products available.

Paint companies manufacture their own line of primers, surfacers, putties and fillers. We recommend that you use one manufacturer's line of these products consistently. Don't use whatever's cheapest or most accessible at the moment.

The body-materials manufacturer designs his products so they are compatible; he uses what is called the *system approach.* For more on this, turn to page 91. Because of this, use one manufacturer's products throughout. If you do, the manufacturer will warrant his products. And, if something goes wrong, he will make it good. If you mix products, one manufacturer will claim it is the other manufacturer's problem. This becomes a vicious

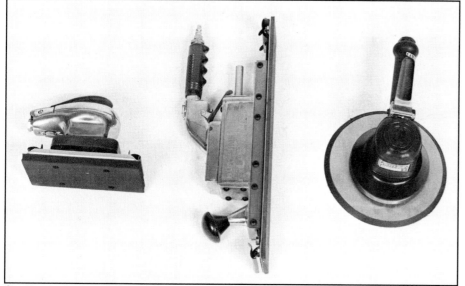

Sanding tools, from left to right: pneumatic orbital sander, or *jitterbug*, block sander, and the invaluable double-action orbital sander (D.A.). Because these tools make a job go considerably faster, they are always found in professional bodyshops. However, you seldom find these tools in a do-it-yourselfer's shop because of their cost.

circle. Save potential headaches. Stay with one manufacturer's products when doing a job.

## SANDPAPERS & ABRASIVES

Although there are many abrasives on the market, we concentrate on *coated abrasives*, commonly called *sandpaper*. Sandpaper's abrasive is glued to a flexible backing of paper, cloth or a combination of the two.

Sandpaper is a misnomer. Rather than sand, common abrasives include natural flint, quartz, garnet and corundum. These materials are all crushed and graded into various particle sizes, or *coarseness*. In addition to these natural abrasives, manufactured abrasives are silicon carbide and aluminum oxide. Those manufactured abrasives are most commonly used in bodywork.

There are a few basics common to all coated abrasives. First, they all are graded by grit coarseness. The smaller the number, the coarser the grit. Conversely, the larger the number the finer the grit.

Grits ranging from #16 to #40 are the coarsest available. These are generally used to remove paint, rust, scale or metal. *Coarse* abrasives range from #40 to #80. These are used for grinding solder and heavy body fillers, or for removing old paint on plastic or lead filler.

A #80 to #120 *medium* abrasive is used to achieve a smooth finish on fillers. This medium-grit abrasive

works well for *featheredging*—blending filler so there's no visible transition after surfacing or painting.

When *medium-fine* paper is required, select a grit in the #120 to #220 range. At the higher end, sanding scratches will be eliminated. At the lower range, old paint can be scuffed in preparation for new paint or surfacer.

*Fine* papers—#220 to #400 grit— are used to prepare the surface just before painting. *Wet-sanding* between coats is done with #400 paper.

*Ultra-fine* paper is in the #400 to #1000-grit range. #600 or #1000 paper is used to *color-sand* prior to rubbing or buffing, page 118. These grits are so fine they actually polish the paint.

**Abrasive Types**—As previously mentioned, silicon carbide and aluminum oxide are the abrasives most commonly used in bodywork. You can recognize these manufactured abrasives by their color: Aluminum oxide is reddish-brown; silicon carbide is black.

Another distinguishing feature of coated abrasives is grain density. In #16- to #120-grit abrasives, the grains are widely spread. Called *open-coat* or *open-grain* papers, they cover approximately 50 to 70% of the backing surface. Open-coat abrasives are for paint removal and grinding down solder and other materials that would adhere to the abrasive particles if closely spaced.

*Closed-coat* or *closed-grain* abrasives have an 85% grain coverage.

These are for work where the ground-off particles are very fine and there is little tendency to *load up* or adhere to the paper.

Finally, coated abrasives come in two styles: *wet-or-dry* or *dry*. As the name implies, wet-or-dry paper can be used with or without water. When used with water, sanding particles are washed away. This helps keep the paper from loading up. Consequently, the paper can be used longer.

Although wet-or-dry papers are commonly available in the #320- to #1000-grit range, 3M's wet-or-dry papers include #150 grit.

Dry paper is the most common coated coarse abrasive. It is used for fast removal of large quantities of materials. Because of its wide variety of uses, it comes in a wide variety of sizes. Most common is 9 X 11 inches. Other sizes include 3-inches wide X 18- to 24-inches long for long-board block sanding; 3-, 7- and 9-inch diameter for disc sanders; 4-1/2 X 11 inches for orbital or *jitterbug* sanders and for various specialty applications.

In addition to coated abrasives, finer abrasives are rubbing compound, pumice, swirl removers, steel wool and corn starch. They are described and demonstrated in chapters 9 and 10.

**Scotch Brite®Pad**—Relatively new to the industry is 3M's Scotch Brite® pad and similar products manufactured under other brand names. Scotch Brite® pads—*Brillo pads* as they are sometimes called—come in three grades: coarse, medium and fine. They consist of interwoven plastic fibers coated with a silicate abrasive. Their great flexibility allows the user to get into areas where sandpaper would certainly crumble, such as in door jams, door pillars and any compound and concave surface that would normally be inaccessible.

Used with the correct solvent, Scotch Brite® pads are excellent for removing road tar and other petroleum-based products from surfaces to be painted.

## TOOLS

There are many tools that make a body-and-paint project go faster and better. For most tools described, there is a hand tool and its electric or pneumatic counterpart. Hand tools are inexpensive and readily available. The pneumatic counterparts are

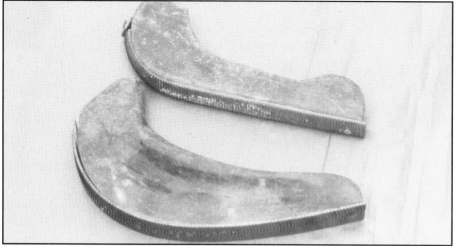

Curved body files were used frequently in earlier days when sheet metal was repaired more often than replaced. Currently, they are only available from the Eastwood Company, a well-known supplier and manufacturer of specialty products for restoration and bodywork use. For more information, contact: The Eastwood Company, 580 Lancaster Ave., P.O. Box 296, Malvern, PA 19355. Tel: 800/345-1178.

expensive—$200 or more. The difference is that the power tool is faster. It is no better, and does no other job. The power tool simply does the job quicker.

**Long-Board**—Of the tools used most widely for leveling a surface, the long-board is the most common. It is also the most important and versatile. The long-board is sometimes referred to as a *block-sander,* because it is used for *blocking* a panel. Blocking is simply leveling the surface.

Although the standard long-board measures 3 X 16 inches, there are many specialty sizes, both shorter and longer. The board is actually cast aluminum with a 1/4-inch-thick foam pad to back up the paper. Two handles on top allow you to manipulate the board with relative ease. Paper grades readily available for the long-board range from #36 to #320 grit.

The pneumatic counterpart of the long-board is the *reciprocating sander.* Although this tool is used in the same manner as the long-board, the base of the reciprocating sander moves— reciprocates—back and forth about 1/4 inch. Other pneumatic counterparts include the orbital sander, the double-action (D.A.) sander and other disc sanders. Primarily, orbital and D.A. sanders are used over old paint where leveling is unnecessary. This sanding removes oxidation and gives the surface the *tooth* needed for the new paint to adhere to.

An excellent hand tool is the rubber sanding block. It fits the hand well and serves many purposes. Measuring 3-inches wide, rubber sanding blocks are available in 4-, 8- and 16-inch lengths. Their rubber construction allows the block to conform to slight surface contours. Because they are solid rubber, rather than foam-type rubber, rubber sanding blocks can be used with water.

For some body contours, there is no sanding block. Generally, these are small-radius concave contours. In this case, you have to make your own sanding block. A 6-inch-long, 1-inch PVC pipe makes a superb block for tight, inside curves. For larger contours, a 6- to 12-inch section of radiator hose works well. Whatever you find lying around that fits the problem contour, wrap a piece of sandpaper around it and go to work!

# SPECIAL TOOLS

You'll need some special tools when you use body fillers. Tools for lead work are the most specialized.

### LEADING TOOLS

**Torches**—First, you need something to melt the lead and heat the sheet metal. The most common tool for this is the oxyacetylene torch—not that it is the only acceptable heat source, just that an oxyacetylene torch is the one most commonly found in body shops. Additional heat sources are propane and MAPP gas. In the very early years of bodywork, the gasoline blow torch was common. This antiquated tool is usually found only in display cases.

**Paddles**—When the metal is heated and the lead melted, something must be used to work the lead. There are many hardwood paddles to choose from. In some tool collections, you can find as many as six different shapes. Old-time bodymen will tell you that one paddle is all you need—usually a flat, stubby paddle that serves only to flatten and move the soft lead.

As any other tool, a leading paddle must be cared for and maintained. This care starts with treating its face to protect it from the hot lead. A tray of beeswax should be kept nearby for this purpose.

To treat it, the beeswax is heated, then the paddle is rubbed across the beeswax. This thinly coats the paddle face. When applied to hot lead, the wax lubricates action between lead and paddle. Additionally, the beeswax is burned away instead of the wood.

Even though beeswax is the best choice, other substances can be used to treat leading paddles, including motor oil, automatic-transmission fluid (ATF), paraffin and even axle grease. The advantage of beeswax is that it has less tendency to carbonize.

**Files**—A body file is the best tool for removing and leveling built-up lead. It is even more effective on lead than it is on sheet metal. If the file is sharp and free of nicks, it will cut lead with little effort.

By selecting and using quarter-round files, you can work in concave areas with the same ease that flat panels and crowns can be worked. We think that filing lead is the best part of the job. It certainly gives the greatest satisfaction.

### PLASTIC BODY-FILLER TOOLS

**Spreaders**—The counterpart to the lead paddle for plastic body filler is the *spreader.* This tool allows you to spread plastic filler in extremely thin, even layers. There are two types of body-filler spreaders: spring steel and vinyl.

**Spring-steel spreaders** are the most effective, and also the most expensive. The excellent flexibility of the steel spreader helps to spread filler accurately. Spring-steel spreaders are usually sold in packs of four, with widths ranging from 1 to 4 inches. This allows you to work many contours.

**Vinyl spreaders** are preferred by many bodymen. As with spring-steel spreaders, vinyl spreaders come in many widths. A vinyl spreader has one great advantage over its spring-steel counterpart: It can be cut to any shape. This allows access to any type of contour you may confront.

Many bodymen think commercially available spreaders are a lot of nonsense. They simply use a putty knife. Like spreaders, they too come in several widths. Because spreaders are inexpensive, try a putty knife and both types of spreaders to determine your preference.

**Surform Files**—Although the standard body file works well for filing lead or plastic, a tool that works better on plastic filler is the *Surform* file. In the slang parlance of the body shop, it is referred to as a *cheese grater* because of its similarity to a common cheese grater. The face of a Surform file has similar perforations that are sharpened to form cutting edges.

Available in many sizes and shapes, a Surform file is used to shape plastic filler by *drawing*—pulling—it across the face of the work. Unlike a body file, pulling a Surform file works better than pushing.

When drawn across filler, the teeth slice off thin shavings that pass through the perforations. This is advantageous because, unlike a conventional file, a Surform file is much less prone to loading up.

The Surform file is used to its greatest advantage immediately after the filler sets up. Used too soon after application, it will only scar the work. If you wait too long, the filler will be too hard to cut.

There is a brief span of 10 to 15 minutes when this file is most effective. Depending upon the temperature, humidity and the amount of catalyst used with the filler, you can begin shaving the plastic four to six minutes after application. Test the filler with a fingernail to see if it has set up. When it has, shave off the excess.

An assortment of Surform files should be in your bodyworking toolbox. They will last for many years. The expense can be justified easily by their durability and quality of work that can be achieved with them.

## TECHNIQUES

Let's look at how to use the mate-

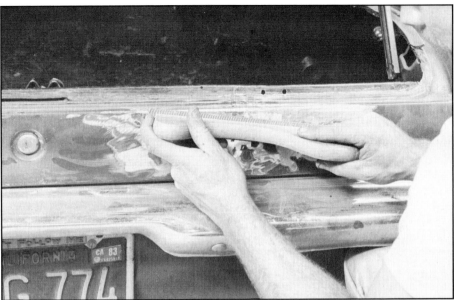

We use Plymouth Barracuda project car from Chapter 4 to demonstrate art of filling with body lead. We start by filing repair area to expose high and low spots.

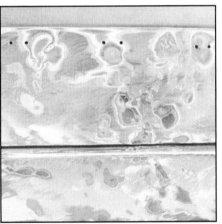

This is about as far as we'll go with the body file. We could work low (dark) spots up a little farther with the pick hammer. However, this is far enough considering we're using lead filler.

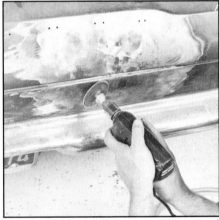

Area to be filled with lead must be ground to bare metal. Three-inch disc sander in electric drill motor is perfect for this grinding job. Tinning, shown on page 69, is next.

rials and tools we've just described. You should be able to finish a panel to look as good as it did before it was damaged. Here, the secret of success is patience—lots and lots of patience. A novice can finish a panel as well as a professional, *if* he has patience and sticks with the project.

The hardest thing for an aspiring bodyman to learn is to rework a panel if the first attempt is not satisfactory. And to give it one more shot before saying, "It's ready for paint!"

As you proceed through the rest of this chapter, you will finally see how it's possible to do a job over and over without satisfactory results. The tendency is to give up and say, "That's good enough." Usually, good

enough is not perfect. Your objective should be to obtain the *perfect panel,* not just "good enough!"

## LEADING

A perfect lead job begins with perfect preparation. The area to be leaded must be absolutely clean and free of foreign material. Select a 3-inch, #80-grit disc for your disc grinder. Chuck it into a 1/4-inch drill motor and remove everything down to the bare metal in the area you wish to lead.

Remove all paint, old filler, primer and all other materials. Heat discoloration of the metal must also be removed. Don't quit grinding until the area is bright and shiny clean.

The reason for all the cleanliness is

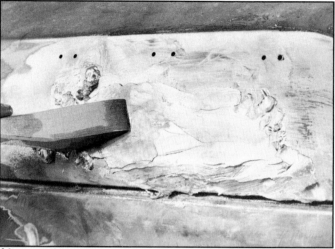

Small piles, or blobs, of lead are melted onto tinned surface by pushing lead bar into panel while heating with torch. When it appears enough lead is on panel to fill area, lead is evenly spread.

After coating wood paddle with beeswax, lead is heated and pushed around until surface is as flat as possible. While we were at it, we leaded both trunk and lower back panel.

### REMELTING LEAD

If you do a lot of lead work you'll be tempted to remelt lead filings and use them again. DON'T! Read again the sidebar on page 69. There's too great a chance to breathe the fumes. Even if you ventilate, the heat will burn away the tin that's part of the lead alloy. You could add tin, but getting the right amount is tricky. Save yourself the trouble and forget it!

simple. Lead will only bond to clean metal. You might be able to cover over a dirty area, but the lead will not stick. So clean it completely.

Next, tin the area to be leaded. Actually, you'll be putting a micro-thin coat of lead and tin on the surface. The lead filler will quickly bond to this area.

**Tinning**—The tools and materials you need to tin a metal surface are tinning compound, coarse steel wool and a heat source. Also, wear a heavy leather glove to shield your working hand from the heat of the torch as shown in photo, page 69.

The tinning compound should be designed for automotive lead work. Plumbers use a tinning compound for *sweat-soldering* copper tubing. This is not satisfactory for your leading needs. You'll find tinning compound for body leading at most good body-shop-supply stores. Purchase a few bars of lead while you're there.

Tinning compound is a mixture of acid, ground lead and tin. When heated, the tin and lead flow, carrying the acid with it. In the process, the acid cleans the metal to which the lead/tin compound must adhere. The thin lead/tin coating keeps the metal clean until you apply the lead filler.

Hold a wad of steel wool about the size of a baseball in your gloved hand. With the torch set at a low, neutral flame, heat the steel wool until it starts to turn red and melt. Quickly plunge the heated steel wool into the tinning compound. This will cover the steel-wool ball with a thick layer of compound.

Heat the panel—not the steel wool—in the area to be tinned. The panel should be hot enough to melt the tinning compound when it contacts the panel. You'll have to experiment to find out how hot this should be. Using the steel wool, spread the compound over the metal surface. Depending on the size of the area to be tinned, you may need to make several applications to cover the work area.

If your technique is OK, the tinning compound will melt and flow over the surface. It will leave the metal bright, silvery and shiny. As the surface cools, the tinned surface changes to dull gray. If heat is reapplied, the surface will turn shiny again. You are now ready to apply the lead.

**Apply Lead**—With a bar of body lead in one hand and the torch in the other, heat the panel until the tin coating melts. Push the bar of lead into the panel while you play the torch

over the area around the lead. The lead will begin to melt and form a small pile on the panel. You will soon discover the correct amount of heat needed to melt the bar—too much and it will fall on the floor. When the pile of semimolten lead is about the size of a half dollar and 1/4- to 3/8-inch high, remove the bar. Move to another area about 3 to 4 inches away. Again, melt a similar pile of lead onto the panel.

Cover the entire area to be leaded with small piles of lead spaced every 3 or 4 inches. Once this is done, you will be ready to smooth the lead.

**Work Lead**—It's time to put a lead paddle to work. Warm the face of the paddle with the torch and pass the paddle over the beeswax. After waxing the paddle, reheat the leaded area. When the lead *just* softens, push it around with the paddle, leveling the piles of lead and filling the voids.

Eventually, you should have all the lead flattened. The entire surface should be covered with a 1/8- to 3/16-inch-thick layer of lead. If you overheat and melt an area so it falls out, reapply lead into small piles as just described.

When the surface is as level and even as you can make it with the paddle, use a body file to file off the high spots.

Skim the file over the surface of the lead until all high spots are removed and the leaded area is completely level. Working around the edge of the lead area, bring it down until it too is level with the surrounding area. While you are doing this, rub your

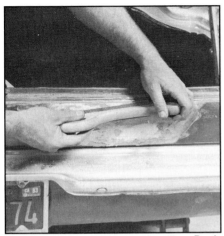

Smoothing lead with body file. Don't remove too much lead. Because it's soft, you can easily file filled surface below level of surrounding sheet metal.

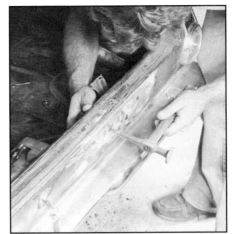

Major advantage lead has over plastic body filler: Lead tolerates some bodywork with pick hammer.

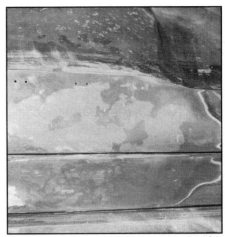

Rubber or wood block wrapped with #80-grit sandpaper is used to remove file marks. Once smooth, *leading acid*—tinning compound—is neutralized with bare-metal cleaner/etcher, or metal conditioner, such as DuPont 5717S. This prepares area for primer/surfacer.

hand across the surface after every few strokes. Feel for high spots, just as you did when you were using the hammer and dolly.

When the area feels level, *stop!* There is a tendency to overfile lead. If this happens you've defeated your purpose, and must start over. Proceed with caution! When the leaded area is leveled, smooth it with #80-grit sandpaper. Wrap the sandpaper around a wooden block and sand the filed area until the sanding marks are uniform and all file ridges are gone.

Clean the area with *bare-metal cleaner/etcher.* You'll find this at a paint shop. All residual lead and acid must be removed from the panel before you proceed. Otherwise, the acid will blister the paint later. When the surface is thoroughly dry, apply three medium coats of primer/ surfacer.

If all has gone well so far, block-sand the filled area and paint the panel. Block-sanding is explained on the following page.

## FILLING WITH PLASTIC

Plastic filler, as we stated earlier, has virtually replaced lead in most body shops. Used sparingly, it works just as well as lead. As with lead, grind down to bare metal the surface to be filled. The surface must be absolutely clean.

**Apply Filler**—Prepare the filler by placing some on a metal, glass or Masonite work board. You'll need enough to cover the area to be filled to a thickness of no more than 1/8 inch. For each golf-ball-size portion of

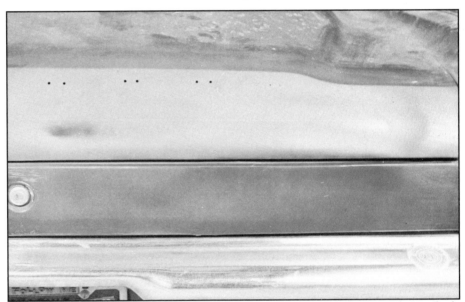

Leaded area is covered with two coats of primer/surfacer. Finishing is done using methods described in following chapters.

Let's complete fender-repair project we left on page 55. First, old body filler, paint and primer is ground away to expose bare metal.

After mixing with catalyst, first application of body filler is laid down. Note that all strokes are in one direction and stop at body line. This helps maintain correct body contour.

75

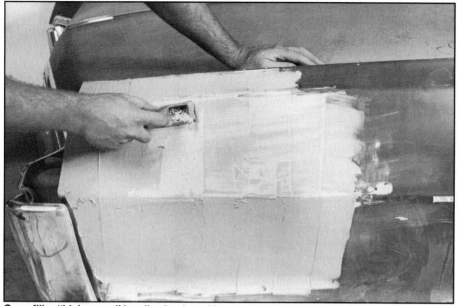

Once filler "kicks over," leveling begins with removing high spots with Surform file.

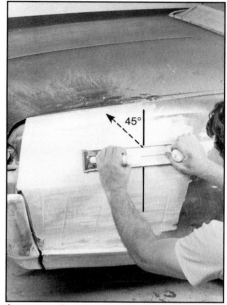

Long sanding board with #36-grit paper finishes leveling plastic filler.

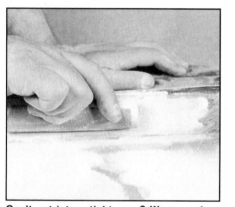

Can't get into a tight area? Wrap sandpaper around 1-inch wood block or PVC pipe and go to work.

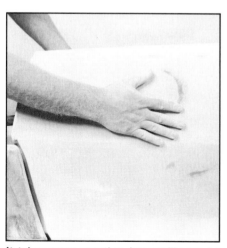

It takes some practice, but you'll soon be able to feel any high or low spots. Close your eyes; you'll concentrate better.

filler, squeeze out a 1-inch *ribbon* of hardener—catalyst. This amount of hardener is only a rule of thumb.

When mixing filler and hardener, use straight strokes with your paddle. Otherwise, you'll create air bubbles and cause pinholes.

Weather conditions, temperature and age of materials will all combine to change the filler-to-hardener ratio. If the filler "kicks over" (hardens) too soon, discard the unused filler. Reduce the amount of hardener for the next batch. If the plastic fails to harden in about 20 minutes, toss it away and start over. Next time, add more catalyst. As you work with filler, you will be able to judge how much catalyst is needed for a given amount of filler.

The correct hardening time allows you three or four minutes to apply the material. It then becomes too stiff to work. In five to ten minutes, the plastic should be hard enough to begin working with the Surform file.

With a plastic or spring-steel spreader, spread the filler over the repair area. Use long strokes *in one direction only*. Don't change directions as you add and overlap filler—it will lift the filler underneath. Fill the area to no more than 1/4-inch thickness. A larger quantity of filler will create a great deal of heat which in turn causes bubbles, just like boiling water. This leaves pinholes in the filler after filing. These will have to

be filled again, defeating the purpose of the original heavy fill!

**File Filler**—Most professional bodymen prefer an 8- to 10-inch curved Surform blade rather than other varieties. This allows for a great deal of control while making each cut. Also, it works equally well on concave or crowned areas.

When the plastic is ready to file, you will be able to draw the file over the surface, cutting off thin curls. If the curls crumble or clog the file-blade holes, the filler hasn't cured enough. Wait a few minutes and try again—but don't wait too long. The material will be too hard to file in as little as ten to fifteen minutes.

Rather than pushing the file, use it in a drawing or pulling fashion for greater control. Carefully level the entire area just filled. Use your hand to find the high spots and shave them down. As with lead, don't overdo it and go to bare metal. Stop when the surface is uniform.

When the *draw filing* is finished, fit a long-board with #36-grit paper and *block* the area.

**Block Sanding**—Blocking, or block-sanding, assures you that the surface will be smooth as well as level. The desired effect is to crosshatch the entire surface of the filler until it is level.

Crosshatching is done by drawing the sanding board across the filler at 45° to the horizontal or vertical, then repeating the process at the opposite 45°

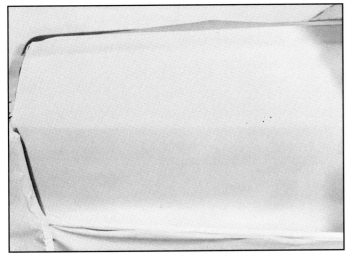
Heavy sand scratches are filled with primer/surfacer.

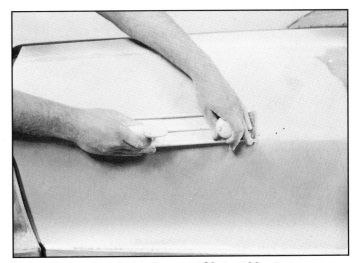
Back to the long board: This time use #80- to #100-grit paper.

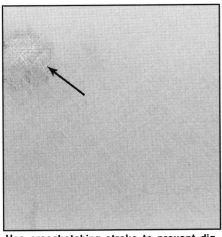
Use crosshatching stroke to prevent digging in with edges of sandpaper. Note high spot in upper left corner (arrow).

Primer/surfacer is next. We use polyester primer/surfacer because shrinkage is minimal. One tube of hardener catalyzes one quart of surfacer. Professional spray gun with pressure regulator for applying primer/surfacer is invaluable.

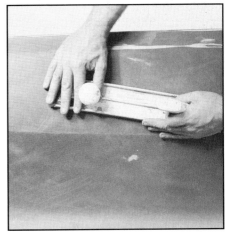
Perfect panel is achieved only by filling and sanding several times. After another application of primer/surfacer, further smoothing is done with #220-grit paper.

angle, or 90° to the first cut. Confusing? Yes, it is a bit hard to describe, but careful attention to the following demonstration should clear it up.

Assume the area being worked is on the side of the car—the surface is vertical. Hold your long-board at the upper right of the area to be sanded, draw the board diagonally across the surface to the lower left. Do this in parallel strokes across the entire filled area until it is covered with scratches from top right to bottom left.

Now, repeat the same process from top left to bottom right. Cover the entire filled area in this direction. The panel should be covered with diamond-shaped scratches, completely crosshatched. Stop sanding when all the high spots are removed.

You block-sand in a crosshatch pattern because if you simply go up and down and back and forth, grooves will form at the ends and edges of the sandpaper. Crosshatching prevents, or at least lessens, this effect. It also makes it easier to maintain the body contour.

Continuously use your hand to feel for high spots. Work these level with the surrounding surface. Don't sand down to the lowest area—you'll just have to build it back up. Rather, mix more plastic and fill the low spots.

Be careful to maintain the contour of the panel as you block-sand. When block-sanding a concave area, wrap the sandpaper around a curved surface, opposite page.

When the panel is flat, the contour correct, and you are satisfied with

your work, change to #80-grit paper. Sand off the coarse crosshatching using the same 45° blocking pattern. Finish off with two or three medium coats of primer/surfacer.

## USING PRIMER/SURFACER

Mix the primer/surfacer according to directions. This is important to get correct flow and drying. The directions will recommend at what pressure to spray the primer/surfacer. Spraying is explained, beginning on page 114.

Spray the entire area, overlapping each successive coat about 5 inches. Spray two or three medium coats, then allow time for *flash-off* between each coat. Flash-off is the time required for the thinner to dry, leaving

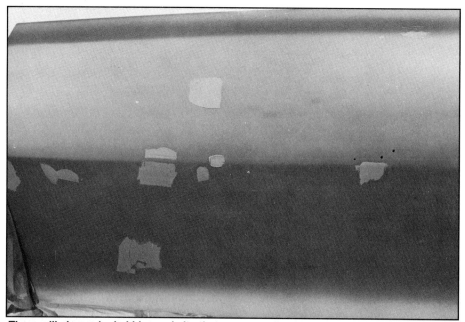

There will always be bubbles and pits that cause small voids in filler. Dabs of spot putty fill these small voids.

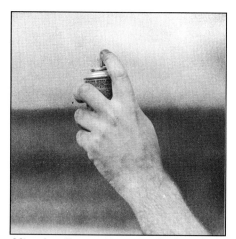

After leveling spot putty, final coat of primer/surfacer is applied. This is followed by the *guide coat*—a compatible, contrasting color lightly sprayed over surface being prepared for paint. We used an aerosol can of silver lacquer sprayed over red-oxide surfacer as the guide coat.

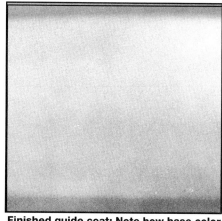

Finished guide coat: Note how base color shows through guide coat.

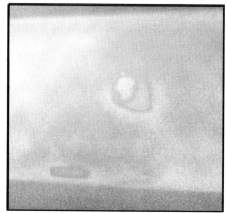

High and low spots become highly visible after a few strokes with sanding board. Guide coat is sanded off high spots; it remains in low spots. Continue sanding until guide coat is removed. What remains will be a level surface.

the surface *tack-free*—not sticky to the touch.

If you use heavy coats of primer/surfacer, the surface will dry quickly. This traps solvents beneath, leaving the area hard on top and soft underneath. Rather, proceed with moderately light coats, allowing sufficient flash-time in between. When the primer/surfacer is thoroughly dry—pressure from the edge of your thumbnail will not dent it—block-sand the area with #180- or #220-grit paper on the long-board.

Continue the leveling high spots with the low areas—low areas that are not pinholes or other voids. Use spot or glazing putty—page 70—to fill these voids. In many cases, the process of building up with primer/ surfacer and blocking with sandpaper will have to be repeated until the panel is perfectly smooth and level. Personally, we feel that if you have time, let the primer/surfacer dry for as long as possible before the final sanding prior to the color coat. Gases continue to escape for weeks. This increases shrinkage which in turn, allows those deep sanding scratches below to show through. Many rod, custom and restoration shops let the primer/surfacer dry for weeks. Make sure you keep everything dry to avoid rusting under the surface if you let it sit.

## USING POLYESTER FILLERS

We described polyester fillers on page 70. Here, we tell how to use

them. Before polyester fillers were available, you had to build up and file down plastic filler or primer/surfacer. Now you can use one of the polyesters to fill the low spots, being assured no shrinkage will occur. This reduces the need to fill and sand, over and over.

Polyester filler is almost a liquid-plastic body filler. One quart of *unthinned* filler is catalyzed with a tube of hardener. The mixture is then sprayed on the area to be filled. Block-sanding is done the same way as with any other filler. One application is usually enough. Although it is not absolutely necessary, apply a coat of primer/surfacer over the *finished* polyester filler.

## USING GLAZING PUTTY & SPOT PUTTY

No matter how careful you are or how good the filler, pinholes and small voids will occur in the filled surface. It is much easier to fill these voids with a glazing putty or spot putty than trying to do it with primer/surfacer.

Apply a *very thin* layer of putty over the void *after* primer/surfacer is applied. Putty shrinks about 50%, so two or three applications may be necessary. Carefully sand between applications to prevent disrupting the surrounding area. And sand only when the putty is thoroughly dry. We

1963 Chrysler Ghia is being prepared for paint. Body was stripped with paint remover; the doors were sent out and dipped.

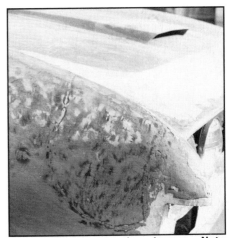
Ghia suffered extensive damage. Note sectioned fender and overuse of plastic body filler.

suggest using a #220-grit dry paper. Finish with a coat of primer/surfacer.

## GUIDE COAT

Of all the tricks used by professionals to achieve the perfect panel, the guide coat is probably the best. It requires patience and the desire to achieve a perfect panel.

After you apply the final coat of primer/surfacer, allow it to dry. Using a compatible lacquer or enamel in either an aerosol can or spray gun, apply a light coat of contrasting color over the primer—light over dark or vice versa. This should only be a *dust coat*—primer should show through the guide coat. Accompanying illustrations indicate correct guide-coat density.

When the guide coat is dry, gently block the panel with a long-board fitted with #220-grit paper. This will quickly reveal the high spots because the guide-coat paint is sanded away, leaving only the primer. Conversely, paint will remain in the low spots.

Continue blocking until all of the paint has been removed, so only the primer/surfacer remains. If any low spots remain, build them up with additional primer/surfacer, putty or, if the low spot is excessive, filler. Repeat the guide-coat, sanding and filling processes until there are no high or low spots. When you've achieved this, you have the perfect panel. A final scuffing with #320-grit (dry) paper readies the surface for paint.

This guide-coat procedure produces show-car quality. However, if you only wish to simulate the original factory finish, stop after the second blocking.

New plastic filler applied and block-sanding underway. Note crosshatching technique.

Ghia begins to shape up. Black guide coat is applied over gray primer/surfacer.

# 7 ALUMINUM & FIBERGLASS REPAIR

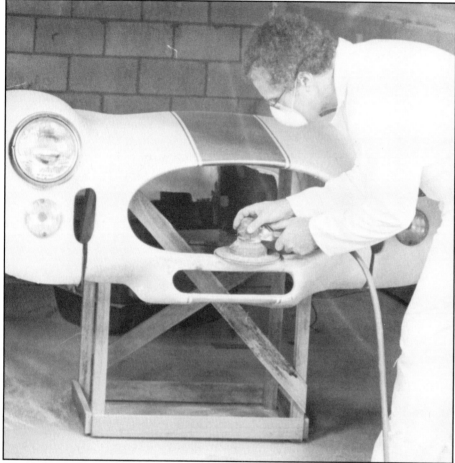

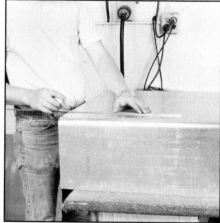

Dave Seward begins layout work on cockpit area of aluminum-bodied dragster.

Fiberglass, such as that used for this Cobra kit-car body or high-production fiberglass-reinforced plastic (FRP) nose and tail pieces, can be repaired in essentially the same manner. Light grinding removes fiberglass "hairs" and levels patched area. See start-to-finish repair job, pages 85—89.

You should become familiar with two more materials used for auto-body construction—aluminum and fiberglass.

Aluminum and fiberglass are being used with increased frequency for trim parts and body panels. Many aftermarket products such as hood scoops, fender flares, air dams and spoilers are constructed from fiberglass. Aluminum, because of its weight advantage, is being used more and more by manufacturers. Custom fabricators use aluminum in bodywork because of its workability.

You should be familiar with these materials, even though you may never work on a Corvette or Ferrari! You may not know what material is used for a body part until you've removed the paint. We describe how to repair aluminum and fiberglass body panels. Pay attention to all safety precautions, especially related to fiberglass.

## ALUMINUM

**Grades & Alloys**—Pure aluminum is of little value for body parts. It is too soft and susceptible to corrosion. To remedy this, other metals and elements are mixed in different proportions with pure aluminum to create aluminum *alloys.* Some *alloying ele-*

*ments* include copper, chromium, iron, manganese, titanium and zinc. Depending on the desired properties, these elements provide strength, toughness, hardness, temper, workability, annealability and corrosion resistance.

Each aluminum alloy is indicated by an *alphanumeric code,* which is a series of numbers and letters. The most-common grade of aluminum used by custom metal fabricators is 3003-H14. The basic number, 3003, indicates that the primary alloying element is manganese, and the H14 suffix indicates the alloy was strain-hardened by cold-working. Cold-working makes aluminum stronger. For more information about aluminum alloys, read HPBooks' *Metal Fabricator's Handbook.*

When ordering aluminum, ask for 0.050- or 0.063-inch-thick 3003-H14. It is easy to shape and weld, and has sufficient corrosion resistance. Let's now look at how to work aluminum.

**Cutting**—Don't use a chisel or cutting torch to cut aluminum. They will damage or deform the metal in the area of the cut. The impact of a chisel blow stretches the material nearest the cut line, pushing it in front and creating buckling. Restoring the metal would require shrinking, which is an involved and difficult process.

Right-hand, left-hand and straight aviation snips work well for cutting aluminum. Right- and left-hand snips have green and red handles, respectively; straight-cut-snip handles are yellow.

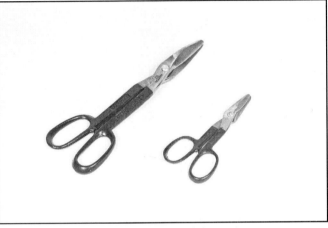

Tinner's snips work well for making straight cuts.

Cutting with a torch leaves a ragged edge and deforms the metal in the area of the cut. However, if you must use a torch, cut about 2 inches away from the finish cut line. Although this will result in wasted material, you can then clean up the cut using aviation snips, tinner's snips or pneumatic nibblers. Tinner's snips are similar to a big pair of scissors. These work great for making straight cuts. *Right-* or *left-hand* aviation snips allow you to achieve a cut line as clean and straight as the one illustrated in the photo. Right-hand snips remove metal to the *right* so you can make a cut curving to the left. Left-hand snips remove metal to the *left* for making right curves.

Pneumatic nibblers, or shears, are similar to air-powered scissors—they shear the metal. Don't confuse these with pneumatic chisels. The subject illustrated is using pneumatic shears. Note how straight and even the cut is, without stretching or buckling.

Be careful when cutting aluminum. The softer it is, the easier it is to cut. Likewise, the easier it is to deform.

### HAMMER & DOLLY WORK

Basically, working aluminum with a hammer and dolly is the same as working mild steel, including work hardening. In some cases, work hard-

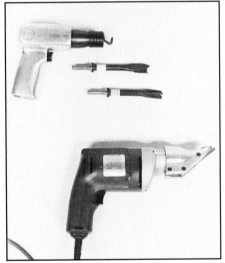

Pneumatic chisel (top) works great for cutting metal body panels. However, a ragged cut results. Nibbler, or cutting head, adapts to 3/8-inch drill motor. It "walks" right through sheet aluminum, leaving a clean cut.

ening is an advantage. It gives aluminum needed strength. However, aluminum must be *annealed*—softened—as it is worked. We explain annealing and how it's done in a minute.

You can metal-finish aluminum easier and quicker than mild steel. However, the ability to anneal aluminum and its resulting softness presents a problem. Forming reduces material thickness—excess forming

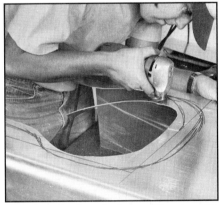

Trimming aluminum is done with pneumatic shears, or nibblers. Although it takes longer, you can achieve similar results with right- and left-hand aviation snips.

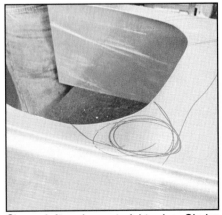

Shears left a clean, straight edge. Circles at corners indicate area that will be raised first. Greatest stretch occurs here.

Dave starts forming metal by bending up sides with his hands.

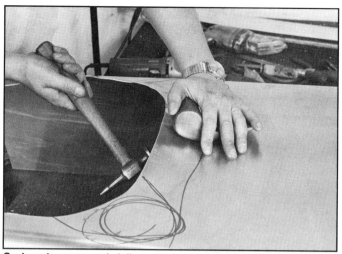
Serious hammer-and-dolly work begins. Note contour of dolly. It matches contour Dave wishes to achieve.

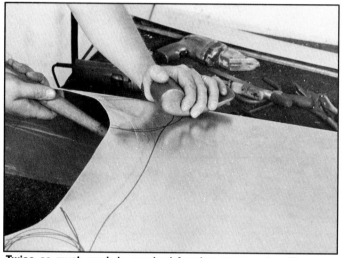
Twice as much work is required forming compound radii versus simple bends.

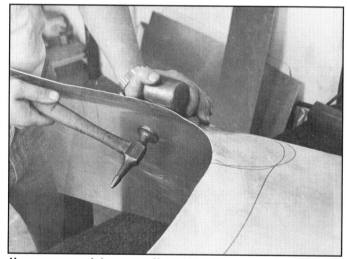
Hammer-on and hammer-off techniques are used to achieve desired contour.

Marks indicate hammer-and-dolly work required to form aluminum. Most work was forming corners, causing considerable work hardening. Such areas must be annealed before additional forming can be done.

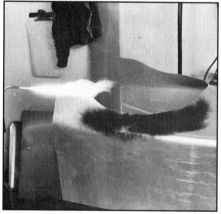
Annealing starts with coating work-hardened aluminum with carbon, or soot. This is done with an acetylene-rich flame.

can reduce aluminum to foil thickness! Consider this as you work a panel. It can be shrunk, but not to the extent it can be stretched. When working out a dent, don't overdo it.

Lift the dent, improve it with the pick hammer, and stop. Underworking aluminum is preferable to overworking.

One way to prevent overworking an area is to have available a variety of dolly shapes. The closer the face of the dolly conforms to the desired panel contour, the less you'll have to work the metal to achieve that contour. Because aluminum works so easily, use a pick hammer when possible. The point of the pick hammer has less tendency to thin metal. In fact, it tends to shrink metal in a manner similar to a shrinking hammer.

Use the pick hammer as described in Chapter 4. With your hands, feel for low spots. *Gently* lift these with the pick hammer. For high spots, work them down with the hammer and dolly. When you can't feel any high or low spots, pass a body file across the surface. This will quickly expose re-

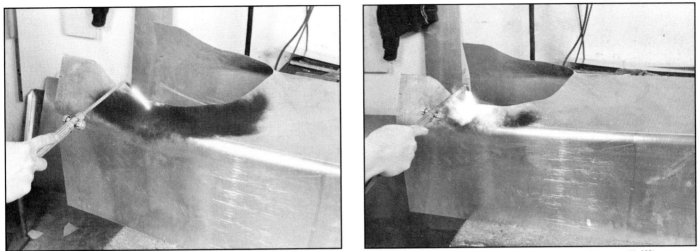

Annealing is done with hotter flame—more oxygen and no smoke. Sooted areas are heated gradually until carbon burns off. When most carbon has been burned off, aluminum is annealed. Before metal cools, it is quenched with water and a sponge.

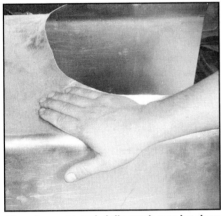

More hammer-and-dolly work can be done after annealing. Dave feels for high and low spots.

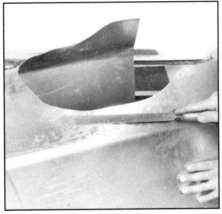

Filing cuts tops off high spots. Go easy when filing aluminum. Material is removed much quicker than with steel.

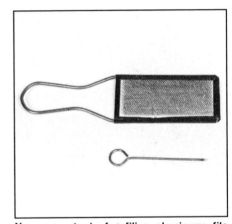

Necessary tools for filing aluminum: file card and pick. File teeth load up with aluminum, reducing file's cutting ability. Use file card—short-bristle wire brush—to remove aluminum particles from file. Remove remaining particles with a pick.

maining low spots and remove high spots. Use the body file sparingly. You can quickly remove a lot of material when working aluminum. So be careful not to remove too much.

Finish off your hammer-and-dolly work with the body file. Smooth the work area by block-sanding with #80-grit sandpaper.

**Annealing**—Annealing is a process that softens hardened metal. It's simple with aluminum. But how do you know when aluminum should be annealed?

As you work an area, you can sense that the aluminum is getting harder with each hammer blow. It gets more difficult to form and the sound of the hammering changes. It will begin to ring as the metal hardens. If you continue forming work-hardened metal, you'll crack it. To prevent this, stop hammering and anneal the area.

Annealing requires a gas-welder.

Light the torch and adjust it to an acetylene-rich flame, using little oxygen. You want a cool, orange flame with lots of soot. Pass this flame over the area to be annealed so black soot covers the surface evenly. Don't heat the metal; coat it with carbon.

When the area is covered with soot, adjust the torch so it has a long blue flame with no soot. This is a cool flame, not hot enough for welding. Pass the torch back and forth over the sooty area to heat it evenly and gradually. As the panel begins to reach annealing temperature, the soot begins to burn off. When most of the soot has burned off, quickly *quench* the area with a very wet, large sponge. This heating and quenching returns the workability of the aluminum and you will have successfully annealed it.

Repeat this process as often as needed. But, be careful not to overwork the area.

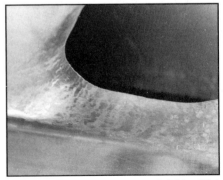

Filing makes high spots bright. Pick hammer raises low spots.

**Shrinking**—If, with all of this hammer-and-dolly work and annealing, you get "more" metal than you started with, it's time to do some shrinking. Unfortunately, you should not heat-shrink aluminum. You'll end up melting a hole through it! Instead, use a shrinking hammer or

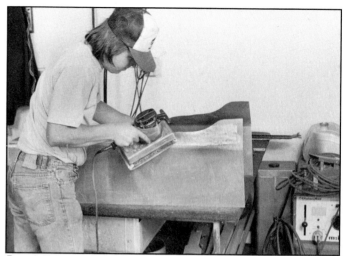

Finish-work in concave areas is done with drill motor and 3-inch sanding disc.

Broad, flat areas finish faster with flat, orbital sander.

Trimming and filling will prepare aluminum panel for paint.

## FIBERGLASS

Aluminum has been used in auto bodies since the early '30s. Fiberglass was first used for Corvette bodies in 1953. Today, there are thousands of those Corvettes on the road. Unfortunately, Corvettes or other glass-bodied vehicles occasionally require the services of a bodyman. We demonstrate how you can repair anything from a crack to replacing an entire fender. These techniques can be used to build kit cars, install aftermarket products or customize a car. A fiberglass panel consists of *fiberglass cloth*—which gives the panel its strength—and *resin*—which bonds fiberglass cloth together and gives the panel its smooth, tough finish. Fiberglass cloth is explained below. Resin is discussed on the following pages.

**Fiberglass Cloth**—Fiberglass, or glass fiber, is molten glass that is extruded into hair-thin fibers. These long, continuous fibers are wound on spools, then spun into multifiber threads. These threads are then woven into a cloth-like material called *fiberglass cloth*.

Fiberglass cloth is available in many *weights*. Generally, 6- to 10-ounce per-square-yard material works best for fiberglass-repair work.

Another type of fiberglass cloth is called *woven roving*. Rovings are numerous strands of glass bundled together rather than twisted into threads. These rovings are then *woven* together. Rovings are loose and bulkier compared to threads. The bulk captures more resin in a given area than does glass cloth. Woven roving is

shrinking dolly as described on page 52. Both work well.

Back the work with a dolly that conforms to the metal contour. Strike the metal with the shrinking hammer, using only enough force to transfer the checkerboard texture of the hammer face to the metal. Excess force warps the metal. Too little force is wasted effort. After a few good whacks at the area, pass your hand over it to determine where and how much to hit it again.

Don't file the surface marks caused by shrinking. Filing makes the metal too thin. Instead, file only enough to establish the correct contour. Then, use plastic body filler or several coats of primer/surfacer to fill the voids

created by the shrinking hammer. Refer back to Chapter 6 for detailed instructions on the use of filler and primer/surfacer.

**Welding Aluminum**—Welding aluminum isn't much different than welding steel. It simply requires practice and some special materials, depending on the type of welding equipment you use: gas or electric. If you chose to gas-weld aluminum, you'll need *aluminum-welding flux* and rod. The flux removes oxides and impurities that naturally form on aluminum alloys. For heliarc-welding, you'll need aluminum rod. See HPBooks' *Metal Fabricator's Handbook* or *Welding Handbook* for more details on welding aluminum.

Mark McConnell's Cobra kit-car took a bump in the nose. Note broken fiberglass at left of racing stripe above bottom scoop—typical fiberglass damage.

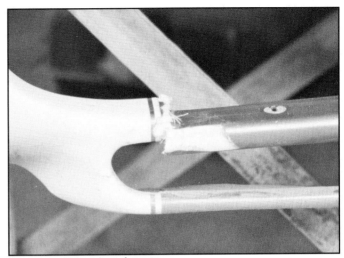

Close-up of fiberglass damage

most commonly found in 24-ounce per-square-yard material.

The third formation of glass fibers is *glass mat*. Mat is *chopped glass*, which is glass fibers chopped into short lengths, with a bonding agent to give body, laid out in a thick, pad-shaped mat. Mat has a lower glass-to-resin ratio than either cloth or roving. The ratio is usually about 25 to 35% glass and 65 to 75% resin. This makes a thick, waterproof, stiff laminate. The area to be filled is thick. Generally, glass mat is used to lay-up complete panels.

Glass fibers come in other shapes and configurations for special applications. *Surfacing mat* is used for the top layer in a laminate. It's thin and smooth, giving an excellent, ridge-free surface. *Chopped strand*, available in 1/4- to 2-inch lengths, is mixed with a catalyzed resin and used to add strength. You can make an excellent paste that will stay in place and not run off by adding a *thixotropic* agent, or thickening powder to the catalyzed resin. These are generally refered to as *microballoons* or *microfibers*. The best of these are West Systems 403 Microfibers, which can often be found in most marine supply stores. If not, contact Gougeon Bros. at: P.O. Box 908, Bay City, MI 48707, (517) 684-7286.

Other glass-fiber configurations are used for producing fiberglass parts, not for repairs.

**Resin**—Fiberglass is saturated with liquid resin during the *lay-up* process—one layer of fiberglass laid on top of one or more layers of resin-saturated fiberglass. Fiberglass cloth is laid in the mold or on the area being repaired and it is saturated with liquid resin. This process is repeated until the desired layers of cloth have been built up. The resin cures, or hardens, to give the part or repair its strength.

Generally, resins used in fiberglass work are polyesters. Although epoxy resins may be used, we limit our discussion to the more popular polyester resins. Polyester resin is a *thermosetting* plastic—the resin sets, or cures, by heat. The heat can be generated from within or externally. We concentrate on heat chemically generated within the resin by the addition of a catalyst. The reaction of the catalyst with an *accelerator* already in the resin produces an *exothermic,* or interior, heat. Heat changes the resin from a liquid to a solid. This is called *polymerization.*

You don't have to remember these terms to do a satisfactory fiberglass-repair job, but, it helps to understand what's happening. Then you'll know why your resin *kicked,* or cured, too quickly—or why it didn't kick at all!

Polyester resins for fiberglass work are designed to cure at room temperature. The slight internal change in temperature when the catalyst is added speeds the cure rate. Resin cures in the can if not used soon enough. Therefore, be sure to buy fresh resin. If a can sits on the shelf too long, it will be too thick to use.

**Laminating & Finishing Resins—** Two types of resin are *air inhibited*—resin which will not fully cure in the presence of air—and *non-air inhibited* —resin which will cure in air. *Laminating,* or *lay-up,* resin is air inhibited. It won't fully cure until all contact with air is removed. This allows one layer to be applied over another so good bonding takes place between the layers. When one layer is covered by another, all the air is removed. The bottom layer then cures fully.

**Finishing,** or *surfacing,* resin is non-air inhibited. Wax, or a similar ingredient, is added to the resin during manufacture. When used, the wax rises to the surface to form a barrier between the resin and the air. This allows the finishing resin to complete its curing process. Before applying primer or paint to finishing resin, the wax should be washed off with acetone.

Another non air-inhibiting resin, *casting resin,* shouldn't be used for repair work. Casting resin is expensive, lacks strength and was designed to do such things as encase roses, scorpions, tarantulas and other items for sale to tourists in the Southwest.

**Resin Catalyst**—Do not use a catalyst intended for epoxy resin or plastic body filler in polyester resin. Such resins are different. They won't work in polyester resin. Use a catalyst specifically formulated for use with polyester resin. This clear-liquid catalyst is called *methyl-ethyl-ketone (MEK) peroxide.*

Directions for its use are on the catalyst bottle and resin can. Usually, catalyst is mixed at a ratio of seven drops per ounce of resin. A little more may be added to speed curing when the air temperature is cold. Less is

To begin repair, Mark aligns break by bridging it with angle iron held in place with C-clamps. Edges of break are tapered with grinder.

Fiberglass mat is used to make repair.

used if air temperature in the working area is hot.

**Gel-Coat Resin**—This is an air-inhibited resin that forms the exterior color coat of many fiberglass products. When laminating an automotive body part, the gel coat is first sprayed into the mold. Usually, it is colored with a resin pigment. Mat, cloth or chopped strands with laminate resin is added. When cured, the part is removed from the mold. The gel coat is now the colored surface of the part. Because no glass was added to this coat, it will be as smooth as the mold in which it was sprayed.

We've covered the two basic components of fiberglass repair: resin and fiberglass. Together, these products form an extra-strong, waterproof, somewhat flexible, composition that can serve as a repair material or actual automotive body part. The next step is to use this material in an actual repair.

First we look at the overall fiberglass repair technique. Then we discuss the specifics of scratches, dents, cracks and other possible damages.

**Safety**—Be careful when working with fiberglass because its resins are flammable in both liquid and solid states. In the liquid state, fumes will ignite with little heat. Therefore, don't smoke while using fiberglass resin. And, if you're working in an enclosed area, open the doors. Extinguish any water heater, clothes dryer, gas-fired-refrigerator or any other pilot lights.

When welding or flame cutting near fiberglass, such as a Corvette frame, keep the heat away. Asbestos panels or several layers of aluminum foil offer protection when placed between the flame and fiberglass panel. The best protection, though, is your own good judgment.

Liquid resin may cause a rash if it comes in contact with the skin. The effect seems cumulative. For most people, occasional contact is no problem. But, constant exposure may cause a severe skin rash. To prevent potential problems, wear rubber gloves when handling resins. Rubber gloves used for washing dishes are adequate for occasional fiberglass use. For doing a lot of fiberglass work, wear *neoprene* gloves. They hold up better against resins and acetone solvents.

If you develop a rash, discontinue contact with the resins and immediately consult a dermatologist. Don't contact any chemicals. Wash the problem area with water and Ivory soap. The dermatologist will prescribe a remedy, if necessary. If you can't find a dermatologist—perhaps it's the weekend—go to a hospital emergency room.

## FIBERGLASS REPAIRS

Although fiberglass has a high strength-to-weight-ratio, it's not as strong as metal. Therefore, don't use it like glue in repair work, trying to imitate a weld.

Fiberglass strength is determined by the number of glass fibers encapsulated in the resin. A repair then, must use a wide, thick piece of cloth, fully impregnated with resin. When possible, place the patch on the back of the repair surface. If the repair must be made on the front surface of a panel, material must be ground away to make room for the thickness of the patch.

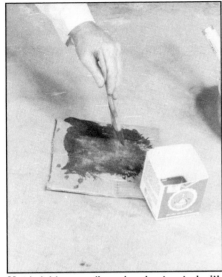
Mat is laid on cardboard and saturated with catalyzed resin.

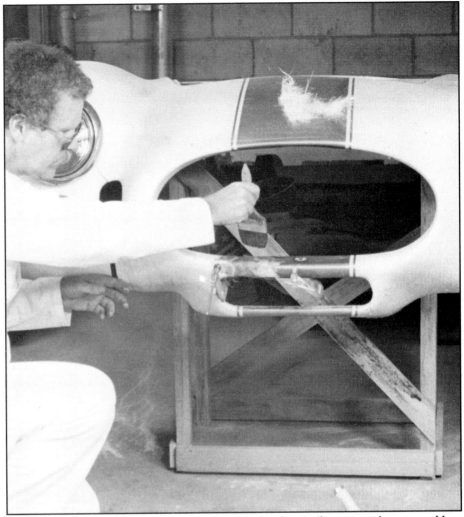
Resin-impregnated mat is applied to break. Mark, why aren't you wearing your rubber gloves?

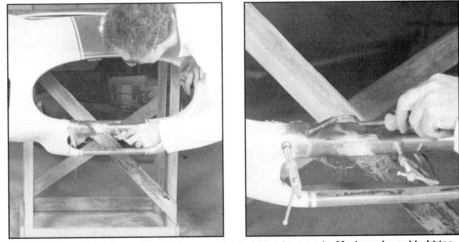
Using roller designed specifically for removing bubbles from resin, Mark works out bubbles.

Another consideration is cleanliness. Fiberglass won't adhere to dirt, grease, silicone or other foreign matter. It will bond to metal, wood, composition materials and other fiberglass. It is extremely important to clean the surface thoroughly. Begin with a soap-and-water wash to remove loose dirt and grime. Follow this with acetone, toluene or MEK. Don't use oil-based solvents because they leave a film. Acetone or similar products removes paint as well as grease, so use them carefully around paint, plastic or other surfaces to prevent damage. Once you've cleaned the surface, grind, file or sand the area you'll be patching.

Be sure to use a filtering or particle mask when grinding fiberglass. Fiberglass dust is extremely dangerous. Inhaling it can lead to silicosis.

**Dents, cracks or pits** in the *gel coat* that have not affected the structural integrity of the fiberglass are easy to repair using plastic body filler. This repair is similar to repairing a surface scratch in a metal body panel. Grind or sand away the surface until the dent, crack or pit is gone. Apply a thin coat of plastic body filler. Block-sand and finish as described in Chapter 6.

**Structural cracks** are more difficult to repair because they've weakened the structural integrity of the fiberglass panel. Begin by cutting along the break line with a hacksaw. Remove any shattered fiberglass pieces. Clean both the top and back of the panel

with one of the non-oily solvents already mentioned. Be sure to remove any sound deadener or undercoating from the panel at least 4 inches back from the damaged area.

Bevel the edges approximately 30° along the edge you cut, using a file or grinder. Now, align the edges, if possible, using a C-clamp. If you can't align the edges with a C-clamp, lay a

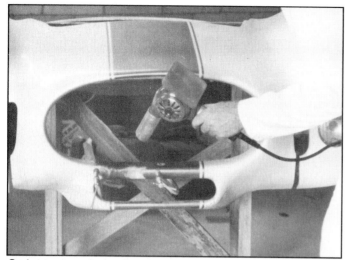

Curing process is accelerated with heat gun. Work should not be overheated, only warmed.

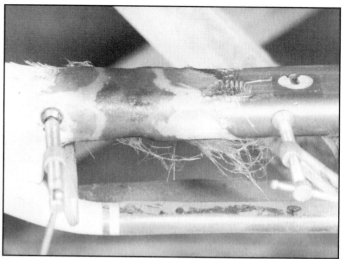

Cured-fiberglass repair patch is ready for filing and finishing.

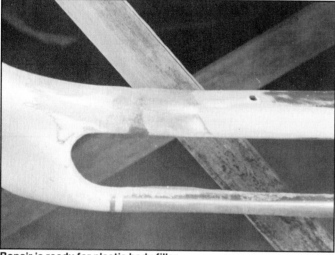

Repair is ready for plastic body filler.

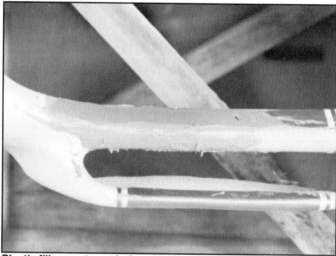

Plastic filler must cure before filing or smoothing.

1/4-inch-thick-steel strap with holes drilled in it over the crack. Bolt one to each side of the panel. This clamping force should align the two edges. When the patch has cured, remove the metal strap and fill the holes.

Once the edges are aligned, cut two or three pieces of glass cloth for a backup patch. Be sure this patch extends at least three inches past each side of the damaged area. Saturate the patch with a catalyzed resin and apply it to the backside of the panel. When the backing patch has cured, turn your attention to the repair of the cosmetic side of the crack.

Chop a few of the glass fibers into 1/4- to 1/2-inch-long strands. Mix these strands with a small amount of catalyzed resin. This forms a paste that shouldn't run when applied to a vertical surface. Fill the crack with this paste. When cured, grind off the high spots, and fill the sanding scratches with plastic filler or two or more applications of glazing putty. The repaired area should now be at least as strong as it was originally.

**Holes** in a fiberglass panel seldom result from impact. What usually occurs is a series of fractures. You must remove shattered material from the fractures to make a good repair. The result is a hole which then must be filled.

Follow procedures described for crack repair to clean and prepare the hole for repair. Be sure to bevel all broken edges. Cut two pieces of glass cloth to cover the damaged area and overlap about three inches of undamaged body. Saturate the cloth with resin and place it on the back side of the hole. Allow the resin to cure.

When the backup patch has cured, cut enough pieces of glass cloth to fill the remainder of the hole from the front, or exterior, side. Saturate these pieces with resin and fill the remainder of the hole, allowing a little overlap. When cured, grind off the high spots, then smooth and finish with a plastic body filler. This works well when you can reach the back of the panel. But what can you do when the back of the panel isn't accessible?

First bevel the edges of the hole

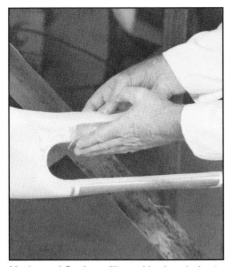

Mark used Surform file and body grinder to level filler. He's smoothing by hand-sanding with #36-grit paper.

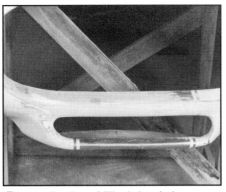

First application of filler is leveled.

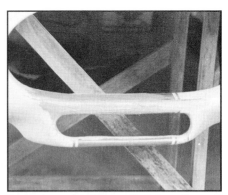

Second coat of filler applied: Leveling and sanding will ready repair for primer/sealer.

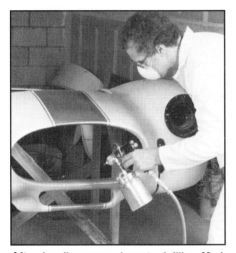

After leveling second coat of filler, Mark applies primer/surfacer.

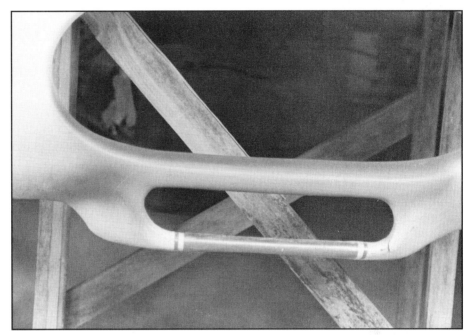

A few dabs of spot putty are needed in voids. After leveling these spots, second coat of primer/sealer will prepare job for paint.

from a featheredge out to about 3 inches on all sides. Over this, lay a double layer of resin-impregnated glass cloth and allow it to cure. When the backing patch is thoroughly cured, fill the hole as described in the previous paragraph. Again, finish with plastic filler to fill any scratch marks left by grinding or sanding.

## FIBERGLASS-PANEL REPLACEMENT

**Bonding Strip—**Between each molded body panel is a backup piece called a *bonding strip*. By cementing the bonding strip into the joint between two body panels, a strong union is formed between two panels. Catalyzed resin is the bonding cement. Locate the seam where the two panels butt.

To separate the damaged panel from the main body structure, cut along the seam line with a saber saw. You will be cutting through the old bonding strip. With a chisel, remove what remains of the bonding strip. You can chisel by hand, or use a pneumatic chisel. Whichever technique you use, be careful not to cause additional damage.

Grind away any remaining bonding strip and bevel the edge. Check that the replacement panel has a beveled edge. If not, bevel it. Fit the replacement panel in place and secure it with 1/4-inch-thick steel straps and bolts as previously described. Thoroughly coat both panels at the seam and the

bonding strip with resin. Join them together. For a better bond, use sheet-metal screws to draw the pieces together. When the pieces are cured, remove the screws and fill the holes.

When the resin is fully cured, use more resin and cloth or chopped-glass fibers to fill the recess on the exterior side caused by the beveled edges. Again, grind, fill and finish.

**Summary—**Cleanliness is the key to quality fiberglass repair because bonding will not take place if bonding surfaces are dirty. Also, you must use sufficient material to build up a patch of equal thickness to the area being repaired. And, be sure to bevel broken edges to give a patch enough surface on which to bond.

# 8 PAINTS & PAINTING PRODUCTS

**Regardless of type of paint used, follow the *systems approach*—all paint products must be compatible. When doing a spot repair such as this, paint products must also be compatible with original paint.**

Painting a car in the '20s started with *the painter* making the paint. Some tree pitch or perhaps tar was thinned with benzene, a pinch of this or that was added, and a measure of lampblack was thrown in. The paint was then spread evenly over the car body with a paint brush. Things are different today. To make paint you must understand the chemistries of ethyl and butyl acetates, toluol and naphtha and such common additives as ethyleneglycolmonethyl ether!

To paint your car, you don't need these skills. You must, though, have a clear understanding of today's paints; what they do, what they're for, compatibility with other materials, and

how they are used. For instance, the wrong thinner used in a gallon of paint that cost over $100 is a major loss.

In this chapter, we discuss today's paints and what is known as *paint systems*. We tell how to select the correct paint for the job you wish to do, how to thin or reduce that paint and under what type of conditions to change the reduction. We also tell about undercoats—the primers, sealers and surfacers that prepare metal to receive paint. Finally, we cover many of the additives and other products associated with achieving a perfect finish, such as rubbing compounds for lacquer, or special cleaners that remove wax and silicone.

## PAINT SYSTEMS

Every paint manufacturer tries to make his paint formula better and less costly than his competitor's. He hires scientists with more degrees than a thermometer to accomplish this. Each scientist, in turn, develops new chemical additives to improve the product. These improvements do such things as increase gloss, improve flow-out characteristics, raise resistance to ultraviolet radiation and provide resistance to chemicals in smog—a special problem caused largely by automobiles.

Then, the manufacturer must consider whether the paint is to be used over bare metal or over an original equipment manufacturer (OEM) paint—a factory paint job. He must also develop paint for different climatic conditions. For instance, painting in July in Atlanta, Georgia, is considerably different than painting in January in Anchorage, Alaska. Temperature and humidity have major affects on a paint job.

A paint system includes paint for specific applications; thinner or reducer to match that paint and allow it to be used under differing weather conditions; and a variety of undercoats—primers—that are compatible with both new and old paint or bare metal.

Together, the paint, thinner or reducer, undercoat and any extra additives become a paint system. You must determine the type of finish you want. The manufacturer has everything you need to achieve your goal. After reading this chapter, you'll be able to discuss your needs with your paint supplier. Here's an extremely important rule: *Select one brand or manufacturer and stay with it throughout a job!*

Each manufacturer compounds his paints and materials a little differently. Consequently, if you mix brands, likelihood of failure is high. And neither manufacturer will warranty his product when used with someone else's. Select the brand that best suits your needs and stick with it. Then, if problems arise, the manufacturer will stand behind his product. There are five or six major manufacturers of automotive paints, all of which are reputable.

The final mirror-like gloss on your car may look great, but it has little to do with safety. Whether you can still breathe after you apply the paint does have to do with safety! Read PPG's (Ditzler) Health and Safety Tips, page 121. Note that there is a 24-hour emergency-information telephone number that can be used for health-related problems. However, prevention beats a cure; the object is not to get to this point.

You must be concerned with fumes emitted from paints and solvents, and particles generated while sanding. Fumes and particles are highly flammable and toxic. They can destroy your lungs or blow up your garage. We don't intend to be fear mongers, but these are real dangers.

---

**ISOCYANATES**

Today's polyurethane paints owe their extremely high gloss and wearability to a linking chemical called polyisocyanate. This chemical is directly related to cyanide, one of the worlds most deadly poisons. Although polyisocyanate is not as dangerous as gaseous isocyanate , it is not something to fool with! *Always wear a respirator when spraying any paint containing isocyanate, such as catalyzed enamels.* To be as safe as possible, you should wear a respirator when spraying *any* paint. Respirators use a fibrous material to filter particles and a chemically charged canister to remove the gases. These canisters begin losing their effectiveness the minute they're exposed to the air. Additionally, they lose effectiveness as they're used. We suggest you keep your respirator in a sealed plastic bag or other airtight container when not in use and change the filters and canisters once a week under heavy use and every other week with light use. Please don't fool around with your lungs!

---

You must allow for sufficient ventilation to carry off fumes from solvent or paint spray as fast as they're generated. The higher the concentration of fumes, the greater the chance of an explosion. *Never spray paint near an open flame such as an appliance with an active pilot-light. Before spraying, shut off all pilot-lights.* Don't forget about water heaters or furnaces with electric ignition. Either may ignite while you are working if you don't unplug it.

The connection should be obvious: Fill a garage with fumes or flammable particles near a furnace or water heater with a burning pilot-light and *boom*—the world's largest combustion chamber! The same problem can arise with a lit cigarette. *NEVER smoke in a painting area or while mixing paints or cleaning equipment.*

Once you're sure there are no open flames, consider your lungs next. Fumes from catalyzed acrylics and polyurethanes are extremely toxic. Wear a canister-style respirator when spraying these paints. The respirator must fit well and not leak. If there is any doubt about the age or condition of the canisters, replace them. The canisters use both a filtration system and a chemical neutralizing action to protect the wearer.

Although a well-fitting, disposable particle mask will afford some protection against airborne particles, (dust, sanding particles, some overspray) it will not protect you from paint gases, such as isocyanates (see sidebar nearby), which can be extremely harmful and even fatal. This is particularly true if you have respiratory problems or will be doing continuous spraying over a long period. In such cases, a canister respirator should always be used.

The disposable particle mask was designed primarily for use while sanding and grinding. So only use one during these operations. It is a single-thickness, filtration mask that will prevent inhaling of large sanding- or grinding-dust particles. This is particularly important when working with fiberglass.

Breathing fiberglass particles can lead to silicosis. The lungs have a thick mucus lining that trap glass particles. Unlike most other particles, glass cannot be coughed out. Once in, they stay.

Some plastic body fillers contain glass fibers. These products, such as *Tiger Hair* (long fibers) and *Kitty Hair* (short fibers), are excellent fillers. While grinding, filing or sanding these fillers or fiberglass, wear a particle mask.

Now that you're totally protected from airborne gases and particulates, take a bit more time to protect yourself from dangerous solvents.

You wouldn't drink lacquer thinner but yet we see painters plunge their hands in it every day, even scrub with it. You, and they, may not know it but the skin will absorb anything placed on it. That's why medical skin patches (nicotine, heart medication, hormones) work. The body accepts the medicine through the skin. We've all heard about the deadly poison of which one drop on the skin will kill you in five seconds. It may be an old wives tale but it does reinforce a known fact: the skin absorbs everything it contacts. We strongly recommend, therefore, that you wear rubber gloves while working with solvents or paints. It may feel clumsy at first but why risk illness or perhaps death? It simply isn't worth the risk.

A particle mask should be worn when performing any sanding operation.

This is what the well-dressed painter is wearing this spring! Note the full cut of his disposable paper suit; the classic lines of his neoprene/rubber gloves; and yes, the brand new, full face, fresh-air mask.

Kitty hair contains short glass fibers. To avoid breathing fibers while sanding, wear a particle mask.

The final safety warning borrows from the old cliche, "A clean shop is a safe shop." As trite as it sounds, it's true. Cluttered work areas are not only dangerous, but they contribute to poor workmanship. You can trip on hoses strung all over the floor; they can also be caught and pulled over fresh paint or filler. And masking paper can mask a lot more than chrome. Masking paper on the floor can hide tools, a can of thinner or box of lead that wasn't put away. Keep your work area clean. Keep your tools clean. You'll work safer and your craftsmanship will reflect your good work habits.

## EQUIPMENT & FACILITIES

The next consideration you must make while selecting a paint system is the availability of equipment and the type of facility you have. We've seen reasonably nice paint jobs done with vacuum-cleaner-attachment guns in all-dirt backyards. However, if your goal is a competition show car, you'll need some professional equipment to handle the more sophisticated paint systems. Much of this equipment can be rented.

You'll need an air compressor, spray gun, and pneumatic or electric hand tools. The cost of these items will be affected by the paint system you choose. The least expensive paint job is with a synthetic, or *alkyd,* enamel. However, it is relatively slow drying. So, you'll have to rent the equipment longer and rental costs will be higher. If you plan a two-tone or base-coat/clear-coat job you'll have to

rent your equipment even longer. At the opposite end of the time scale is acrylic lacquer. Lacquer is the fastest drying of all the paints. It can be masked over within an hour for a second color application. Therefore, rental costs will be lower.

About the facility: If you are fortunate enough to have access to a spray booth, you'll be able to work any paint system. But, you should be prepared to be in and out of the booth in a reasonable amount of time. A professional cannot tie up his equipment for long periods.

Will you be stripping all the old paint off and doing a complete rework or do you simply need to repair a panel? The first requires an area where you can make a mess. The latter won't be as messy, but requires products compatible with the existing finish.

Consider then, your equipment and facility. There is a system to match what you have access to. You can't get a show-car finish using aerosol spray cans.

## TIME & COST

Paint costs vary greatly. Synthetic enamel is the least expensive; and the most expensive is catalyzed urethane. In most cases, a paint system in between will do. However, don't just consider the cost. For instance, some expensive paint systems work so quickly that the time saving is worth it. If you rent a spray booth, time saved is money that doesn't leave your pocket.

Paint booths do more than protect new paint from contamination. They provide excellent lighting and filter out airborne particles.

Larger than home work-shop compressors, these two-stage, intercooled "industrial-strength" beauties can keep up with any spray gun.

Here's a tip on how to save a lot of money on paint. Paint suppliers have a problem. When they mix a batch of paint for a special order, they sometimes goof and the paint does not match. Consequently, the customer refuses the order.

These paints are nearly impossible to sell because they were mixed to match a specific color. If your heart is not set on an exact shade, you may be able to buy one of these paints for one-half to one-third the regular price. So, if it would normally cost $150 a gallon, getting it for $60 or $75 would be a terrific buy.

Another tip: Use wash thinner or a cheap bulk thinner to clean tools. Discount paint stores sell bulk lacquer thinner for half the price of high-quality thinner used for reducing color-coat lacquer. Bring your own 1- to 5-gallon can to put it in and label it as such. Just remember never to use cheap thinner for thinning paint. Only use it as a cleaning solvent.

If possible, paint your vehicle in a booth. This minimizes paint contamination, allowing you to use inexpensive synthetic enamels.

## SUBSURFACE COVERAGE

You must also consider whether the paint works with or against the surface you want to cover. A common example is that you can't spray lacquer directly on enamel. Most of us have learned this the hard way. Lacquer thinners dissolve and lift enamel— separate the enamel from the surface it's applied to. This causes total failure of the paint. Enamel, however, has no effect on lacquer— unless it is catalyzed urethane on fresh lacquer.

You must also consider whether you will be painting bare metal, and if it is ferrous or non-ferrous, or galvanized steel. ABS, fiberglass, nylon and other body materials present yet other considerations. Fortunately, these are problems only if you let them be. There are primers for each of these applications.

If this book does not answer a question you have, your best friend may be the manager of an automotive paint-supply store. If he can't help, ask the factory representative. The paint-store manager will have the factory rep's phone number. The answer to your question will be a phone call away.

Let's review the major points to consider when deciding on a paint system. First is safety. Next are the facilities and equipment. Think also about cost and time. Even if you're a home craftsman, your time has value. Finally, there's the surface to be covered. The primers, sealers or surfacers must be compatible with the subsurface and final paint. When all of these requirements are met, you have a paint system. Now, let's look at auto paints and how they developed over the years.

# HISTORY & BACKGROUND OF PAINT FINISHES

## EARLY PAINTS

The earliest paints were not really paints, but dyes. From European caveman to Southwest Indian, people colored their bodies and decorations with these pigmented dyes made from berries, roots and herbs. For a *binder*—something to hold it together—they used mud. Water or blood was used for thinning. This didn't give a satisfactory or long-lasting job. By the time fire was used for heating and cooking, they discovered that the dyes became part of this material when heated.

These would be known as *thermosetting* paints in today's terms. The Japanese and Chinese developed "real" paint. They used an excretion of the Lac bug to develop a hard shellac—read *shel-lac*. When pigmented with various natural dyes, this gave a long-lasting, colorful paint. Shellac was used to decorate their art. Some museums exhibit Japanese and Chinese shellacs dating back to 1000 B.C. Today we no longer call them *shellacs;* we call them *lacquers*. And we no longer make shellac or lacquer from bug droppings. We still, however, make a nitrocellulose lacquer that is a product of the cell walls of wood fibers. Most modern lacquer is acrylic lacquer—a product of petrochemical advances. But, we're getting ahead of our brief history lesson.

Before the '20s, manufacturers painted cars with varnishes consisting of different formulas of pitch, tar, solvents and color pigments. Applied with a brush and drying by evaporation, it took about a month to paint a car. The finished product was beautiful, but the paint had a very short life.

Nitrocellulose coatings were introduced between 1922 and 1924. Hard resins, plasticizers and nitrocellulose composed the formulas. They dried much faster, but were limited mostly to dark colors, and a few light colors. Chalking and dulling was rapid. Between 1926 and 1928 a white pigment that reduced chalking was developed. The '30s saw great improvements in paints. Synthetic enamel was introduced, as was the baking process for alkyd melamine enamel. Enamel used on the produc-

Some paint stores sell inexpensive dual-purpose thinner, such as this from Pap's. It is both wash thinner and primer thinner. Look for an equivalent thinner at your local paint store.

tion line at that time contained either a melamine or urea resin, so that the film could be cured by baking for 30 minutes at 250F. From 1930 to 1960, Ford, Chrysler and American Motors used this type of enamel. Continued improvements took place in the last part of this period, resulting in the so-called *super enamels*.

Between 1957 and 1959, General Motors introduced a new type lacquer in the form of the thermoplastic-acrylic lacquer. Later, they changed from a rubbing and polishing formula to a *reflow* formula. It was first baked and then reflowed at higher temperatures after imperfections were sanded out in the coating.

In the early '60s a thermoset acrylic enamel was adopted by Ford, Chrysler and American Motors. In 1970, a new type of reflow thermoset acrylic enamel was used.

Another type of coating system was introduced in 1971, and adopted by General Motors, Ford, Chrysler and American Motors. This coating was dubbed *Non-Aqueous Dispersion* (N.A.D.). Basically, this means that the resin and pigment are dispersed in a non-solvent, similar to gasoline. It was applied to the car, then heat from baking fused the particles.

Research is being conducted all the time. Much of this research is aimed at reducing harmful emissions and

fire hazards. General Motors is using waterborne coatings that eliminate organic solvents. Water is used as the carrier and is forced out through high-temperature baking.

## MODERN PAINT

Although we've come a long way in the development of paint finishes, there is still a long way to go. Tons upon tons of thinners, reducers and solvents evaporate daily into our atmosphere. Continued research will bring more water-based paints. Attempts are being made to produce a satisfactory and economical powder coating. Powder will be applied to bare metal and melted by heat or electricity to produce a high-gloss, ceramic-like hard finish.

Today, we have four basic types of paints: acrylic lacquer, acrylic enamel, synthetic enamel and two types of catalyzed enamels: acrylic urethane and polyurethane—which are highly resistant to acids, fuels, and chemicals. All are available in clear or color.

**Acrylic Lacquer**—In the past, acrylic lacquer has been the choice of most professionals to refinish show cars. In the '50s everyone wanted "15 coats of hand-rubbed lacquer (nitrocellulose)." However, due to recent environmental laws, lacquer's glory days may be numbered. As much as 85% of thinned lacquer paint evaporates into the air. But it is still the easiest paint to spray, which makes it a good choice for beginners and do-it-yourself enthusiasts. Lacquer dries quickly, and can be applied in thinner coats to avoid drips and sags.

With today's lacquers, 15 coats are not necessary to build *depth*. Usually, four coats are sufficient, depending on the color. Yellow and white, because of their weak pigmentation, often require more coats. In the early years, one or two coats were sprayed on the car. The surface was sanded—usually with #400-grit paper—until all the *orange peel* was removed. Orange peel is the effect paint displays when, instead of flowing out level, it tends to dry bumpy, similar to the surface of an orange.

When all orange peel was removed, or as much as possible, another one or two coats were applied. The same sanding operation was repeated. This cycle was repeated until the painter

Orange peel usually results from using a thinner or reducer that evaporates too quickly, preventing paint flow-out.

Enamel reducers and lacquer thinners are available in three evaporation rates: slow, medium and fast.

had built sufficient depth to: fill imperfections in the subsurface; remove all traces of orange peel; and leave enough paint to keep color after rubbing with compound for the final finish.

These operations have been reduced considerably with the use of acrylic lacquer and thinners that have varying evaporation rates. By thinning the lacquer with a medium- or fast-evaporating thinner for the first two or three coats, color may be applied one coat over another with no drying time in between. The final coat is thinned with a slow-evaporating thinner. This allows the lacquer to *flow-out,* nearly eliminating the orange-peel effect. The higher-quality binders and pigments give sufficient depth over old-style lacquer, so these three or four coats are sufficient to hold up under color sanding and buffing.

Acrylic lacquer is also used widely for spot repairs because of its fast-drying capability. Scratches, nicks and surface imperfections may quickly be repaired by a water wash, followed by a solvent wash. The damaged area is featheredged and primed with several coats of primer/surfacer. After the surface has dried, the top coats are spotted, melted or blended into the original finish surrounding the repaired area. The repair is finished after sanding and buffing.

Some of the drawbacks to acrylic lacquer have already been explained. To achieve the final surface finish, a long operation of sanding and buffing must follow. Second, lacquer is generally more expensive than acrylic

enamel and always more than synthetic enamel. Usually, lacquer thinners are more expensive than enamel reducers. And they are more volatile than enamel reducers.

Use lacquer if you must spray your car in a garage or on a driveway. Its fast-drying quality reduces dust and other contamination. If something does land on the freshly applied surface, you can repair it easily. Allow the paint to dry for five minutes. With the corner of a piece of #400-grit paper, remove the bug or dust particle and sand the area smooth. Give the sanded area a little shot of paint and everything is fine again. If you don't have a power buffer, not to worry. Every paint manufacturer makes hand rubbing compound. It takes a lot of time and muscle, but there is no reason why you cannot do a professional-looking job if you are willing to invest the time and material.

**Synthetic Enamel**—Synthetic enamel, or *one-part enamel,* is the least expensive of the five paints. This is not to say it's cheap. Synthetic enamel just doesn't cost as much as the others. It requires fewer top coats than acrylic lacquer. It is very slow drying—up to 24 hours—but dries to a high gloss. No sanding or buffing is required. This slow-drying process allows synthetic enamel to flow-out, minimizing the orange-peel effect.

These reasons are why many professional refinishing shops—those with high-quality spray booths and banks of infrared heat lamps—prefer synthetic enamel to other paints.

The heat lamps give the customer the *baked-enamel* surface that has become synonymous with durability and high gloss. Baking temperatures range from 140 to 200F. These temperatures are achieved through the use of infrared heat lamps in large banks of reflectors that extend the length of the car. This is an advantage because rapid surface drying by solvent evaporation prevents dust penetration and it further minimizes orange peel.

Although amateurs can use synthetic enamel, it should be applied and dried in a booth. If baking facilities are not available, paint your car in a booth on a weekend morning and leave it for 24 hours before introducing it to the dusty outdoors.

**Additives** or rapid-dry reducers will speed drying time, but compare costs with other systems. The additional cost of additives may negate any savings gained by using synthetic enamel.

Another problem with using synthetic enamel is overspray. Because of the slow drying rate, overspray that settles on appliances, the kids' bikes or whatever, it will be difficult to remove. Unlike lacquer overspray that

For that "baked-enamel" finish, you'll need heat lamps or a gas oven such as this.

Select a paint system, such as Martin Senour's, and stay with it. Disregarding this rule will guarantee paint failure.

dries before settling and can be wiped off like dust, enamel overspray settles wet—it sticks. It makes a mess.

If you must use synthetic enamel outside a spray booth, be sure to spray when there's no wind. Also, pray for bright sunlight to speed drying. Wet down the work area—driveway, street, lawn or wherever—to hold down dust. Caution: Don't get water on the car. And don't work under a tree, carport or other overhangs. These have things that will fall into your paint.

The best way to use synthetic enamel is to do all bodywork and preparation as we've described. Do masking and chrome removal yourself. Buy your own paint. Then, take it to a high-production paint shop. They will spray it for you in their booth, pass it through their dryer and charge a minimal fee. The price and time will be less than if you use acrylic lacquer—without all the hassles.

**Acrylic Enamel**—Although it costs more, acrylic enamel has greater durability and higher gloss than synthetics. Acrylic enamel has many other advantages. It dries to a harder finish than synthetic enamel. Acrylic enamel also dries faster and without the need for baking, although baking accelerates drying. It resists chalking and fading better than synthetic enamel or lacquer. Acrylic enamel

also has excellent flow characteristics and greater flexibility than lacquer.

Lacquer, if applied too heavy, will crack and is highly susceptible to stone chips. These problems are largely overcome by acrylic enamel.

Acrylic enamel is one of the best for *polychromatic*—metallic—colors. Aluminum particles in synthetic enamel cause quick pigment fading and chalking. These are not problems with acrylic enamels. Acrylic enamels are available in a broader range of colors than are synthetics, too.

This color availability makes acrylic enamel more popular for repair and refinishing of complete sections, such as doors, hoods, fenders and deck lids. Most OEM paints have a color code. By cross-referencing a paint code, paint stores can mix an acrylic-enamel formula for matching the OEM paint. If the original paint has faded, a good paint mixer can change the formula to match the faded paint. Then, a good painter can apply it to match the rest of the car body so it will be indistinguishable. We discuss paint matching in Chapter 10.

Acrylic enamel should be sprayed in a booth. However, if you can't, add hardener and use a medium-fast reducer—weather permitting—to accelerate drying time. If the weather is very hot or dry, avoid fast reducer. Instead, use a medium or slow reducer.

Acrylic enamel can be two-toned or recoated within the first six hours of drying. After six hours, a recoat sealer—clear—should be used.

Acrylic enamel is easy to apply and dries quickly to a deep luster and high gloss, requiring no buffing. Its porcelain-like finish is extremely durable. Cost is slightly higher than synthetic enamel, but less than acrylic lacquer.

**Catalyzed Acrylic Enamel**—As far as we're concerned, the "King Of The Road" paint is catalyzed acrylic enamel that uses a urethane catalyst. It is one of the most modern and sophisticated finishing systems available.

In addition to having all the advantages of acrylic enamel, urethane hardener makes it highly resistant to many chemicals, stone bruises, nicks and scratches. It also produces a tough, mirror-like finish that retains its gloss longer than synthetic or regular acrylic enamel. Two-toning and recoating can be done anytime.

We think that a five-year-old could satisfactorily spray a job with this combination. By using a *three-coat system* consisting of *fog coat, color coat* and *gloss coat,* you don't have to worry much about runs or sags. The three-coat system is explained in Chapter 9.

Think of the catalyst for acrylic enamel the same way you think of body-filler catalyst or fiberglass-resin catalyst. A chemical reaction between the two of them—acrylic enamel and the catalyst—creates a finished product harder than either individually. As the old saying goes, "The whole is greater than the sum of its parts."

Because catalyzed acrylic enamel cures so hard, it can be color-sanded and buffed the same as lacquer. And the finished product looks similar to the very best lacquer job. This allows you two options: You can spray it and leave the surface as is. Or, if you find excess dirt or other foreign matter in the surface, or—heaven forbid—a run, the problem area or complete surface may be sanded out and buffed. This results in one of the most beautiful finishes possible.

Color-sanded and buffed catalyzed acrylic enamel rapidly is becoming the top choice in show-car finishes, even over acrylic lacquer. Again, the polychromatic range is greater and the paint is more durable. Special colors for custom work, such as pearls and iridescents, last longer.

Here's an example of how durable catalyzed acrylic enamel is: If a custom-car builder or an automotive-restoration shop doesn't have access to a powder-coating facility for painting a frame, catalyzed acrylic enamel is used—even if lacquer is used for the body.

Unfortunately, catalyzed acrylic enamel is expensive, generally costing about 30% more than acrylic lacquer. In many cases, the additional expense is well worth it.

**Base Coat/Clear Coat**—For the ultimate in automotive finishes the base-coat/clear-coat system gives the greatest "wet" look. This is the latest factory finish. One or two light coats of paint are applied to give the car its color. Then, for gloss and depth, a clear-coat is sprayed over the color-coat. The color-coat need not be glossy because the clear-coat gives the gloss.

Three clear-coat systems are available in the aftermarket: acrylic-lacquer clear-coat (used by many Japanese manufacturers), acrylic-enamel clear-coat (used over acrylic enamel), and urethane-enamel clear-coat (used over lacquer).

Clear-coating is an additional step to consider. This is another reason why it's important to stay with one system. Use materials supplied by one manufacturer so they will be compatible.

If you wish to repair a base-coat/clear-coat finish, consult your paint supplier. He should know which system will be compatible with the paint on the car. However, if you are starting from scratch, any of the three—acrylic lacquer, enamel or urethane—will give you a job that should last for years.

Base coat/clear-coat combination we used on our project car.

Base-coat/clear-coat systems work well. Unfortunately, we managed to developed a *curtain*—series of runs—in clear coat.

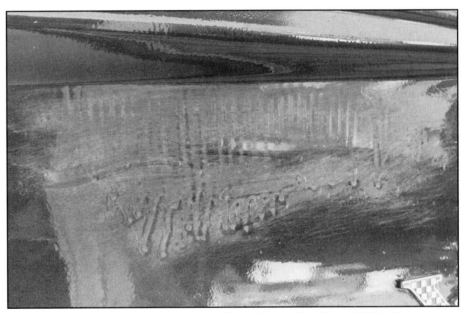

To repair runs, sags or curtains, start by sanding off tops with #80- or #100-grit dry paper.

Hint: One great use for clear urethane is to bring a high gloss to a dull finish where buffing is impractical.

During the restoration of an antique or special-interest car, the standard practice was to spray the exterior of the car with lacquer. However, door jams, engine compartment, body-pan underside and other areas were painted with acrylic enamel; it usually didn't match. The enamel gave gloss where buffing was impractical or very difficult. It was necessary to spray the enamel first, then mask it to prevent lifting by the lacquer. Several steps are eliminated and a better job is produced using the latest approach.

Now, exterior, interior and underside areas are all sprayed with lacquer. The areas previously painted with acrylic enamel need only enough paint to color the surface. To give those areas gloss, they are given a catalyzed-urethane clear-coat. No masking is required because the lacquer will be sanded and buffed. Also, clear urethane will not lift or damage the lacquer. The result is the best of both worlds—and with much less work.

A bonus is that clear-coat urethane resists fuels, acids and other chemicals. Where best to use it than in an engine compartment or the underside of a body?

Now you know about the various paints available. Discuss the project with your supplier. He'll help you make the right decision on what materials to use.

Finish by wet sanding with #400, then #600-grit paper.

Each major manufacturer offers a refinishing guide at minimal cost—sometimes it's free. Even if there's a charge, it's well worth your investment. The guide tells about the materials the manufacturer sells and describes how to use, mix and match them. With the directions in this book and the manufacturer's product-user directions, you will have all the information necessary to give your car a professional-looking paint job.

## THINNERS & REDUCERS

Most materials used to thin paints to spraying consistency are called *thinners* or *reducers*. Actually, they are both thinners because thinners and reducers change the consistency of paint to make it thinner. However, thinners generally refer to solvents that thin acrylic and nitrocellulose lacquer. Solvents used in acrylic, synthetic and urethane enamel are *reducers*.

**Retarders**—Another thinning solvent falls into a category called *retarders*. There are two types of retarders: *Universal* retarders are for lacquers and enamels. Urethanes, require their own retarder.

As the name implies, a retarder slows something. In this case, it's paint drying time. See charts, pages 114 and 121 for retarder use.

Part of choosing a paint system is selecting the thinner or reducer that will assist paint *flow-out* characteristics. Flow-out determines the shine or gloss of the final coat. It also determines the amount of orange peel in lacquer and in some enamel paints.

Thinners and reducers are only two of several factors that influence paint flow-out. Others include air pressure at the gun, quality and style of the gun, hose size and others. These are detailed in Chapter 9.

**Lacquer Thinners: Acrylic & Nitrocellulose**—We include nitrocellulose lacquer because it is used in many applications, particularly for antique cars. It is used primarily on those cars that were originally painted with nitrocellulose lacquer to maintain their originality. *Warning: Do not use thinners specified for acrylic lacquer in nitrocellulose lacquer or vice versa.* These thinners are not interchangeable. It will destroy the paint. You'll get something that looks like curdled milk!

**Thinner Drying Rate**—Lacquer thinners come in as many as five drying, or evaporation, rates, depending on the manufacturer. The three common drying rates are fast, medium and slow.

Two considerations when selecting a thinner's drying rate are weather and which coat of paint you're applying. Let's look at the weather first. The basic rule is that drying rate should be the inverse of the temperature: slower drying rates for warmer temperatures; faster drying rates for colder temperatures.

Thinner evaporating rate helps determine the paint flow-out. If the weather is hot and dry, and you use a fast-drying thinner, you'll only spray powder. The paint will evaporate before it reaches the car's surface. If you use a medium-speed thinner, it will reach the surface, but so little thinner will be left that the paint will not bond well. A slow-drying thinner allows the paint to leave the gun, "melt" into the previous coat and flow out smooth.

On a cold, wet day, that same slow-drying thinner will not evaporate fast enough. This will cause the paint to run and allow it to absorb moisture from the air. And moisture causes paint to *blush,* which is a milky white haze that appears on the surface as the paint *tries* to dry. A fast-drying thinner in this temperature and humidity extreme avoids these problems.

Another consideration when selecting a lacquer thinner is the particular coat of paint you're preparing to spray. The first few coats should dry as quickly as possible, without a dusty overspray. This prevents dust and bugs from contaminating the fresh paint. Then the final coat should be thinned with a very slow-drying, high-gloss thinner. This allows the last coat to "melt" in heavily and flow out smoothly. Some professional painters spray the final coat with almost pure thinner, consisting of 90% thinner, 10% lacquer. This is a difficult process. We suggest that you don't try it. Using this much thinner can lead to runs and sags that will require a lot of repair time.

The manufacturer's refinishing guide will suggest which thinner to use at what temperature. Some paint shops have wall-mounted thermometers that indicate directly on the face of the thermometer what thinner/reducer to use at which temperature!

When finished sanding, there should be no evidence of the run, sag or curtain.

Buff sanded area with power buffer or rub it by hand to bring back gloss.

*Do not thin paint with thinner that's been in use for more than 30 days. Use fresh thinner.*

**How Much to Use?**—Additionally, the manufacturer's guide tells you—as do the directions on the paint can—how much thinner to add. It is as important to use the correct amount of thinner as it is to have the correct evaporation characteristics because it also determines paint flow-out characteristics. Primarily, the percentage of thinner used determines how the paint comes out of the gun. Incorrectly thinned, paint will come out in globs, strings or as dust.

Thinning rates are generally given as percentages. For example, the directions may say **Reduce by 150%**. This means use one-and-a-half parts of thinner to one part of paint. In other words, if one gallon of paint is thinned with one gallon of thinner you reduced the paint 100%. If you use a gallon-and-a-half of thinner to one gallon of paint, you've reduced the paint 150%. To make it easier, use the following chart as reference.

**Enamel Reducers: Synthetic & Acrylic**—Most that applies to thinners applies to reducers. Temperature affects reducer drying rate just as it does thinners. However, total drying time is different because enamel dries by evaporation *and oxidation*. Although we don't go into a discussion of oxidation or *polymerization*, you should understand that enamel must *cure* or *set up* after the solvents—reducers—have evaporated.

Select a reducer carefully. The directions on the label suggest a variety of compatible reducers and how to use them. Always follow the manufacturer's directions. Just as acrylic-lacquer thinner is different from nitrocellulose lacquer, so is acrylic-enamel and synthetic-enamel reducer different. If the wrong reducer is used, you'll probably have to throw out the whole mess and start over. We've seen the wrong reducer used when it wouldn't mix with the paint. It simply floated on top of the paint like oil in water!

**Urethane-Enamel Reducers**—Some urethanes must have their own reducers. They cannot be reduced using acrylic- or synthetic-enamel reducers. Urethane reducers are available in slow, medium and fast evaporation rates. This evaporation-rate selection is satisfactory because urethanes are more forgiving than lacquers. If you use urethane correctly, it's unlikely you'll have a failure.

**Wash Thinner**—We mentioned wash thinner earlier as a money-saver. Now let's look at what wash thinner does. Wash thinner dissolves almost any paint. It must be used for washing equipment. The key word is *equipment. Never use wash thinner on the surface of something you intend to paint.* Contaminants in wash thinner will ruin any subsurface. Therefore, only use wash thinner to clean spray guns, plastic-filler tools, spills and other *equipment.*

We recommend that after washing a spray gun with wash thinner, to run some fast-drying thinner through the gun to clear the wash thinner. This will prevent contamination of the next cup of paint sprayed.

| Parts by Volume | | | Volume Measure | |
|---|---|---|---|---|
| Percent | Paint | Reducer or Thinner | Paint | Reducer or Thinner |
| 12 1/2% | 8 | 1 | 8 oz. | 1 oz. |
| 25% | 4 | 1 | 8 oz. | 2 oz. |
| 33 1/3% | 3 | 1 | 8 oz. | 2 3/5 oz. |
| 40% | 5 | 2 | 8 oz. | 3 1/5 oz. |
| 50% | 2 | 1 | 8 oz. | 4 oz. |
| 75% | 4 | 3 | 8 oz. | 6 oz. |
| 100% | 1 | 1 | 8 oz. | 8 oz. |
| 125% | 4 | 5 | 8 oz. | 10 oz. |
| 150% | 2 | 3 | 8 oz. | 12 oz. |
| 200% | 1 | 2 | 8 oz. | 16 oz. |

Note: For volumes greater than 8 oz., multiply the reducer or thinner amount by the same number as the increase in volume. For example, for a 25% mixture of 16 oz. of paint, you'd add 4 oz. of reducer or thinner. Chart courtesy Martin Senour

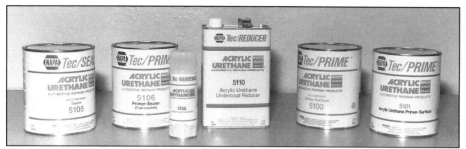

Here are six of over a dozen primers formulated for specific applications.

Excellent product, catalyzed polyester primer doesn't shrink. This eliminates additional filling, thus saving considerable time.

Let's now look at what should go underneath all of the expensive paint and thinner.

## UNDERCOATS

At last count there were about 16 types of paint undercoats, including primers, primer/surfacers, sealers, primer/sealers and adhesion sealers. Among each of these categories are sub-categories for lacquer, enamel and urethane. Let's look at a few.

**Primers**—Primers do one thing: prepare a bare surface for receiving either a surfacer or sealer. They do little or no filling because they have minimal solids. There are more primers designed to cover metal, plastic or fiberglass. *Metal primer* is available for most metal sufaces, such as aluminum, bare steel or galvanized steel. Generally, primers are lacquer-based. There are also excellent enamel-based primers. Polypropylene primer for priming polypropylene plastic is special because it is neither lacquer or enamel.

**Primer/Surfacers**—Primer/surfacers prepare bare surface for paint, and fill small voids. Typically, lacquer or enamel primer/surfacers are available in light gray, dark gray and red. Acrylic urethane primer/surfacers are available in beige and gray. Many of these, such as Martin Senour's TEC Prime 5100, may be tinted to the same color as the finished coat of paint. On color coats that tend to be a bit transparent, such as maroon, this is a real advantage.

**Sealer (Barrier Coat)**—A sealer, or *barrier coat,* seals, or *barricades,* the old coat from the new. This prevents color-bleeding of old paint into the new. Old maroons and burgundies are notorious for this. And, sealing an old finish prevents it from being lifted by the new finish. This is particularly important where lacquer is put over enamel. Without a sealer, the old enamel will surely lift.

Sealers are usually clear or have gray pigment. Pigmented sealer helps you see whether the surface being sealed is completely covered. In addition to clear and pigmented sealers, most manufacturers provide *sanding sealer* or *non-sanding sealer.* Non-sanding sealer is useful in areas where it's difficult to sand, such as inside door jams. Sealers come in lacquer and enamel.

**Primer/Sealers**—Unlike primer/surfacers, primer/sealers are not for filling. Rather, they prime bare surfaces and seal old finishes.

The priming ability of primer/sealers can come in handy. Suppose you featheredge a scratch in an OEM paint job. Sanding may take the paint and primer down to bare metal. If you plan to shoot acrylic lacquer over the area, seal it with primer/sealer to prime the bare spot and seal the featheredge against lifting.

We mentioned waterborne, or water-based, coatings on page 95. The only waterborne primer/sealer we're aware of is available from Rinshed-Mason (R-M) Paints. This is an outstanding product. When we first saw it demonstrated, we thought the factory rep had lost his mind. He sanded the area to be covered with #80-grit sandpaper! He shot his waterborne primer/sealer directly over this surface to fill and level the scratches, and prime the bare surface. After drying, we wet sanded the area with #400 paper and finished it with acrylic lacquer. It worked! We now strongly recommend waterborne primer/ sealer because of its leveling characteristics and priming and sealing abilities. And it is environmentally safe!

**Adhesion Sealers**—Except for a few differences, *adhesion sealer* is similar to other sealers. It comes ready to spray and requires no thinning. An adhesion sealer works well when applying acrylic lacquer over old paint. Keep in mind acrylic lacquer's tendency to lift anything but other acrylic lacquer.

**Summary**—There are many undercoatings to select from. Many are so specialized that even the professional rarely uses them—such as clear polypropylene primer. It is important to be aware of these products so you can solve specific problems when they arise.

## PAINTER'S HELPERS

There are dozens of products for solving specific painting problems. We'll cover some here. New products are being introduced constantly, though. Even though we don't mention a product, don't assume it doesn't exist.

**Flex-Agent**—Flexible vinyl or urethane is used frequently on front and rear bumpers and for panels that install between bumpers and body panels. The paint on this flexible material must match the body paint and be flexible so it will withstand bending and flexing without cracking or chipping.

A *flex-agent* additive allows the paint to cure and harden to a high gloss, but remain flexible. The flex-agent is compatible with all paints. You don't have to choose from a variety of flex-agents to match a particular paint.

Flex-agent can also be added to acrylic lacquer for painting interior parts, such as vinyl trim and upholstery where flexing is necessary. Flex-agent works well when reconditioning the interior of an older car where the vinyl has suffered from sun fade.

**Flattening (Sunburn) Agent**—If you want to turn a high-gloss finish into a semi-gloss or flat finish, yet retain a smooth surface, use flattening agent. Like flex-agent, flattening agent is compatible with all paints. The container directions tell how to use it for the desired effect—the more agent, the less glossy the appearance. Typical uses for flattening agent is in engine-compartment paint or for restoring a musclecar hood to its original semi-gloss black.

**Texturing Agent**—Texturing agent, when combined with paint, causes the paint to gather thicker in some areas and thinner in others. The action is similar to water beading on a waxed surface. This produces a bumpy texture that can be controlled by the amount of agent used. Besides vinyl-top repairs, it makes a nice texture on interior-trim parts on older-model cars.

**Suede Base**—Suede base was designed to achieve the flat, non-reflective original suede-like finish used on instrument panels and other interior parts. It is compatible with both enamel and lacquer. To use it, add the base to the paint at a ratio of about 25%. Follow this with the recommended thinner or reducer.

**Fisheye Eliminator**—Fisheyes are those little, round, imperfections found in the paint *after* the paint has been applied to what you thought was a perfectly clean surface. Surprise! It wasn't clean. A speck of silicone left from a wax job done months, or even years, ago will cause fisheyes. The result is small, round spots, reminiscent of a fish's eye, over which the paint will not flow or adhere to.

Fisheyes can be corrected without redoing the subsurface. Adding *fisheye eliminator* to the paint for the next coat. The directions on the container tells you how much to use.

The types of fisheye eliminator include a universal product and one for enamels only. Use the universal type if you're spraying acrylic lacquer.

**Cleaners**—If you sand a surface before cleaning it, you'll force wax

and silicone into the subsurface. Clean it first with a *wax and silicone remover*, such as R/M Pre Kleeno. In California and some other major states the Environmental Protection Agency is pushing the use of low VOC (Volatile Organic Compound) cleaners. These environmentally friendly, water-based cleaners, do an excellent job and help keep some of

---

**VINYL-TOP REPAIR TIP**

Here's a fast vinyl-top problem solver. Add two ounces of flex-agent to one quart of acrylic lacquer and four to six ounces of texturing agent. Thin to spraying consistency. Spray this combination over a scratched, burnt and peeling vinyl top. The result, from ten feet away, will look like a new vinyl top.

---

**PAINTING PLASTIC BODY COMPONENTS**

Plastic body components used in late-model vehicles are handled differently than steel, fiberglass or aluminum body materials. First, you must determine what family of plastics a particular component is made from. Then, you can determine what painting method or additive to use. Below is a listing of parts, their plastic type and code, and how they should be painted.

| EXAMPLE | PLASTIC TYPE (CODE) | PAINT PROCEDURE |
|---|---|---|
| 1. Bumper fillers and Guards | Semi-Rigid Vinyl (PVC) | Use Flex-agent |
| 2. Fascias | RIM Urethane (PUR) | Use Flex-agent |
| 3. End Caps, Soft (same as RIM) | Thermoplastic Polyurethane (TPUR) | Use Flex-agent |
| 4. Nose Cones (Hard), End Extensions, Spoilers | Fiberglass-Reinforced Polyester (UP) | Same as Steel |
| 5. Ash Trays | Phenolic (PF) | Same as Steel |
| 6. Louvers, End Extensions | Nylon (PA) | Same as Steel |
| 7. Louvers, Garnish Instrument Panels, Trim Panels | ABS | No Flex-agent |
| 8. Garnish Moldings Cowl Trim Panels | Polypropylene (PP) | No Flex-agent |
| 9. Dash Cover | Flexible ABS | No Flex-agent |
| 10. Bumper Fillers | Ethylene Propylene Monomer (EPM) | Use Flex-agent |

Beginning in the early '80s, auto manufacturers began coding plastic components as shown above. However, to determine which plastic is used on earlier models, cut a sliver from a hidden area. With long-nose pliers, insert it into a match flame. Watch how it burns, then compare it to the following:
● ABS burns with heavy black smoke.
● Polypropylene burns with little or no smoke.
● Vinyl burns with a blue-green tint.
Note: If you're unable to cut a sliver from what you think is vinyl, heat a copper wire red-hot. Immediately apply the wire to the vinyl in a what will be a hidden area of the plastic. A small glob of plastic will adhere to the wire. Use a match to burn this glob to determine the plastic.
Rigid ABS does not require primer. Paint will adhere directly to this plastic.
1. Wash the part with wax and silicone remover.
2. Color coat the part.
3. Allow it to dry and install.
Soft exterior plastic parts flex. Therefore, flex agent must be added to paint.
1. Wash part with wax and silicone remover.
2. Sand part with #400-grit or finer sandpaper.
3. Use flex agent in the following manner:
  a. One pint acrylic lacquer, one pint flex agent and 1-1/2 pints suitable thinner makes 3-1/2 pints prepared finish material.
  b. Mix lacquer and flex agent. Then add thinner.
  c. Apply eight to 10 double wet coats at 30 to 35 psi. Allow flash time between coats.
  d. Air dry approximately four hours at 70 to 85F before installing.
  e. Allow a minimum of two weeks before sanding and buffing.

There are a variety of buffing compounds from which to select.

Vinyl and plastic dyes allow you to change color of plastic and vinyl interior parts. This is great stuff for restoring color of vinyl crash pads.

the "crud" out of our atmosphere. Martin Senour makes a fine product called Kleanz-Easy II. Use a water-based, low VOC cleaner as you would any cleaner. On bare metal surfaces, however, be sure to dry thoroughly.

Never use lacquer thinner as a *wash*—cleaner. It will only spread around the contaminants, and won't remove them as does wax and silicone remover.

First clean the surface to be painted by washing it with mild detergent and water to remove dirt. Follow this with a wash using wax and silicone remover. You can now begin sanding. With this procedure, you'll have few problems with fisheyes.

**Buffing Compounds**—As with sandpaper, machine-rubbing and hand-rubbing compounds smooth the paint surface and remove orange peel and imperfections. Machine-rubbing compound is for use with power buffers. It comes in fine, medium and coarse grades. Hand-rubbing compounds are for those craftsmen who think that only hand work can bring out the real luster. Hand compounds generally come in fine and coarse grades. They do an excellent job.

The use of buffing, or rubbing, compound is explained in Chapter 9, beginning on page 119.

**Miscellaneous Products**—There are dozens of miscellaneous products available to the craftsman.

If you're into doing a super show job, start with bare metal. This means removing all the old paint by grinding it off or using a chemical paint remover. We recommend paint remover. Of the dozens on the market, select the strongest paint remover you can find.

After you've removed the paint, you must *condition* the metal to neutralize the remover and protect the metal against corrosion. There are many products for different metals, such as plain steel, galvanized steel and aluminum. Be sure the conditioner you select neutralizes *and* protects because there are products that do either but not both. Read the directions to be sure.

Although we discussed plastic body fillers in Chapter 7, little was said about the different *types* of fillers. To strengthen plastic fillers, some manufacturers add short or long fiberglass strands. These fillers work well with fiberglass products and are strong. But they are difficult to finish. They require a good surfacer to fill the voids created by the strands.

Powdered aluminum is another plastic-filler additive. This is used where rust removal is necessary and welding is difficult. An example of this is the rust that forms under a vinyl top around the rear-window reveal molding. It's a make-do fix. We don't recommend it, just acknowledge its existence.

Today good vinyl dyes are available. A few years ago, we would have said "less-than-adequate vinyl dyes." With proper cleaning of the material to be dyed, vinyl dyes are satisfactory products. Interior color changes are made easily.

A great new product and time saver is 'Slime.' It gets its name from its color and consistancy: green, thick and gooey. Slime may be sprayed or brushed onto surfaces which must be protected from overspray, such as tires, windows, or body panels when doing spot repairs. Apply it and allow it to dry then do your paint work. Later it may be hosed off after the job is done, leaving a clean surface free of overspray.

These are a few of the many products to make the painter's life easier. If you have a problem, we suggest that you talk to the paint-store manager or directly to a factory representative.

# 9 PAINTING EQUIPMENT & TECHNIQUES

Dave Gauthier installs headlight eyebrow on freshly restored and painted '56 Thunderbird. Immaculate paint reflects meticulous preparation.

The final phase of a paint project is applying the finish paint coat. Eight chapters are devoted to preparation; one to the finish coat. This eight-to-one ratio also holds true for the amount of preparation work. If you apply eight times more effort to prepare the surface than you do to finish it, odds are your job will be a success.

Throughout this book we've stressed that good paint will not make up for poor preparation. If you've prepared the surface correctly, the paint will reflect the time, effort and expense. Poor preparation will be reflected with even greater clarity.

In this chapter, we discuss the minimum amount of equipment you must have and how to use and maintain it. We also demonstrate and discuss paint application.

We include a section on painting problems, their causes and remedies. Before we start the final step, we'll say it again: If your preparation is careful and correct, you've eliminated most of the potential problems.

## SHOP EQUIPMENT

**Compressors**—A compressor must be able to develop and maintain sufficient pressure and volume. Pressure is expressed in pounds per square inch (psi) and volume in cubic feet per minute (cfm). The pressure is needed to atomize the paint, and volume is needed to evenly distribute it. Although there are several types of compressors, such as piston, diaphragm and blower, we'll cover only the piston style. There are single-stage and two-stage piston compressors.

**Single-stage compressors** use an electric-motor-driven crankshaft and one connecting rod and piston to compress air. The electric motor is usually 1/3 to 2 horsepower (HP) at 110 to 220 volts on a single-phase circuit. This is the type of electric current usually found in the home garage and small shop.

As the motor rotates the compressor, it drives the piston up and down.

103

| SIZE OF AIR HOSE INSIDE DIAMETER | AIR-PRESSURE DROP AT SPRAY GUN (PSI) | | | | |
|---|---|---|---|---|---|
| | 10-Foot Length | 15-Foot Length | 20-Foot Length | 25-Foot Length | 50-Foot Length |
| **1/4 inch** | | | | | |
| At 40-psi pressure | 8 | 9-1/2 | 11 | 12-3/4 | 24 |
| At 50-psi pressure | 10 | 12 | 14 | 16 | 28 |
| At 60-psi pressure | 12-1/2 | 14-1/2 | 16-3/4 | 19 | 31 |
| At 70-psi pressure | 14-1/2 | 17 | 19-1/2 | 22-1/2 | 34 |
| At 80-psi pressure | 16-1/2 | 19-1/2 | 22-1/2 | 25-1/2 | 37 |
| At 90-psi pressure | 18-3/4 | 22 | 25-1/4 | 29 | 39-1/2 |
| **5/16 inch** | | | | | |
| At 40-psi pressure | 2-3/4 | 3-1/4 | 3-1/2 | 4 | 8-1/2 |
| At 50-psi pressure | 3-1/2 | 4 | 4-1/2 | 5 | 10 |
| At 60-psi pressure | 4-1/2 | 5 | 5-1/2 | 6 | 11-1/2 |
| At 70-psi pressure | 5-1/4 | 6 | 6-3/4 | 7-1/4 | 13 |
| At 80-psi pressure | 6-1/4 | 7 | 8 | 8-3/4 | 14-1/2 |
| At 90-psi pressure | 7-1/2 | 8-1/2 | 9-1/2 | 10-1/2 | 16 |

Use table to determine pressure drop at gun for a given pressure at compressor, and hose ID and length. Table courtesy of DeVilbiss Company.

Combination pressure regulator and two-stage water trap; water is removed in first trap, pressure regulated by valve in center, and remaining moisture is removed by second trap.

On the downstroke, air is drawn into the cylinder. On the upstroke, this air is compressed and stored in a tank.

In most cases, the compressor head and electric motor are mounted on top of the storage tank. The volume of the tank ranges from 8 to 12 cubic feet. The single-stage, 1-1/2-horsepower, 12-cubic-foot compressor that develops 100 psi is the smallest compressor you should consider for simple painting projects. This gives you just enough volume and pressure to spray primers, surfacers and lacquers on small panels or areas. On a cool day, it can give sufficient air to spray a full car in lacquer. It will, however, tend to overheat because it will run continuously.

**Two-stage compressors** have either two or four pistons. The first, or largest piston, compresses air the same as the single-stage. This compressed air is then passed through an *intercooler* and into the second, or smaller cylinder. The air is further compressed in the second stage and stored in the tank.

The smallest two-stage compressor is 1-1/2 HP, 110 to 220 volts, single- or double-phase, on a 12-cubic-foot tank. There are models up to huge industrial-type compressors, too many to be covered in this book. The smallest two-stage compressor will serve your painting needs better than the largest single-stage compressor. Generally, a two-stage compressor will be able to stay ahead of the painter. It will also supply enough air to operate many of the pneumatic tools we discussed earlier. To select the right compressor, you need to determine what you need in terms of pressure and volume.

**Pressure**—In the single-stage-compressor discussion, we said the minimum pressure requirement was 100 psi. This arbitrary figure is based on what is generally manufactured. Most single-stage compressors have a minimum pressure of 100 psi. The compressor has an automatic "cut-off" switch that turns off the motor when 100 psi is reached. Similarly, it "cuts-in" at about 80 psi. Lacquers are generally sprayed in the 30- to 45-psi range. When pressure falls to 80 psi in the tank, the desired spraying pressure will barely be reached at the gun due to pressure drop in the hose and at the couplers.

**Volume**—The smallest compressor we will discuss develops about 10.5 cfm at 100 psi. A good, professional spray gun requires about 8.5 cfm. The key here is 10.5 cfm at *100 psi*. As pressure drops, so does air volume. With only a 2-cfm difference, a 10- to 12-cubic-foot storage tank will empty quickly.

If you're looking for a compressor, buy the largest you can afford. Base this on the cubic-foot-per-minute consumption of the tools you wish to use and the length of continuous time you'll be using them. It's extremely frustrating to run low on air while you're trying to lay out large quantities of paint, or to have a circuit breaker open because the compressor motor overheats. Remember that too much air is better than not enough. You can certainly spoil a job with too little air.

**Hoses & Couplers**—The standard air-hose inside diameters (ID) are 1/4, 5/16 and 3/8 inch. The larger the hose, the less air-pressure drop between tank and gun. Preferred hose size in most paint-and-body shops is 5/16 inch; 3/8 inch is heavy and hard to drag around; and 1/4-inch hose can't carry the volume. If the 1/4-inch hose must be used, it shouldn't be longer than 12 feet. The accompanying table gives air-pressure drop for various-length 1/4- and 5/16-inch-ID hoses at different pressures.

Quick couplers and other connectors should have a minimum 5/16-inch ID. A smaller ID excessively restricts airflow. One restriction causes pressure loss equal to the smallest passage.

**Filters & Traps**—Moisture is a constant problem. It gets into the paint and causes bubbles, water spots and lifting. Because moisture is in the air being compressed, even when the humidity drops to 3 or 4%, it means every cubic foot of compressed air contains eight or nine times the water contained in the atmosphere. This water gradually condenses in the tank and gets drawn into the line.

To prevent water in the tank from reaching the paint gun, you must use a trap to collect water in a glass or metal canister so it can be drained off. Again, select the best moisture trap you can afford. The trap should be compatible with the compressor—the larger the compressor, the larger the trap.

Air drawn into the compressor must be filtered. This prevents dust and dirt from wearing the cylinder-

Standard professional spray gun of auto-paint industry; external-mix, syphon-fed gun made of brass, steel and aluminum.

Through air line at base (arrow), gun constantly swirls paint inside cup. This keeps metallic particles, such as those in polychrome paints, from settling to cup bottom.

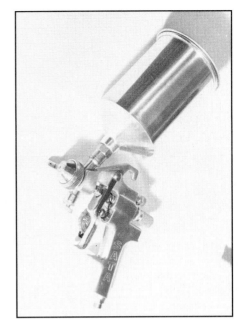

Gravity-fed gun is rapidly becoming favorite of auto-paint industry.

bore walls. Generally, this is an oil-soaked vinyl or felt filter that is positioned just inside the compressor intake. Be sure this filter is clean, oiled and in place. Compressor vibrations sometimes move filters out of position, so check it periodically.

**Maintenance**—Lines and compressors should be serviced on a daily basis. Begin by draining the compressor tank before each use by opening the small petcock at the bottom of the tank. Let the compressed air blow out the collected water. Drain the *transformer*—water trap—after every paint session. If the humidity is high, drain it several times in one day during use.

Inspect the compressor before you start spraying. Check the oil in the compressor sump. Change it every 60 to 90 days. Inspect strainers and filters to be sure they're in place and clean. Check for leaks in lines, connectors and valves. At 60-psi pressure, a 1/32-inch-diameter hole will leak 1 cfm, or 60 cubic feet per hour. This amounts to holding an average paint gun wide open for three hours. The result will be added wear and strain on the compressor.

Buying a proper compressor can be the most expensive part of a home paint job. To reduce this cost, consider renting one. They can be rented in almost any size.

You may also consider buying a used one. You can often find a great

deal, especially if the compressor has a slight problem. A leaking connection is easy and inexpensive to fix, and there are gasket kits readily available. Sometimes, it's even profitable to have the compressor rebuilt, but replacing an electric motor is another matter. Often, the motor is the most expensive item, and it costs a much to repair one than to buy a rebuilt replacement.

**SPRAY GUNS**

Just as it's important to have a good supply of air, it's equally important to have a good gun. The spray gun should be designed specifically for professional auto painting. Many spray guns are available at department stores, but even the best of these are unsatisfactory. Buy a *professional* spray gun, such as Sharpe or DeVilbiss, at a paint-supply store. You'll be assured of a quality tool specifically designed for paint spraying.

**Gun Types**—One basic type of professional spray gun incorporates a one-quart-cup paint container as an integral part of the gun. Another uses a separate one- to 10-gallon canister, with a hose connecting the gun to the container. These two types can be subdivided into *bleeder* and *non-bleeder, internal-* and *external-mix,* and *pressure-, gravity-* or *siphon-feed* guns.

The standard is the one-quart cup, non-bleeder, external-mix, siphon-fed

spray gun. The others have special painting uses.

**Bleeder** spray guns are used generally with small, diaphragm-type compressors. A constant stream of air passes through the gun. This prevents pressure buildup and consequent damage to the compressor diaphragm. The gun trigger controls only the flow of material, not airflow.

**Non-bleeding** spray guns control airflow with a shut-off valve at the trigger. This allows you to control both air and material with one trigger.

**Internal-** and **external-mix** guns are named for where the paint is mixed with the air. Internal-mix guns have pressurized cups that mix the paint and air *internally.* The material is then released from the gun in spray form. This is unsatisfactory for automotive work, but is OK for around-the-house painting.

External-mix guns are the norm of the auto-paint industry. Material is fed to the tip from the cup or tank by siphon or pressure. Air pressure from the sides of the nozzle atomizes the paint and shapes the spray pattern.

**Pressure-feed** guns are used mainly with large paint tanks. Material is placed in the separate canister or tank. The tank is pressurized and the material flows through a hose to the gun.

**Gravity-feed** guns have the paint container, usually a one-quart cup, sitting on *top* of them. Gravity forces

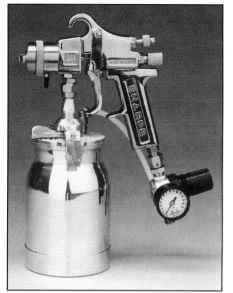

Sharpe's most current HVLP gun. Note the fluid pressure regulator and the air hose going to the cup. It's the pressure in the cup that forces the paint to the tip.

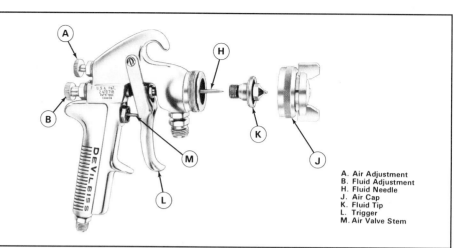

A. Air Adjustment
B. Fluid Adjustment
H. Fluid Needle
J. Air Cap
K. Fluid Tip
L. Trigger
M. Air Valve Stem

Figure 1. Knob A adjusts shape of spray pattern and B regulates material flow from cup. Drawing courtesy of DeVilbiss Company.

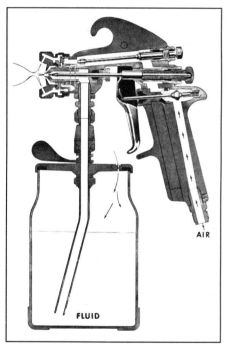

Cutaway of typical siphon-feed gun. Drawing courtesy of DeVilbiss Company.

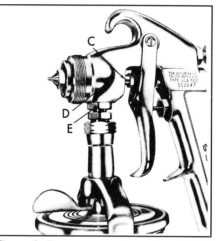

Figure 2. Passageway at needle valve C must be clean and oiled to prevent air leakage into material passage. Drawing courtesy of DeVilbiss Company.

the paint to the gun where it is mixed externally with air.

**Siphon-, or suction-feed,** guns are the most common and recognizable. These have the cup mounted below the gun. A metal pipe draws the paint from the cup into the gun.

All three feeding-system types are used in the auto-painting industry. Pressure-feed models work well for large-volume work with one color. A major advantage of the pressure-feed gun is it can be used upside-down. Gravity- and siphon-feed guns will not work in the inverted position.

**High volume low pressure guns** (HVLP) have been introduced to help meet the latest VOC levels mandated by recent environmental laws. Rather than using 45 to 60 lb. of air pressure to atomize the paint, the HVLP gun uses from 1 to 10 lb. maximum at the tip. However, this low pressure must be backed up by 12 to 18 cfm volume of air! As a rule of thumb, one horsepower will deliver about 4 cfm, so you'll need a minimum 5 HP compressor. From the compressor to the wall mounted regulator, 3/4-in. minimum pipe must be used, and no less than a 5/16 in. hose, which should be 25 to 50 feet long. Do *not* use a "cheater valve" with an HVLP gun. A cheater valve is an air pressure control valve at the gun. The valve and pressure gauge seen on the illustrated gun is the fluid pressure regulator. This provides pressure to the cup and is an integral part of the system. Conventional spray guns waste 70 to 75% of the material being sprayed. The HVLP system reduces this by 30 to 50%. These guns may be found in four basic types: conventional pressure-assisted siphon feed, air conversion units, turbine units and gravity feed.

**Low volume low pressure** guns are being developed for the home craftsman to meet these same requirements. They're for the occasional user rather than the production shop as they deliver paint quite slowly. It adds an additional 45 minutes to a full paint job.

Now that you know about the styles of paint guns, we'll confine further discussions to the standard siphon-feed, external-mix, non-bleeder gun.

### OPERATION & MAINTENANCE

To operate the gun, fill the cup with paint thinned or reduced to the manufacturer's specifications. Set air pressure to that recommended by the manufacturer. Some guns have a built-in pressure gage or an add-on pressure gage. Gages at the gun work better. Otherwise, you must determine gun pressure by compensating for pressure loss due to hose length and diameter, then set pressure at the compressor. If there are no air leaks, you can make the two standard adjustments by rotating the knurled-knobs A and B, Figure 1.

Figure 3

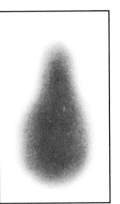

Figure 4

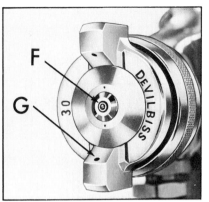

Figure 5. Position and cleanliness of wing-ports G determine spray pattern of material exiting port F. Wing-ports must be absolutely clean before satisfactory spray pattern can be achieved. Drawing courtesy of DeVilbiss Company.

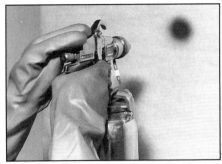

To adjust spray pattern begin by closing both the air and fluid adjustment knobs (clockwise). Turn air adjustment knob counterclockwise until a small dot appears when the trigger is pulled full back. You may have to open the fluid adjustment just a crack.

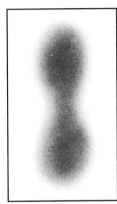

Figure 6

Figure 7

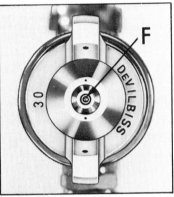

Figure 8. Straight-on view of nozzle. Restriction at position F causes spray pattern shown in Figure 9. Drawing courtesy of DeVilbiss Company.

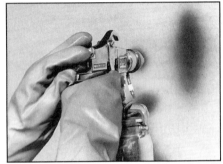

Begin opening the fluid adjustment until the pattern increases in size and volume.

Figure 9

Knob A governs the shape of the spray pattern from a tight, circular pattern to a wide, vertical, fan pattern, Shown in Figure 3.

Knob B governs the amount of material flowing from the cup. This can be turned off or opened completely. Regulate material flow to conform to the type of substance being sprayed and the desired width of spray. As pattern width increases, more material must be allowed to pass through the gun to compensate for the larger area to be covered.

Professional painters set spray pattern and volume each time by spraying a pattern on masking paper cover-

ing a window or other large expanse. Experiment the same way. Tape about 10 feet of masking paper to a wall or the inside of the garage door and make some test patterns. You'll be a proficient gun handler in no time.

**Correcting Spray Patterns—** Sometimes a pattern will be correct, but the gun will spit and splatter. To correct this malfunction, be sure everything is perfectly clean. The gun may have dried packing around the fluid needle valve, which allows air to enter the fluid passageways, C in Figure 2. Back out the nut and place two drops of machine oil in the packing. Replace and finger tighten the nut.

Another problem could be dirt between the fluid tip and gun body, K in Figure 1. A loose fluid tip will do the same thing. Remove the tip, then clean it and the gun body. Replace the tip. Or, there could be a loose or defective swivel nut, E in Figure 2.

If a poor pattern is the problem, one of the following remedies should cure it and give a pattern as shown, Figure 3. If your pattern looks like Figure 4—fat in the middle—or splatters, atomizing pressure is not high enough. Increase pressure at the tank or at the gun.

A split pattern, as shown by Figure 6—heavy at the ends and weak in the middle—is the result of atomizing pressure being too high. This is opposite of Figure 4. To correct a split pattern, reduce pressure until the pattern is the correct shape. If this doesn't do it and air pressure is OK, a split can be caused by too-wide a spray. To correct, turn material-control B counterclockwise. At the same time, adjust A clockwise to reduce the height of the pattern.

Figure 7 *half-moons* to the right because wing-port G is clogged. If the pattern half-mooned to the left, the other wing port would've been clogged. Cure this by removing the air cap, J. Soak it in thinner and clean the part. *Do not use any wire or metal instruments.*

If the spray pattern looks like Figure 9, there's a restriction around

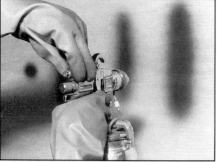

Increase size of pattern with the air adjustment knob. Continue increasing both fluid and air until the size and volume you wish to use is reached.

When setting an HVLP gun start by opening the fluid pressure regulator (with the trigger in the full on position) until the desired amount of paint begins to flow.

Look familiar? Here's the '64 Plymouth Barracuda used for leading project, page 73. Don's son, Steven, will do his first paint job while we shoot photos.

Molding must come off so peeled and chipped paint can be taken down to metal.

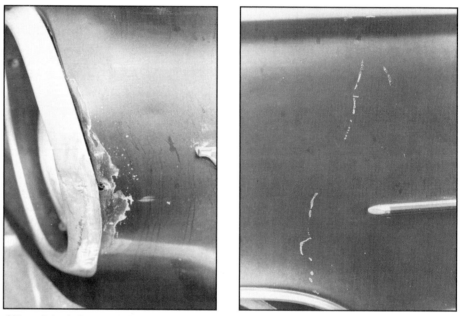

Although body has no major damage, paint is rough. Finish is peeling above wheel opening; fender is damaged at headlight; and there are miscellaneous scratches and abrasions. Featheredging with sandpaper and some minor filling will correct such damage.

the fluid tip at the position of F. If the restriction were at the bottom, the pattern would be heavy at the top. Remove the air cap and fluid tip. Wash them in thinner and replace.

**Setting The HVLP Gun**—Start by setting this regulator to 55 to 75 psi. This pressure is determined by the paint manufacturer's recommendation. Now, with the fluid pressure regulator in the full off (counterclockwise) position, pull the trigger full on. (Half on begins the air flow, full on adds the material flow.) Nothing but air will pass the tip until you begin to turn the fluid pressure regulator in the clockwise position. At about 2 to 3-lbs. of pressure the gun will begin to spray. Slowly continue turning knob clockwise to increase cup pressure until desired fluid delivery and atomization is achieved. Do not exceed 15 psi or you'll damage the cup. Now, shoot a test pattern. This pattern may be adjusted as you would with a standard gun.

**Maintenance**—The best way to ruin a gun is to not clean it *immediately after use.* Some catalyzed enamels and urethanes will set up in six hours. If this happens, you can just about kiss your gun goodbye. Hardened paint anywhere in an orifice or packing area reduces performance of the gun.

Fill the cup about 1/4-full of wash thinner and rinse out the excess paint. Pour this out and add another 1/4 cup of fresh wash thinner. Clamp the cup to the gun. Shake and swirl the thinner around in the cup, then spray it out the nozzle. Next, place a finger over the nozzle and pull the trigger. This will back-flush the gun. *However, never back-flush an HVLP*

*gun.* This will blow out the gaskets and seals. Empty the remaining thinner, add clean thinner and repeat the process. When the thinner is expelled, wipe off all surfaces with clean thinner. Next, remove the air cap, J. Clean this with a stiff bristle brush and thinner. *Never use wire, a knife or hard instrument to clean out air passages G and F.* Finally, put the air cap into the cup, add 1/2 inch of thinner, and clamp the cup onto the gun. This prevents any missed paint from hardening in the air cap or fluid passages.

Always hang up the gun when you're changing the cup. Never lay a spray gun on its side. Material will flow into the air passages and conta-

With bodywork finished, Steve goes over car with D.A. sander using #220-grit sandpaper.

minate the air on the next usage. To lubricate the gun, place a drop of oil on the air-valve stem M and packings at C, A, B and H. Finally, be sure the air-vent in the cup-lid is open. If you're renting a booth in a paint shop you'll probably find a gun cleaning cabinet. Again, environmental controls require dumping less VOC's into the atmosphere. Certainly, spraying lacquer thinner directly into the air does affect air quality. With a cabinet, the gun is disassembled, placed in the proper location, the lid closed, and cleaning takes place. By the time you lift the lid the gun is dry and ready for use. When cleaning an HVLP gun in the cabinet, don't forget to remove the fluid pressure regulator first.

**Paint Booth**—You may be able to rent or use a paint booth. There are two types: dry and air washer. Dry paint booths are found in most paint shops. The dry booth is a completely sealed chamber, large enough for a car and painter, who must be able to move about freely. A large fan draws fresh air into the booth through large, disposable filters, much like those found in household furnaces and air-conditioners. Contaminated air is expelled directly into the atmosphere. The air-washer type is found in production facilities and is similar. However, contaminated air is drawn through a curtain of water and baffles before being expelled into the atmosphere. This removes solids.

The hot set-up today is the *down-draft* booth. Filtered fresh air is drawn in from the top of the booth and expelled out holes in the floor. This prevents much of the overspray and

dust problems normally associated with spray booths. If your shop really has the big bucks, then the fresh air being drawn in can be temperature and humidity controlled!

Cleaning is the first step in using a booth. All the interior surfaces must be free of dust, dirt and overspray. The floor is swept and washed to remove as much dust and dirt as possible. To remove remaining atmospheric dust, the fans are turned on with the doors closed. The car is blown-off and tacked-off. Then it is rolled into the booth. Once in, the car is again washed with wax and silicone remover and given a final tacking.

## SURFACE PREPARATION

If your car required bodywork, that part of the car should be ready for paint. This being the case and you're going to paint all of the car, it must now be made ready to receive the final color coat. On the other hand, if no bodywork was necessary, you must decide how extensive surface preparation will be. This can range from complete paint removal to as little as lightly sanding the old paint.

**Remove Paint**—Most people who begin by removing all of the paint wish they hadn't. So, don't remove it unless you have a good reason. Two reasons are that it has too many coats of paint, or there is rust under the old paint. If you decide to remove the paint, be forewarned. There could be surprises waiting for you.

Good plastic filler work may be hidden under the paint. If you remove the paint, you also remove much of the filler. Consequently, you must redo the filling work. Removing paint by grinding or sandblasting roughens and removes the metal, which must then be treated and smoothed. Grinding into good lead work is a sad happening. You can't replace it easily.

We recommend considering complete paint removal only as the beginning of an extensive bodywork project, not as surface preparation for paint. If you decide to remove all the paint, follow the recommendations in Chapter 6 and work from there.

If you use paint remover, use a good *neutralizer* on the bare metal afterwards. To prevent rust, follow this by *immediately* priming the metal. Grinding and sandblasting also require immediate priming of the metal.

**Wax, Oil & Polish Removal**—If you don't plan bodywork and wish only to prepare your car's surface for immediate painting, begin by totally removing the wax and oil.

Paint will not bond to silicone or oil. Thoroughly wash the car with water and detergent to remove surface dirt. Then wash the car with wax and silicone remover. Remember, it's extremely important to use wax and silicone remover *before* you begin sanding. Disregard this and you'll drive the wax and silicone *into* the paint. When the car is completely clean, you can begin sanding.

## SANDING

The entire surface to be painted must be sanded. This removes oxidized paint and remaining road film, provides a *tooth* for the new paint, and helps level the surface. The easiest way to sand is with a D.A. (dual-action) sander as shown above.

Place a #320-grit disc on the D.A. pad and go over the entire surface you are preparing for paint. Keep the pad flat to avoid gouging. Finish by hand sanding those areas where the D.A. missed with #400-grit wet-or-dry sandpaper.

If you don't have a D.A., you can do the job just as well by hand. Your paint supplier can provide you with a foam-rubber pad around which you can wrap a half sheet of sandpaper. The pad will spread the force of your fingers so you won't sand shallow grooves in the paint. It also gives you something to hold on to so it has less tendency to slip out of your hand. Use plenty of water to wash out the sanding particles while sanding. The sandpaper will last longer and cut better.

## DOOR JAMBS, TRUNKS & HOODS

**Tight Areas**—If planning a complete color change or just a thorough job, you should paint the door jambs, under the trunk lid and under the hood. These areas are difficult to clean and sand. You'll have trouble getting into all the tight contours with sandpaper, so use 3M Scotch Brite® pads, page 71. Their great flexibility will allow you to sand any contour.

As on the exterior surface, begin by washing with wax and silicone remover. Use one of the coarse- to medium-grade Scotch Brite® pads.

Begin masking job by outlining area to be masked with tape. Paper is temporarily placed over window opening.

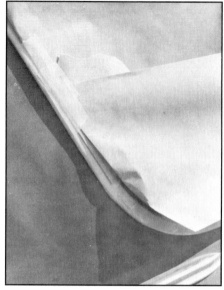

Fold paper under to form neat edge.

Bottom paper tacked in place and ready to be sealed with masking tape.

Final job should be neat appearing and without crevices which trap dust.

These surfaces are generally in poor condition and require a lot of work.

Another product that works quickly and well in tight areas is *liquid sandpaper*. It cleans like wax and silicone remover, and etches the paint. Etching creates a tooth similar to that obtained with sandpaper. Use liquid sandpaper like wax and silicone remover. Wash the area and dry it.

**Maintain the Surface**—After the car has been cleaned completely and sanded, you must keep it from being recontaminated. Wash the car one more time with clear water. From this point, *do not touch the surface with any part of your body*. Oil from your skin acts like silicone, preventing good adhesion of the paint.

When the surface dries after the water bath, go over it again with wax and silicone remover. This time, be absolutely sure to use *new, clean, cotton towels*. A dirty towel will cause contamination. Either the paint supplier or the hardware store can supply you with new cheesecloth. It is an inexpensive, uncontaminated cleaning medium made from cotton.

We stress cotton because it is soft. Polyester scratches, so don't use old T-shirts or other undergarments. They are usually made of at least 50% polyester.

**Tack Rag**—When all of the wax and silicone remover has evaporated, use an air nozzle to blow any remaining dust out of cracks and crevices.

You're now ready to wipe the car down with a *tack rag*.

You can get tack rags at a paint-supply store. Varnish-impregnated, cheesecloth, tack rags come in their own packages. Remove the tack rag from its package and carefully unfold it until it's one flat sheet. Wad the tack rag into a large fluffy ball.

Gently wipe off—tack—car with the tack rag. The varnish in the cloth picks up small bits of dust or dirt. Caution: *Never leave the tack rag on the car.* The varnish in the tack rag will quickly adhere to the paint. If left for long, it can even etch the paint. After you've completely tacked the surfaces to be painted, mask the surfaces that won't be painted.

Sanded and masked car is ready for primer. Note plastic trash bags over tires; they work as well as tire covers used by professional bodymen. If this were a restoration, all chrome would've been removed rather than masked.

Rick Talamentes prepares Porsche for masking by blowing off dust and tacking.

Now that we've seen a do-it-yourselfer masking job, let's look at how it's done in a professional piece-work paint shop. We visited our local Maaco Auto Painting and Bodyworks for this.

**Masking**—Masking is critical, because if it isn't done correctly, it may ruin an otherwise good paint job. Work to achieve an accurate edge. When the tape is removed, there should be no new paint on the chrome or rubber. And there shouldn't be old paint peeking through where the tape edge covered a surface that should've been painted.

Masking tape and masking papers come in many widths. The narrower the tape, the easier it will form for going around curves. The wider the tape, the greater the coverage. Paper comes in three or four widths. Select paper wide enough to do the job, but without waste. Never use newspaper

for masking. It is too porous and will allow wet paint to bleed through. Also, the black ink will bleed onto the surface and contaminate it with an oily film.

Whenever possible, it is better to remove a piece of trim than to mask it. This lets you check for hidden rust, protects beneath the trim and gives a more professional appearance. When time, or other considerations prohibit the removal of a piece of trim, mask it.

Begin by masking all exterior trim, such as door handles, antennas, moldings and logos. On inside curves, it is often best to use short pieces of tape, shaping them like a fan, one over the other, until you've gone around the

corner. On side trim, open the door and wrap masking tape across the ends of the trim. Move next to the door glass.

Don't start by masking with paper. Run a strip of tape around the trim or glass itself, in the case of a hardtop or late-model car. Now you can use the paper. If you have access to a paper-and-tape machine, your job will be easier. The machine automatically applies the masking tape to the edge of the paper as you unroll it. If not, don't worry. Although it won't be as fast, you can do just as well without.

Lay a strip of paper along an edge that is outlined with masking tape—it doesn't have to be pretaped. If the paper is not pretaped, hold it in place with short pieces of tape. Fold the

Rick begins masking by outlining first. Avoid getting tape on surface to be painted.

Rick places paper, then trims it to fit with razor blade.

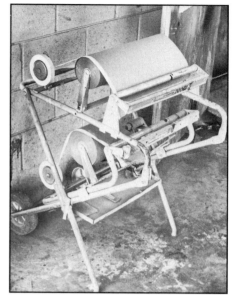

Professional masking-paper/tape dispensers automatically apply strip of masking tape to edge of paper. This speeds masking job considerably.

ends of the paper *under* to match the contour being masked. This gives a nice, neat job where dust and overspray can't collect. When the paper is shaped to the contour of the window, run another strip of tape over the paper and tape the edges. This seals the area, preventing overspray from blowing underneath. If you use two pieces of paper, be sure to seal this opening by taping them together.

Windshields and rear windows are protected in much the same manner. Be sure all edges and seams in the paper are sealed.

If you're doing jambs, trunk or hood, you'll have to mask off the interior. The entire opening need not be masked. Just run wide strips of paper along the masked edge. By controlling the gun's spray pattern, you can work into the jambs, drip channel or fender flanges with little or no overspray.

Under the hood, lay a drop cloth over the engine to prevent overspray from falling on it. Run a piece of paper along the inside edges of the fender and cowl to prevent overspray into the engine compartment and onto the fire wall.

On cars without body-colored engine compartments, fender bolts are *unpainted*. If you're painting one of these cars, back the fender bolts out and mask them; you don't have to remove the bolts. After you've finished painting, remove the tape and run the bolts back in. This leaves the bolt heads unpainted as they came from the factory.

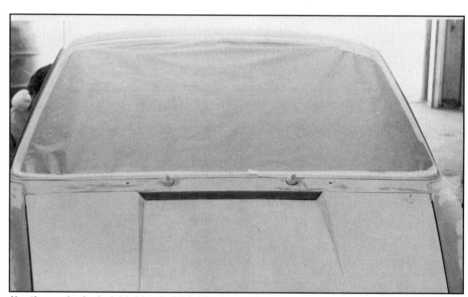

Neatly masked windshield, windshield-wiper-drive studs and radio antenna.

## MASKING TIPS

1. After laying down piece of tape, go back and press it tight to prevent paint from blowing underneath.
2. If tape won't stick to a surface, wash surface with wax and silicone remover. If used sparingly, you can also use wax and silicone remover on rubber surfaces.
3. When doing two-tone paint, follow the paint manufacturer's directions so you will know when fresh paint may be masked.
4. Never leave masking tape on a job for more than a few days, particularly if car is left in direct sunlight. Tape will dry out, adhere to the surface and is difficult to remove.
5. Do not remove tape from a wet paint job. Give lacquer an hour to dry. Enamel should dry at least six to eight hours, such as overnight.
6. When practical, cut tape. Tearing tends to lift and stretch the ends.
7. Never pull "up" on masking tape when removing it. It will lift fresh paint. Peel it back away from paint and over itself. This prevents lifting fresh paint.

Rubber strip on color-keyed bumper is masked.

Outlining tape must be applied carefully.

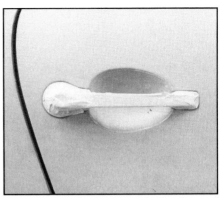
Door handles require careful attention and a lot of tape.

Mask off the inside edges of the trunk and use a drop cloth to prevent overspray from getting on the trunk floor, spare, carpet, etc. Mask off rubber seals around the trunk. Painted rubber seals look bad and tend to stick when trunk is closed. The same applies to door-jamb seals.

Mask the headlamps as you did the windows. On older-model cars, such as our '64 Barracuda, wrap the bumpers with paper. On later-model cars, the bumpers will require careful tape-and-paper work. If the bumpers are body-color, paint them later with paint mixed with flex-agent additive.

Again, give your masking job the same professional care you've used for other steps thus far. Keep it neat. Don't touch your skin to areas to be painted. And don't be afraid to go back and rework an area that you're not satisfied with. You're now ready for the final coat of paint.

# PAINTING TECHNIQUES
## GENERAL INSTRUCTIONS

*Follow the paint-manufacturer's instructions!* They are on the can. Almost everything you'll need to know about the paint will be there. Although we give general techniques, the manufacturer gives instructions on how to use its specific paint.

**Measure**—One of the cheapest pieces of equipment—and a necessary one—is a simple measuring cup. If the directions say to reduce the paint 150%, mix one cup of paint with one-

Masking completed, all that's needed to ready Porsche for paint booth is a drop cloth over engine and covers on wheels and tires.

and-a-half cups of reducer. See the chart in Chapter 8, page 99.

To achieve best results, measurements must be accurate. Do not use the "by-guess-or-by-golly" approach when preparing or applying paint materials. If you don't follow directions, the least that will happen will be runs, dry spots or excess orange peel. At worst, the job will be a total failure, requiring that you start over.

**Open the Can**—After you remove the paint-can lid, there's a little trick you can do to make mixing and pouring neater and cleaner. With a hammer and small nail—about a six penny—drive the nail through the can *trough* in several places. The trough is immediately inside the lid sealing edge. These holes allow paint caught in the trough to drain back into the can, keeping the rim clean. The holes are sealed when the lid is replaced.

To keep overspray off suspension, driveline and body underside, hang a skirt of masking tape and paper from body.

Thin, rough or dry coat may be caused by too little fluid, gun too far away, paint too thin, excess air, stroke too fast, or not enough overlap. Drawing courtesy of Ditzler Automotive Finishes.

| Variable | Lighter | Darker |
|---|---|---|
| **SHOP CONDITION** | | |
| A. Temperature | Increase | Decrease |
| B. Humidity | Decrease | Increase |
| C. Ventilation | Increase | Decrease |
| **SPRAYING TECHNIQUE** | | |
| A. Gun Distance | Increase | Decrease |
| B. Gun Speed | Increase | Decrease |
| C. Flash Time | Increase | Decrease |
| D. Mist Coat | (will not lighten color) | Use Wetter Mist Coat |
| **THINNER USAGE** | | |
| A. Type Thinner | Use Fast Thinner | Use Slow Thinner |
| B. Reduction of Color | Increase Amount of Thinner | Decrease Amount of Thinner |
| C. Use of Retarder | (Do Not Use Retarder) | Add Retarder to Thinner |

- Chart courtesy of Martin Senour Paints -

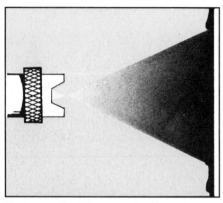

Heavy coat with sags, ripples or orange peel may be caused by dirty air nozzle, gun too close, paint too thin or thick, low air pressure, stroke too slow and too much overlap. Drawing courtesy of Ditzler Automotive Finishes.

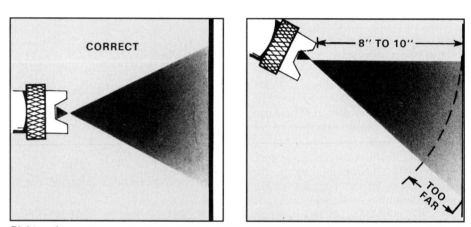

Right and wrong way to use paint gun: Hold gun eight to 12 inches away and move it back and forth square to surface. As shown, fanning gun will result in outboard spray being too far from surface. Drawings courtesy of Ditzler Automotive Finishes.

**Stirring & Thinning/Reducing**—To assure the paint and its pigments are thoroughly mixed, the paint must be shaken on a machine at the paint store. If the paint can sits undisturbed for more than 48 hours, return it to the paint store to be shaken again. Careful and complete mixing of all the paint components is a must to ensure consistency throughout the spraying process. Be sure to stir the paint well just before pouring it into the paint cup.

To save time, most professional painters thin or reduce a complete gallon at one time. To do this, you'll need an empty *clean* can. Buy one at the paint store. After thoroughly stirring the paint, pour enough in the clean can to make a thinned or reduced gallon. Add thinner or reducer to complete the gallon and stir.

For example, if directions call for 200% reduction, each cup of paint will require 2 cups of thinner or reducer. A fully prepared gallon requires 5-1/3 cups of paint plus 10-2/3 cups of thinner or reducer. You must be accurate. Remember, the thinning or reduction of paint determines how well it flows when applied. Flow equals gloss—no flow, no gloss. On the other hand, excess flow produces runs. Follow the directions!

Once paint is mixed, fill paint cup and make some practice runs.

**SPRAYING PAINT**
**Adjust Gun**—To adjust the gun, follow the directions given on pages 106-108. Test the spray pattern on a piece of paper. Adjust the spray, adjust the material and set the atomizing pressure to the paint-manufacturer's specifications.

If you've never painted before, buy a quart of inexpensive paint and practice. This is the best way to perfect your technique. Use paper strips or scrap parts. Mistakes made here are of little consequence. Practice until you have the feel of it after reading the following.

**Technique**—Spray guns are designed to give the best performance when held eight to 12 inches from the surface to be painted. If held closer, air pressure ripples the fresh paint. Hold it farther away and the paint will go on too dry, causing orange peel or dry film. It will also affect the color. A slower-drying thinner or reducer will allow more leeway in spray-gun work. It will, however, cause runs when too close and excessive overspray when too far away. Try to maintain the eight- to 12-inch working distance.

One of many paths can be used to paint a car. Here are two popular ones: Start at roof and finish on driver's side; or start at right fender and finish on driver's side. Regardless of pattern used, establish it in your mind *before you start spraying*—otherwise you may drag a hose through fresh paint. Drawings by Tom Monroe.

Car is primed and ready for sanding.

If a primer/sealer was used, don't sand through it. Reseal such spots if this occurs.

Begin the first stroke outside of the boundary of the surface to be painted. Pull the trigger and start the airflow. Just before you reach the edge of the surface to be painted, pull the trigger all the way in to release the material.

Pass across the surface in one full, long stroke. Keep the gun equal distant from the panel all the way across. Do not *fan* it—keep the gun square to the surface. Lock your wrist and arm, using your body and shoulders to pull you across the surface. This forces you to maintain the distance and angle from the beginning of the stroke to the end.

Move at a rate of speed that will put down a full, medium-wet, coat. If you go too slow, the paint will run. If you work too fast, the paint will be too thin and dry. The illustrations on page 114 show correct and incorrect procedures.

Similar to mowing grass, the next pass begins where the first pass ended. Again, air first, then material just before you reach the edge of the surface to be sprayed. On the second pass, overlap 50% of the first pass and direct the center of the spray fan at the lower or nearest edge of the previous stroke.

This process is repeated over and over as you work: Move left to right, then right to left, covering 50% of the previous pass, working from top to bottom or farthest to nearest.

**Application Procedures**—When you think you have the technique mastered, you're ready to begin painting for real. Again, read the manufacturer's recommendations to determine how many coats to apply and the waiting time between coats. Called *flash time*, this is the time required for sufficient evaporation of the thinner

or reducer. Waiting during the flash-time period prevents runs when the next coat is applied. If instructions on number of coats to apply and flash time are omitted, here are general rules:

1. Enamels typically get three medium coats: *tack coat, color coat* and *gloss coat.*

2. Lacquers are usually sprayed two medium coats at one time until the desired coverage is achieved.

3. Flash time is determined by touching the freshest paint on a masked area. If you apply a little pressure and your finger comes away clean, the surface is ready for another coat.

**Spray Car**—Spray the door jambs first. Reduce air pressure to 20 psi and adjust gun to a round spray. This should eliminate overspray on the upholstery. To prevent the seals from

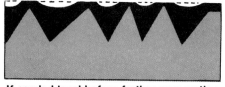

If sanded level before further evaporation, additional shrinkage will cause sanding marks to show through. Drawing courtesy of Ditzler Automotive Finishes.

Primer/surfacer applied over sanded metal simulates contours of metal, shrinkage being more over deep voids. Drawing courtesy of Ditzler Automotive Finishes.

First coat of metallic blue looks good.

Sight down side of car and observe light reflections. Make sure bodywork looks straight from this angle. Check every body panel using this method.

Remember Morgan Nokker demonstration, page 47, and lead work, page 73? Here are the results—straight trunk lid and lower back panel.

sticking to the door jambs, close the doors to the first catch. Now, return the atomizing pressure to manufacturer's recommendation and spray inside the trunk lid, under the hood, along the front-fender flanges and similar areas.

Next, move to the outside of the car. The illustrations on page 115, show two popular working patterns for painting a car. Choose either or make up one that works best for you.

These are the basics of spray painting. Followed carefully, they will produce professional-quality results. Now, we'll look at some specific types of paint and how they're applied.

# TECHNIQUES FOR SPECIFIC PAINTS

To recap, excellent results can be obtained if you follow the manufacturer's directions and:

1. Reduce paint correctly.
2. Use correct air pressure.
3. Use correct amount of material.
4. Select correct reducer, based on temperature and humidity.
5. Adjust gun correctly.
6. Maintain correct flash time between coats.

Let's look at some specifics for each type of paint:

## ACRYLIC LACQUER
**Reduction**—Most acrylic lacquers are thinned 125 to 150%. Any more thinning will cause excess overspray. The last coat may be thinned 200% with slow-drying thinner.
**Air Pressure**—Acrylic lacquers spray best between 35 and 45 psi. Like enamels, excess pressure causes overspray and orange peel.

**Number of Coats**—To achieve enough buildup for sanding and buffing, at least four or five double coats are needed. Some colors require as many as six or seven double coats.

## SYNTHETIC ENAMELS
**Reduction**—Synthetic enamels require the least reduction. Some are reduced by 15 to 20% while other synthetic enamels may require up to 33%, or one quart of reducer to three quarts of paint. Regardless, always reduce enamel according to manufacturer's directions.

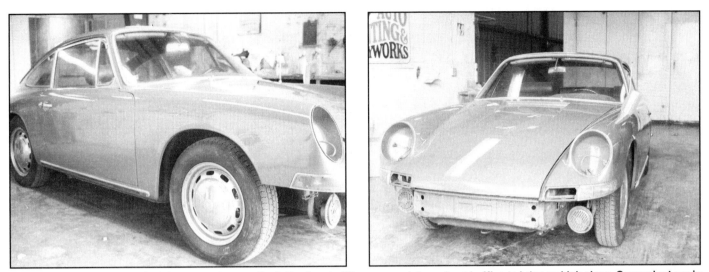

Here's how the Porsche paint job came out—excellent. Fresh out of the oven, paint needs no buffing to bring up high gloss. Our project car is another matter because it was sprayed with clear acrylic urethane.

**Air Pressure**—Gun pressure should be maintained at 55 to 60 psi to correctly atomize the paint. If you're using a *pressure pot* or remote-cup gun, use less pressure.

**Number of Coats**—Don't apply too much enamel in an effort to achieve good flow-out characteristics. This is unnecessary and wastes paint. It also encourages runs. Normally, two medium coats will hide most colors. If the old color shows through, apply a third coat. Honor the flash time, which ranges from 10 to 30 minutes, depending on temperature and humidity. Keep the gun square to the surface and about 10 inches away.

**Reducers**—There are many reducers for synthetic enamels. Select according to temperature and humidity.

**Hardeners**—Hardeners may be added to most synthetic enamels. Consult your paint supplier if you think a hardener is needed for your job. Usually, one pint of hardener is needed for one gallon of paint. Although a hardener reduces drying time, tape time and recoat time, it also increases cost.

## ACRYLIC ENAMELS

Acrylic enamels are similar to synthetic enamels. For better color *hold out*, a primer/sealer should be used before applying the acrylic enamel.

**Spraying Technique**—Spray one heavy *wet coat*—caused by a slow-drying thinner or reducer—or two medium wet coats. Allow about 20

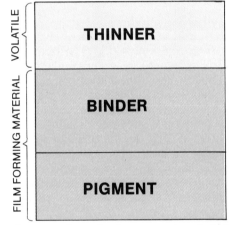

One ingredient of paint evaporates. Called *volatile*, it is the thinner or reducer. Two ingredients, *binder* and *pigment*, remain in paint film after drying.

minutes flash time before applying the second or third coat.

Metallic colors can be controlled by applying the third coat with the gun held at a distance of 12 to 15 inches. Read more about applying metallic paint on page 127.

**Hardeners**—Acrylics work well with hardeners. These additives improve gloss, eliminate the recoat period, cure harder and give better flow-out characteristics. Add one pint of hardener to one gallon of acrylic enamel. Then, reduce this mixture 50%.

## POLYURETHANE

**Reduction**—Polyurethanes are normally mixed with equal parts of catalyst and reducer. Follow the manufacturer's directions—there is little room for error.

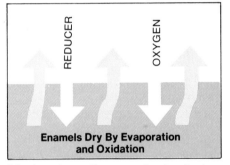

Alkyd and acrylic enamels dry in two stages; first by evaporation, then by oxidation. Heat speeds drying, however longer drying results in tougher paint. Paint should never be dried with a heat gun or fan as blushing or wrinkling may result. Artificial drying should only be done with heat lamps or in an oven.

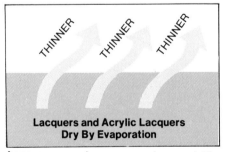

Lacquers remain more or less soluble. Therefore, when covered with like material, new coat bonds with old.

**Number of Coats**—Apply similar to other enamels. Usually two full wet coats with at least 15 minutes flash time will give good coverage.

**Air Pressure**—Spray with a gun pressure of 55 to 60 psi.

## ACRYLIC URETHANE (COLOR)

**Reduction**—Most acrylic urethanes are mixed with equal parts of catalyst. Solid colors are then reduced at a ratio of four parts of catalyzed color to one part of reducer. Metallics are reduced in a ratio of two parts of catalyzed color to one part of reducer.

**Number of Coats**—For good coverage, apply acrylic urethane with two or three wet double coats with a short flash time between double coats at moderate temperatures.

## ACRYLIC URETHANE (CLEAR)

**Reduction**—Except for the catalyst, clear acrylic urethane comes ready to spray directly from the can. Add one-half to one pint of catalyst for each gallon, depending on the brand used.

**Number of Coats**—Usually, two wet coats will give sufficient depth and gloss. If you plan to color-sand and buff the clear coat, we recommend that you apply three coats.

## REMINDERS

These are some of the specifics of painting with particular types of paints. Remember: You must follow the manufacturer's directions; stay with one manufacturer's products throughout the project; and double check the specifics—reduction, air pressure, number of coats and flash time.

When you've finished painting and the paint has hardened according to label instructions, you can begin color-sanding and buffing, if that was the plan. Although some painters prefer removing masking tape for color-sanding, we recommend that you leave it on the trim. This prevents the trim from being scratched accidentally. If you're not going to color-sand, remove the tape. If you're going to use a *guide coat* to assist with color-sanding, page 79, don't remove any masking.

**WARNING:** You must wear a respirator while spraying polyurethane. Polyurethanes contain *polyisocyanates*—a base similar to cyanide.

After adding white racing stripes and three coats of clear, Steve color-sands car prior to buffing. He's using ultra-fine (#1000-grit) sandpaper wrapped around a foam-rubber sanding block.

## COLOR SANDING & BUFFING

Nitrocellulose and acrylic lacquers were meant to be *color-sanded* and *buffed*. Without these treatments, they remain flat, with little or no gloss and a great deal of orange peel. All of the other paints may be sanded and buffed if they, by the manufacturer's direction, use a hardening catalyst. The remainder, such as synthetic and acrylic enamels, may be sanded and buffed if a hardener was added. Buffing enamel that wasn't cured with a hardener will ruin it.

**Color-Sanding**—Color-sanding is so named because the color coat is sanded rather than the primer coat. Beyond that, it is similar to any sanding operation, but with a few major differences. The idea of sanding before buffing is to remove all the orange peel. All peaks are removed so only a flat surface remains.

Color-sanding requires ultra-fine sandpaper—1000- to 1200-grit wet-or-dry paper, used wet. All sanding must be done by hand—no pneumatic sanders. When sanding, use a rubber sanding pad between your hand and the sandpaper. Half a sheet of sandpaper is wrapped around the pad.

**Process**—Sand in one direction only. This will help hide any sanding scratches. If you go any which way, even after buffing, the sanding scratches will still show.

If you want a show-quality finish, use a guide coat. Using a compatible paint in a contrasting color, spray a

Thinner in lacquer or acrylic color swells primer/surfacer. Drawing courtesy of Ditzler Automotive Finishes.

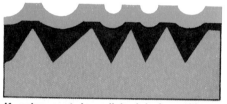

If color coat is polished before thinner evaporates from primer/surfacer and color coat, scratches will appear as evaporation and shrinkage continues. Drawing courtesy of Ditzler Automotive Finishes.

thin *dust coat* over the entire surface to be sanded. The contrasting color will remain in low points as you color-sand. When all the guide coat has been sanded off, you can be assured that the paint surface is perfectly level and free of orange peel.

Once you're finished color-sanding, you can remove any remaining masking tape and paper.

**Buffing**—A power buffer must be used to buff paint after color sanding—a pneumatic power buffer is preferable. Use a top-quality buffing pad if you're doing a lacquer job. If you're buffing urethane, use a polishing pad. You'll need about one quart of machine buffing compound and a brush to apply it. Finally, you'll need a spray bottle filled with clean water.

Using the brush, dab on two or three ounces of rubbing compound. Without turning the buffer on, use the pad to work the compound around the area to be buffed. Buff about three or four square feet at a time. Generally, the start-to-finish pattern will be the same as your painting pattern.

Start the buffer pad moving slowly. Work the compound around into a smooth, even film. Never apply pressure to the buffer. It will cause excess heat buildup and burn the paint. Let it work under its own weight. You may even want to lift the buffer a bit when you're "working up" the final gloss.

Increase buffer speed a little and work it back and forth, and around in circles within the area you are working. As the compound begins to dry,

After color-sanding, paint is buffed using a good buffer, buffing compound and top-quality, clean buffing pad.

Heat quickly dries buffing compound. Don't add more compound. When it dries, spray a little water on area and continue buffing.

spray some water on the surface to dampen the compound. Continue this operation until you can see gloss begin to appear. When this happens—after two or three wet-downs—increase buffer speed and buff the area to a high gloss.

Be careful around sharp body edges. The paint is thin here, and is easily worn through. Approach a sharp edge, such as a door line, with the buffer rotating in the direction away from the edge. If the pad is rotating into the edge, it will catch and abrade the paint at the edge.

When you've buffed the complete car to your satisfaction, finish by using a *swirl-mark*—buff- or wheel-mark—remover.

**Remove Swirl Marks**—Because buffing compounds are oil-based, a film is left after buffing. Within this film are swirl marks from the buffing pad. A good swirl-mark remover will produce a beautiful satin luster to a buffing job. Remove the buffing or polishing pad from your machine and install a foam, *glazing pad*. Using your buffing or polishing pad will only continue to add swirl marks.

Here's our project car finished and ready to drive to school in the fall! Compare "driveway" job with professionally done Porsche.

| Problem | Contamination: air lines, compressor, tools or original finish | Offset of old finish or repair | Excess film thickness | Exposure to harmful chemicals | Flash-off too short or too long | Improperly dried with heat gun or fan | Improper cleaning or preparation of substrate | Incorrect use of additives (type or amount) | Material not properly mixed | Piling-on of heavy, wet coats | Poor shop temperature, too hot or too cold | Washed too soon or with untried detergents | Wrong gun technique or adjustment | Wrong reduction or thinning; amount or grade |
|---|---|---|---|---|---|---|---|---|---|---|---|---|---|---|
| 1. Adhesion loss and chipping |  |  |  |  |  |  | 1 |  | ✔ |  |  |  |  | ✔ |
| 2. Bleeding |  | 2 |  |  |  |  | ✔ |  |  |  |  |  |  |  |
| 3. Blistering | ✔ | ✔ |  |  |  |  | 3 | ✔ |  |  |  |  |  | ✔ |
| 4. Blushing |  |  |  |  |  | ✔ |  |  |  |  | ✔ |  | ✔ | 4 |
| 5. Checking |  | ✔ | ✔ | 5 |  |  |  | ✔ | ✔ |  |  |  |  |  |
| 6. Cracking |  | ✔ | 6 | ✔ |  |  |  | ✔ | ✔ |  |  |  |  |  |
| 7. Cratering |  |  |  |  |  | ✔ | 7 |  |  |  |  |  |  |  |
| 8. Crazing |  | ✔ |  |  |  |  |  |  |  |  | 8 |  |  | ✔ |
| 9. Featheredge Cracking or Splitting |  |  |  |  |  | ✔ |  |  | ✔ | 9 |  |  | ✔ | ✔ |
| 10. Fisheyes | 10 | ✔ |  |  |  |  | ✔ |  |  |  |  |  |  |  |
| 11. Lifting | ✔ | ✔ |  |  | 11 |  | ✔ |  |  |  |  |  |  | ✔ |
| 12. Mottling |  |  |  |  |  |  |  |  | ✔ | 12 | ✔ |  | ✔ | ✔ |
| 13. Orange Peel |  |  |  |  |  |  |  |  | ✔ |  |  |  | 13 | ✔ |
| 14. Runs or Sags |  |  |  |  | ✔ |  |  |  |  | 14 |  |  | ✔ | ✔ |
| 15. Water Spotting |  |  | ✔ |  |  |  |  |  |  |  |  | 15 |  | ✔ |
| 16. Wrinkling |  |  |  |  |  | ✔ |  |  |  | 16 | ✔ |  |  |  |

✔ = primary problem and remedy number
✔ = additional causes

**Remedies**

1. Remove finish around an area considerably larger than the affected area and refinish.
2. Apply two medium coats of a sealer designed for this specific problem.
3. Sand area affected to a smooth finish. In extreme cases, remove material to bare metal, neutralize and refinish.
4. Decrease humidity. Add retarder to reduced color coat and apply two wet coats.
5. Color-sand and buff. If.extremely bad, sand and refinish.
6. Sand and refinish. Extreme problems may require stripping to bare metal and refinish.
7. Sand and refinish.
8. Reduce by 200%. Blend with retarder. Apply double wet coats until crazing disappears.
9. Sand and refinish.
10. When dry, apply double coat of color containing fisheye-eliminator additive.
11. Sand off all old finish and repaint.
12. When color coat has set, apply another double coat using fast thinner or reducer at higher than normal pressure.
13. Color-sand and buff.
14. When dry and hard, sand flush with paint surface. Buff to proper gloss.
15. Color-sand and buff. Extensive damage may require refinishing.
16. Sand and refinish.

# HEALTH & SAFETY TIPS
from Ditzler

For best results when using paint products, you must be thoroughly familiar with them and follow proper handling procedures and safety and health precautions.

**Warning Labels**—All paint products should carry warning and caution information which must be read and understood before use. Material-safety data sheets and other technical information are available through paint-products salesman.

**Proper Use**—Some paint products may contain heavy metals such as lead or chromium. Consequently, they should not be used on household articles such as childrens' furniture or toys.

**Health Considerations**—Good practice requires limiting exposure to vapor, dust and mist to the greatest extent possible through good ventilation and personal protection such as:
● Respiratory protection programs for qualifying and training personnel and selecting and maintaining equipment.
● Protective eyewear to prevent mechanical or chemical injury.
● Proper clothing to prevent skin contact which may result in irritation or dermatitis.

**Safety Considerations:**
● Work areas must be clean and properly designed for use and storage of flammable liquids.
● Paint and solvent products should be kept away from all sources of ignition, including open flames, sparks and static electricity generated by liquid transfer.
● Spray equipment, particularly high-pressure airless types, are hazardous if improperly used. High pressures may inject coating into the skin, causing serious injury requiring immediate treatment.
● Proper fire extinguishers and other extinguishing devices are prudent in all operations involving flammable liquids.

Materials used in paint products are subject to workplace regulation such as those of the Occupational Safety and Health Act (OSHA).

**For emergency information 24 hours/day call (412) 434-3131.**

Remove swirl, or wheel, marks left from buffing paint using a wheel-mark remover such as these.

Finished Barracuda project car in color

Apply the swirl-mark remover directly from the bottle. Using a clean, damp cheesecloth, wipe down a three- or four-square-foot area. When the swirl-mark remover dries, wipe it off with clean cheesecloth.

You should now have paint with a beautiful, deep-luster, satin gloss. Don't do anything with the paint job for a minimum of 30 days—wait 60 days if it's enamel. This allows solvents in the paint to finish evaporating. If you wax the paint before they've evaporated, the remaining solvents will be trapped between the paint and the wax. This will soften the paint surface, killing the gloss.

Finally, don't wash the paint with high-pressure water, such as in pay car washes. If the paint hasn't had time to cure, you blow off the paint. Instead, wash the paint with a soft sponge, mild soap, clean water and a garden hose.

# METRIC/CUSTOMARY-UNIT EQUIVALENTS

| Multiply: | by: | to get: | Multiply: | by: | to get: |
|---|---|---|---|---|---|
| **LINEAR** | | | | | |
| inches | X 25.4 | = millimeters(mm) | X 0.03937 | = inches |
| feet | X 0.3048 | = meters (m) | X 3.281 | = feet |
| **AREA** | | | | | |
| inches$^2$ | X 645.16 | = millimeters$^2$(mm$^2$) | X 0.00155 | = inches$^2$ |
| feet$^2$ | X 0.0929 | = meters$^2$(m$^2$) | X 10.764 | = feet$^2$ |
| **VOLUME** | | | | | |
| quarts | X 0.94635 | = liters (l) | X 1.0567 | = quarts |
| gallons | X 3.7854 | = liters (l) | X 0.2642 | = gallons |
| fluid oz | X 29.57 | = milliliters (ml) | X 0.03381 | = fluid oz |
| cups | X 0.2366 | = liters (l) | X 4.227 | = cups |
| **MASS** | | | | | |
| ounces (av) | X 28.35 | = grams (g) | X 0.03527 | = ounces (av) |
| pounds (av) | X 0.4536 | = kilograms (kg) | X 2.2046 | = pounds (av) |
| **TEMPERATURE** | | | | | |
| Degrees Celsius (C) = 0.556 (F - 32) | | | Degrees Fahrenheit (F) = (1.8C) + 32 | | |
| **PRESSURE OR STRESS** | | | | | |
| pounds/sq in. | X 6.895 | = kilopascals (kPa) | X 0.145 | = pounds/sq in |

Conversion chart courtesy of Ford Motor Company.

# 10 SPOT REPAIRS, COLOR MATCHING & CUSTOM FINISHES

**1955 Thunderbird with spot-repaired hood-to-grille filler panel. Paint was lifting immediately left of center, following photo.**

By now you understand how to do body repair and painting. However, if you only want to repair a scratch or nick, this won't require pulling a dent—and you certainly don't want to paint the whole car!

Small repairs are called *spot repairs.* They allow you to refinish a small area on a fender, door or any other body panel. Spot repairs are relatively easy to do if the paint is new. But what about paint that is six-years old and faded?

To help you match old paint, we include a section on matching colors, pages 127—129. You can match paint by mixing different tints with a base, or by controlling the spray at the gun. Or, both methods can be used.

If you want to go beyond the standard paint job, the last section of this chapter discusses custom finishes and specialty paints, pages 130—134. Here, we get into glamour colors such as *candy apple, metal flake* and *pearlescent.*

Let's start by looking at how the professional makes spot repairs look invisible.

### SPOT REPAIR

A spot repair begins with featheredging the paint immediately around the damaged area. Featheredging removes paint in a gradual manner from bare metal at the point of damage, and radiates out about eight- to 10-inches into the old, undamaged

**Spots where paint lifted must be repaired to return car to perfection. Let's look at spot-repair process.**

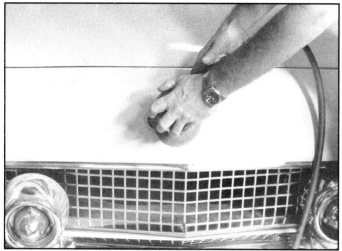
Don featheredges lifted paint with D.A. sander.

Result of featheredging

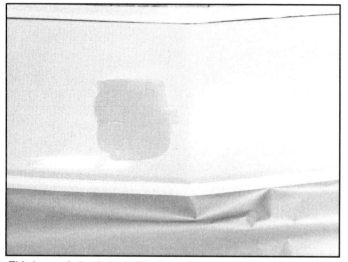
Thin layer of plastic body filler is applied over featheredge area.

Using #80-grit paper wrapped around stirring stick to block-sand body filler.

paint. See the spot-repair sequence pictured on pages 124—126.

After featheredging the paint around the damaged area with #80-grit paper on a D.A. sander, go back over the area with #120 grit to remove coarse scratches. About two feet around the featheredge, block-sand the area with a #400- to #600-grit wet-or-dry paper. This removes oxidation and adds tooth. Now, spray the sanded area with a good *lacquer* primer/surfacer using two full wet coats.

When the primer is dry, go over the area with a glazing putty to fill remaining scratches. When dry, block-sand with #220-grit dry paper. Two more full wet coats of primer/surfacer should fill any remaining sand scratches. A final block-sanding with

#360-grit paper will make the area ready for paint.

**Blending**—Now come the "tricks." The human eye is very discerning, but it can be fooled. If you can see a definite division between the old and new paint, the repair will be apparent. If, however, there is a transition, or *blending*, of the old into the new, the eye should pass over it, not noticing a change in tone or tint.

Have you ever noticed when comparing colors that you must have the two close together, whether they are on a car, house, fabric or other item? Separate the colors and you can't judge the match. This, then, is what you are doing when you blend paint. You're increasing the distance between new and old paint so the colors cannot be compared directly.

If you are going to use enamel, sand the repaired area with #400-grit wet-or-dry paper. Sand out about one foot into the old paint. For lacquer, use a finer-grit paper to prevent sand scratches showing through. We recommend *ultra-fine*—#1000- to #1200-grit—paper. Or, use non-sanding sealer to accomplish the same.

Although it costs more, you'll get the best job with a good non-sanding sealer before you apply the paint. Then you can eliminate sanding with ultra-fine paper. The sealer will fill sand scratches caused by #400-grit paper. When the area is sanded and sealed, you're ready to paint.

If the original factory paint is one- or two-years old, a paint dealer should have a match in either lacquer or acrylic enamel. If the paint is older or

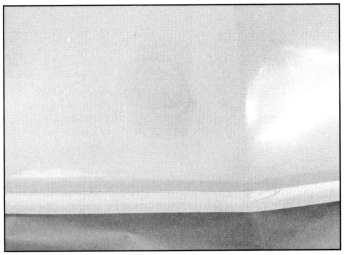
Featheredging shows through thinly sanded filler.

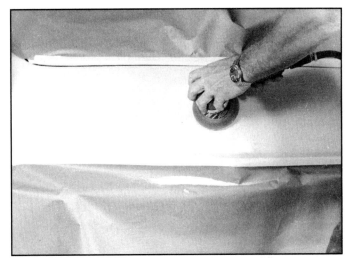
Further work with D.A. sander using #320-grit paper prepares area for primer.

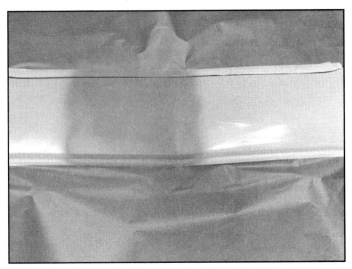
After masking, immediate vicinity of repair is primed—no more.

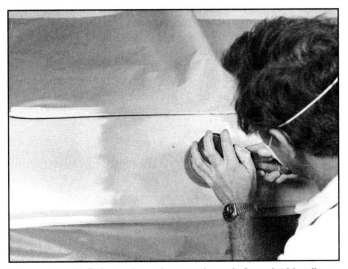
More work with D.A. sander makes repair ready for paint blending.

chalked and faded, take a small part of the car, such as a wind-vent or fuel-tank-access door, to the paint supplier for matching.

A good paint matcher can come close to a "perfect" match by mixing a variety of tints with a base color. Unfortunately, there's no such thing as a "perfect" match.

Blending involves spraying heavy coats over the primed area to give it full color. Then, blend outward onto the old paint surface by using a progressively thinner coat of paint, or dust coat. This makes the gradual transition from new paint to old. Here's how it is done.

**Mix** the paint according to manufacturer's directions. Unless you're using lacquer, add hardener to the paint. This allows you to color-sand

and buff the new paint, should it be needed to match the gloss of the old paint.

**Spray** one full wet coat at the recommended pressure over the primed area. Allow for correct flash-off, then spray a second coat. Bring this coat out into the blend area by simultaneously easing off the trigger and pulling the gun away from the paint surface. The pass should end in a fog coat, or *fade-out*. Blend the entire periphery of the spot repair using this technique. If you're spraying a solid coat, this is as far as you go. If spraying a metallic, finish by applying a clear coat. Read more about metallics on page 127.

**Clear coats** are used by many spot painters regardless of the paint used—acrylic lacquer, enamel, ure-

thane or polyurethane. In many cases, the repair will be over an OEM base coat/clear coat. If this is the case, it, too, requires a clear-coat finish.

Spray the clear coat over the color coat within the time prescribed by the manufacturer. This will be termed *recoat period* on the label. Blend the clear into the old paint using the same technique you used to blend the color coat. Don't work all the way across the panel. This defeats the purpose of blending. You'll then have to move into the adjacent panel to achieve a proper blend.

**Color-sand** with ultra-fine sandpaper after allowing 24 hours for the paint to cure. Finish by machine or hand buffing. Be careful not to sand or buff through the clear coat. If you do, *rings* will appear where the color coat

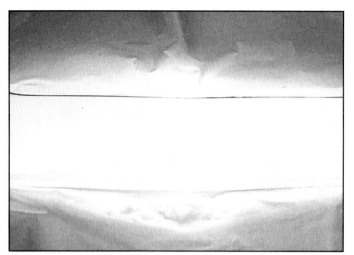

Three-coat system is used to blend. First coat only covers primer; second coat moves out a little farther; and third coat is blended using blending process discussed in this chapter.

Color-sand spot-finished area with ultra-fine sandpaper.

Buffing completes spot-repair job.

Compare spot-finished area with original paint. They are indistinguishable.

was penetrated.

Blending metallics can be a real problem. The blend edge will tend to mottle. The color can change from light to dark, *flip-flop,* page 129, and do many strange things. A clear coat will correct most of these problems. So, spend the extra bucks and time, and clear-coat.

**Backtaping**—It can be difficult to blend from a damaged area that's at the edge of a large panel, such as the edge of a hood or trunk. Because the damage is at the edge of the panel, blending must involve the adjacent panel/s. In this case, it's best to work to an edge along a crown of the adjacent panel, such as the top of a fender, as in the case of the edge of a hood.

Mask along the fender crown and you'll get paint buildup, resulting in a distinct edge. You'll be able to see and feel it because there will be no blend. To eliminate this problem, many professionals use *backtaping,* which eliminates edge buildup and, even though it's small, gives the needed blend area to fool the eye.

To backtape an edge, run a strip of masking tape along the crown edge, but allow half the width of the tape to stand up—the half that's toward the repair area. In opposite terms, only half the width of the tape will be sealed down—the half that's *away from the area to be painted.* The other half will be a little wall standing up along the crown edge. When you spray up to this "wall" formed by the tape, the paint will bounce off and onto the crown. Because there is no tape edge on which to build up, there will be no paint edge to distract the eye once the tape is removed. And, even though this gives a small blend area, it will be enough to fool the eye if the paint match is close.

## FURTHER THOUGHTS ON BLENDING

A chalked, dull finish is difficult to blend into. It won't reflect light the same as the high gloss of fresh paint. To help this situation, machine-buff the area that you'll be blending the paint into. Do this *before* you paint.

After buffing, clean the area with wax and silicone remover to remove the residue left by the buffing compound. If you don't, the paint won't stick. When the area is buffed and cleaned, blend in the spot repair as described earlier.

**Metallics**—Earlier, we mentioned how metallics tend to "misbehave." Let's take a look at some of these problems and how to overcome them or, possibly, use them to our advantage.

Metallics tend to be darker when applied in full, wet coats, and lighter when applied in *drier coats*—caused by fast reducer or thinner. When the paint is applied wet, using a slow reducer, the metallic particles settle to the bottom of the paint film. When applied dry, the metallic particles are trapped evenly and closer to the outer surface throughout the paint film.

When the metallic particles are covered by a full film of opaque color, they reflect little light. This tends to make the paint appear darker. When the particles are near the surface, as in a dry application, they'll reflect a great deal of light. This makes the paint appear lighter. Following are some things you can do to control this color change, regardless of whether the paint is metallic.

Lighten color:
- Increase air pressure
- Use faster-drying thinner
- Increase distance from gun to surface
- Increase thinning

Darken color:
- Reduce air pressure
- Use slower-drying thinner
- Reduce distance from gun to surface
- Decrease thinning.

If you are careful and follow these directions, you should be able do a successful spot repair.

Priming fender on restored Thunderbird prior to painting: If production color was used and paint is in top condition, paint store should have information needed to mix paint to match. Otherwise, color-matching process must be used.

## COLOR MATCHING

We could write a separate book on the complicated subject of matching colors. Considerable practice and experimentation with the way colors change when mixed is required. We can give a general description of how color matching is done. If you get deeply involved in painting, practice mixing and matching colors. Before you dump one gallon of paint into another in an attempt to color match, watch your paint dealer do it and ask questions.

Regardless of who does the color matching, the first thing to do is get the factory *paint code,* usually found on the car's vehicle-identification tag. You'll find this tag on the fire wall,

driver's door jam, door post or on top of the dash at the base of the windshield.

Normally, the paint code will be a letter, number, or combination of letters and numbers. Take this *alphanumeric* code to the paint store. This code, along with the year, model and make of your vehicle, will help the paint supplier match the color.

When he finds the paint code, it will tell him exactly how the paint was blended, or *compounded*. He will then blend those tints and base in the exact proportions *by weight*. The resulting blend should be identical to the original factory mix—a "perfect" match to the original paint. Many paint suppliers who've been in business for two or three generations can mix and match colors that go back to the '30s and '40s.

If the paint is faded, your supplier should be able to match a color sample of the old paint *if he has a good eye and knows what components to mix together.* This is what we'll look at: how to mix the required colors to get an exact match for a particular paint.

**Color Perception**—To match colors successfully, your vision must be correct. Sorry guys, women have a better eye for color than most men. They are relatively free from a problem that plagues one out of every 12 men—color blindness! If you are concerned about your ability to *see* colors correctly, don't attempt to color match. Leave it to someone else. However, if you have a good eye for color, learning to match colors is simply a matter of being careful, having patience and remembering what happens when a particular color is introduced to another.

**Tinting**—As discussed in Chapter 8, components that go into a paint must be compatible with that paint. This holds true with tinting. Lacquers must be tinted with lacquer tints, enamels with enamels, and acrylics with acrylics. There are about 40 shades of tints available for each paint category. However, a good basic selection requires only nine shades each. These are:

| | | |
|---|---|---|
| White | Black (strong) | Oxide yellow |
| Black (weak) | Rich | Oxide red |
| Blue | Brown | Burnt |
| | Green | sienna |

We have found another helpful shade: violet. It can change the tint when others seem to do nothing. So, add violet to the list of basic tints.

**Color**—Before you can tint a paint, you must first understand the vocabulary. Following are the terms used to describe a paint-color change:

A. Lighter or Darker (called depth)
B. Cast differences
    1. Redder
    2. Bluer
    3. Greener
    4. Yellower
C. Cleanliness
    1. Grayer (dirtier or more muddy)
    2. Brighter (cleaner appearance).

If you have a car such as this J2X Allard, the only way to match the original paint is through mixing and matching, not with a paint code. The same goes for custom-mixed paint. Take a small panel, such as a fuel-filler access door, to the paint store so the paint can be matched directly. It's the only way to get an accurate color match. Photo by Tom Monroe.

Begin checking tint by spraying a small area with the prepared paint. When it's dry, stand back and look at the paint. Compare it to the paint you want it to match. If a tint change is needed, use one of the words listed above to describe the desired change. Example: "The color I've just sprayed is _____ compared to the original paint." Or, "The color I've just sprayed is _____ on the original paint." This gives you a starting point to add tints or adjust for *depth.*

**Adjusting Color**—The first step in adjusting a color is to correct depth. Here, you have determined whether the new paint is lighter or darker than the original paint. Refer to chart, page 114, to make corrections:

These are the variables that lighten or darken the overall appearance of a paint. Another way to obtain lighter or darker paint is to allow the thinned mixture to sit for about ten minutes first. Afterwards, pour off the top half into a clean can. Stir what is left over and test it by spraying. The color should be lighter. If you want darker paint, test the portion you poured off—it should be darker.

When you think you have the correct color depth, which is neither too light nor too dark, you're ready to adjust the *cast,* or color.

Even though you need one quart of paint, begin with 1/2 pint so you won't end up with a gallon of unusable

paint. By starting with 1/2 pint and carefully measuring and recording the tints used, you can simply transfer these proportions to the remaining paint once you achieve the desired cast.

**Cast Differences**—Each color can only differ in two directions: A color may be either greener or redder; yellower or bluer; yellower or redder; and bluer or greener. The colors that are either greener or redder include:

| | |
|---|---|
| Blue | Purple |
| Yellow | Beige |
| Gold | Brown |

For variations of the following colors add yellow or blue:
    Green
    Maroon
    White
    Black
    Grey or silver

For variations of the following colors add yellow or red:
    Bronze
    Orange
    Red

For variations of the following colors add blue or green:
    Aqua
    Turquoise

Determine what the overall cast of the sprayed paint is. Then refer to the following "kill chart" to correct cast. Add 1/2 teaspoon of the "kill" color at a time.

| COLOR | ADD | to kill CAST |
|--------|--------|------|
| Blue | Green | Red |
| Blue | Red | Green |
| Green | Yellow | Blue |
| Green | Blue | Yellow |
| Red | Yellow | Blue |
| Red | Blue | Yellow |
| Gold | Green | Red |
| Gold | Red | Green |
| Maroon | Yellow | Blue |
| Maroon | Blue | Yellow |
| Bronze | Yellow | Red |
| Bronze | Red | Yellow |
| Orange | Yellow | Red |
| Orange | Red | Yellow |
| Yellow | Green | Red |
| Yellow | Red | Green |
| White | Yellow | Blue |
| White | Blue | Yellow |
| Beige | Green | Red |
| Beige | Red | Green |
| Purple | Blue | Red |
| Purple | Red | Blue |
| Aqua | Blue | Green |
| Aqua | Green | Blue |
| Gray | Blue | Yellow |
| Gray | Yellow | Blue |

Chart courtesy of Martin Senour Paints

When you've obtained the desired depth—lightness or darkness—and cast, you're ready to adjust for *cleanliness*, or brightness of the paint. Unfortunately, you cannot brighten a color without changing depth and cast. The only way a color can go is to the grayer side. To gray a color, add about 1/4 teaspoon per reduced quart of white, and only a drop of black—no more. For colors such as brown, gold and yellow, use gold to muddy the color.

**Tinting Metallics (Polychromes)—** The values in the following chart are based on one quart of reduced paint. Light, medium and dark metallic refers to the base color, not the amount or size of the metallic particles.

LIGHTER—Add Ultra Polychrome
Light Metallic = 8 tsp
Med Metallic = 4 tsp
Dark Metallic = 2 tsp
REDDER—Add Violet
Light Metallic = 1/4 tsp
Med Metallic = 1/2 tsp
Dark Metallic = 2 tsp

GREENER—Add Yellow/Green
Light Metallic = 1/4 tsp
Med Metallic = 1/2 tsp
Dark Metallic = 2 tsp
YELLOWER—Add Indo Yellow
Light Metallic = 1 tsp
Med Metallic = 6 tsp
Dark Metallic = 15 tsp
BLUER—Add Green/Blue
Light Metallic = 1/4 tsp
Med Metallic = 1/2 tsp
Dark Metallic = 2 tsp
GRAYER—Add Carbon Black
Light Metallic = 1/4 tsp
Med Metallic = 1/2 tsp
Dark Metallic = 2 tsp
BROWNER—Add Gold
(DIRTIER)
Light Metallic = 1/2 tsp
Med Metallic = 1 tsp
Dark Metallic = 4 tsp

*tsp = teaspoon; Med = medium
Chart courtesy of
Martin Senour Paints

**Flip-Flop—** Another problem associated with polychromes is called *flip-flop*. This phenomenon occurs in polychromes when angle of view or light striking the paint surface makes color depth change from light to dark and back to light again as one of these angles changes. Flip-flop works like this: A painted panel viewed from the front of a car grows darker as you walk to the rear. As you return to your original position, the surface lightens. This effect occurs most frequently in transparent pigments such as gold, silver and light polychromes.

**Cause & Correction—** Flip-flop results from the amount of metallic particles oriented in a particular direction and their depth in the paint film. As the direction of light or viewing changes, so does the amount and quality of reflected light. Remember, light is diminished the farther it travels through paint the film—both in and out. The result is darker-appearing paint. And, the shorter the distance, the lighter the paint. This can be controlled, somewhat, with the spray gun.

Spraying the area a little wetter will darken a metallic paint when it's viewed square to the paint surface. When viewed from an angle, the paint will tend to lighten. This is a result of the metallic particles lying deeper and flatter within the film. To reverse this effect, spray a slightly dryer coat.

Both techniques are a compromise and will only make minor changes. If greater changes are required, you must resort to more involved measures, such as tinting with white.

**Tinting with White—** To correct severe flip-flop, you have to add a small amount of white. This eliminates the sharp contrast when the panel is viewed from an angle. White reduces paint-film transparency, cutting the transmittance of light through the paint film.

Be careful when adding white. A little white goes a long way. Too much will ruin your paint. In one quart of reduced color, use the following amount of white: 1 teaspoon in light metallics, 1/2 teaspoon in medium metallics, and 1/4 teaspoon in dark metallics.

These are the methods used by professionals to match colors. To be successful, you must be patient, mix in small batches before attempting large quantities, and proceed in an organized, step-by-step manner. Correct first for depth, then cast and, finally, for cleanliness.

### SPECIALTY PAINTS & CUSTOM FINISHES

It's difficult to define specialty paints and custom finishes. This is because they fall into the same categories as the paints we've discussed throughout the second half of this book. They are lacquers, acrylics, enamels, urethanes and polyurethanes. The difference is in the way specialty paints and custom finishes are used and applied—and, often, how much they cost!

Polychromatics are used in every production shop in the world. Add a little metallic to the enamel and spray away. There are, however, specially formulated polychromatics. They have a high metallic content and a semitransparent base color. In acrylics, they generally are used with a catalytic hardener. These specially formulated polychromatics are called *glamour colors,* and are usually for custom finishes.

Here's an example of how paint use puts it in the custom category. Suppose two quarts of white alkyd enamel are divided into three parts, and each part tinted with varying amounts of blue tinting base. This material is then used to spray three stripes down the sides of a car. Although alkyd enamel has been available since the '50s, this particular use makes it custom paint.

Custom paint may refer to how paint is applied, not to the paint itself. Such is the case with this Harley-Davidson show bike and its ornate graphics.

Graphics on Baja Bug required many talents. These include accurate masking, spray-gun control and pin striping by hand.

Larry's T-bucket on display: Following photos show how flame paint job was done.

It is usually *how* a paint is applied that determines whether it is a specialty paint or custom finish. There are, however, some readily recognizable speciality paints.

*Candy apple, pearlescent* and *metal flake* are synonymous with specialty finishes. However, they are simply acrylic lacquers sprayed in *three-part systems.* This simplifying discussion is not designed to denigrate or lessen the beauty of specialty paints. The purpose is to remove some of the mystery. Standard polychromatics have already been covered. The metallic is added directly to the color. Not so with the system referred to as *candy apple.*

## CANDY APPLE

Candy-apple colors are probably the most widely recognized and used colors of the specialty group. The unusual brilliance, depth and dimensional *candy* appearance make it a favorite, especially for smaller jobs such as motorcycles, street rods and street-machine graphics.

Candy colors have expanded from the basic red, green and blue of the early '50s to dozens of colors and shades. To achieve brilliance, a three-part system uses base, or ground coat, color coat, and several clear coats.

**Composition**—Candy colors generally are formulated from acrylic lacquer. And, because each manufacturer has its own formulation, stick with one manufacturer's system! Doing this will avert a disaster caused by material incompatibility.

**Ground coats** used for candy colors are generally silver or gold-bronze. Aluminum or bronze particles in these ground coats are extremely fine. Other base coats may be used. They will, of course, change the final appearance. We've seen white, black and blue used as ground coats.

**Color coats** are transparent. This allows light to pass through and be reflected by the ground coat. Clear acrylic is formulated with only color pigment. No white or black is added to provide opacity. If you spray the color coat over an imperfect base, imperfections will show through.

**Clear coats** of acrylic lacquer or urethane create the final depth and gloss. We prefer urethane because of its durability and ultraviolet protection. The clear coat is color-sanded and buffed. The finish looks like you could swim in it!

**Application**—To apply candy apple, prepare the surface as you would for any other paint. Sand the final primer/surfacer with #360-grit dry paper or spray it with a non-sanding sealer. Reduce the gold or silver base coat according to the manufacturer's directions. Use a thinner that's compatible with weather conditions. Spray two full wet coats. Check the finished surface and be sure you have complete, even, coverage of the area being worked. This is very important because the color coat won't hide anything.

Let's depart from the typical manufacturer's directions and look at some tricks. Spray one or two more ground coats. This time, reduce the base coat about 150% with a fast-evaporating thinner. Increase gun pressure to about 50 to 55 psi. When spraying, hold the gun between 18- and 24-inches away from the surface and apply a full mist coat. Here's why:

If you apply the gold or silver ground coat wet, the metallic particles will settle to the bottom of the paint film and flatten out. In some instances, the super-fine particles will clump together, giving a mottled, black appearance. By using a fast-evaporating mist coat, the metallic particles will position themselves at random and not so deep in the film. By presenting more surface to the light, you'll get more sparkle, more-even coloration and little chance of flip-flop.

Allow the base coat sufficient flash time before applying the color coat. Warning: *Never touch the base coat with your skin.* Body oil tarnishes metallic particles, leaving finger prints visible through the color coat.

Apply the color coat as soon as possible. Leaving the base coat exposed to the elements courts disaster.

Spraying the color coat presents only minor problems. Strive for even coverage. Don't worry about gloss. Gloss is obtained with the clear coat. Thin the color with a medium-to-fast thinner according to label directions. Spray single, even coats, with *little or no overlap.* Apply only enough coats to give the color depth you want. The more material you apply, the darker the finish becomes. Avoid runs. They cannot be sanded out without changing the appearance of the sanded area. Stop spraying when you think it's "almost" right. The color will be a little darker once it dries.

Allow the color coat to cure at least 24 hours if you will be clear-coating

**Metal flakes and graphics are used in conjunction with conventional paint to create striking effect. Be careful when using metal flake. It's easy to overdo it.**

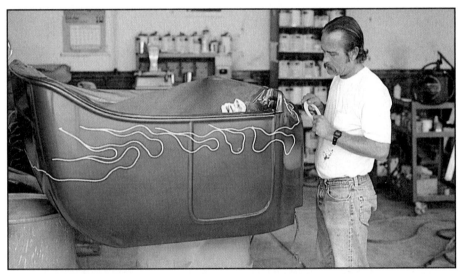
**Ed Hopkins, known to his friends as "Trip," begins layout of flame job on Larry's roadster.**

**Careful placement of 1/4-inch masking tape provides "drawing" of flames. Narrow tape is easy to bend in a tight radius.**

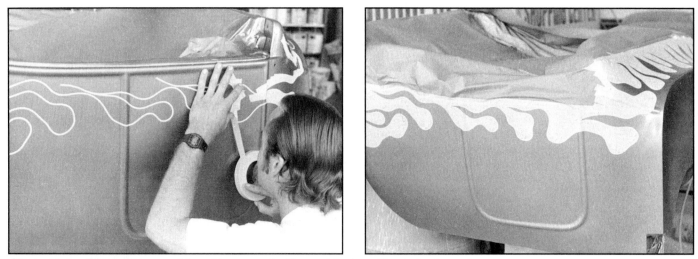

After outlining, Trip continues masking with paper and wider masking tape. Flames begin to take shape.

Careful gun work is required to apply silver over blue body at mask.

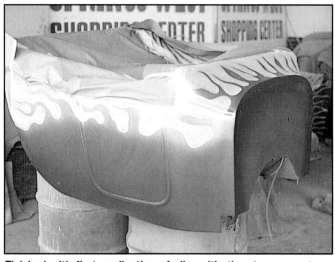

Finished with first application of silver, it's time to remove tape and paper.

with catalyzed urethane. If using a lacquer clear coat, spray it as soon as sufficient flash time has passed.

Apply three or four full, wet coats of clear. Allow the recommended time for flash-off between coats. After 24 hours, color-sand and buff.

This type of candy-apple application will give you the greatest brilliance, deepest color and highest gloss. Don't be afraid to experiment with various undercoats, mixing of top coats and learning to develop your own custom colors.

## PEARLESCENTS

Pearlescents were introduced in the early '50s, soon after candy apple. Mother-of-pearl was ground into a fine powder mixed with the ground coat. A clear, nitrocellulose lacquer was then sprayed over the ground coat. Unfortunately, the clear coat turned yellow within six months and ruined the entire effect of the paint. But it was great while it lasted!

Today's pearlescents last as long as a polychrome paint. Dozens of colors, tints and tones are available. Like candy apple, pearlescent is a three-part system.

**Application**—The ground coat has a great affect on the final appearance of a pearlescent paint job; more so than other three-part systems. This is the result of the *very* transparent color coat. Generally, pearlescent base coats are white. In an effort to be unique, many people use other light-colored ground coats. For an ex-

traordinary effect, a *black* ground coat is sometimes used. In bright sunlight the effect is dramatic.

To determine which ground coat to use, visit a paint distributor who has a complete line of paint chips showing pearlescents and the other commonly available specialty paints.

Once you've selected a ground coat, prepare the surface, thin the ground coat and apply three coats. Because the ground coat is a conventional opaque color, use the painting techniques described in Chapter 9. When the base coat dries according to the manufacturer's recoat recommendation, turn your attention to the pearl coat.

The pearl coat is a clear coat with "pearl" powder added. Manufacturers

**Easy on tape removal, Trip. Don't lift paint!**

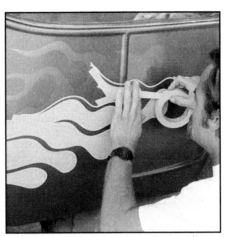

**Second set of flames go down after a 24-hour drying period. This prevents masking tape from lifting fresh paint.**

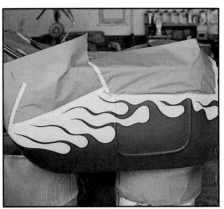

**Body is now ready for metallic violet.**

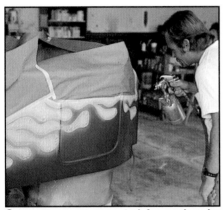

**Same steps are repeated for each color application. Off comes this masking, on goes the next.**

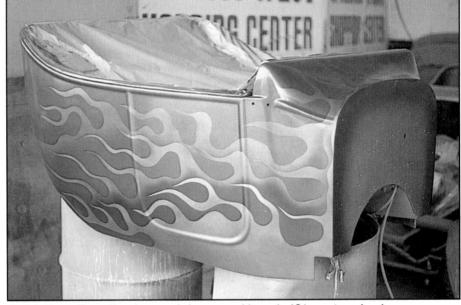

**Finished job: Now, all we have to do is reassemble car in 48 hours to make show.**

no longer use ground Mother-of-Pearl for this. Instead, they use a *mylar* compound. Although not as glamorous sounding, mylar lasts longer, provides a greater range of tints and is much cheaper! Today, there are many tones to select from such as red, green, blue, gold and platinum.

Some manufacturers supply the pearl coat ready-mixed. Others provide you with a can of clear and a bottle of pearl flakes so you mix your own. Either way is OK.

As with candy apple, apply the pearl coat at 50 to 55 psi and hold the gun back from the paint surface 18 to 24 inches. Because pearls work much like the metallics, use a mist-coat application. This arranges the pearl particles in a random, yet even distribution.

For the third coat, we recommend a catalyzed urethane. Apply three wet coats, allow adequate curing time, then color-sand and buff.

## METAL FLAKE

Metal-flake paints use flakes that are larger than those in polychromes, with one difference. They're not metallic. Instead, they are mylar-plastic flakes. The mylar flakes come in three sizes—small, medium and large; and usually three colors—silver, gold and bronze. Using metal-flake paint is similar to using pearlescent paint. Base coat goes on first, "metal" flake mixed with clear is next, and final clear coat gives the gloss.

**Application**—The second coat is applied over a light or dark ground coat, which usually is black to give a high-contrast background for the bright flakes.

After you've decided on background color, you must choose metal-flake size. Small- and medium-size flakes can be applied with a standard gun and tip. You'll need a special gun and tip for spraying large flakes. The air cap has a port opening that's almost 1/8 inch in diameter. The fluid tip and fluid needle are designed to compensate for increased material flow.

The second coat—clear with metal flake—will have a distinct texture, especially with medium and large flakes.

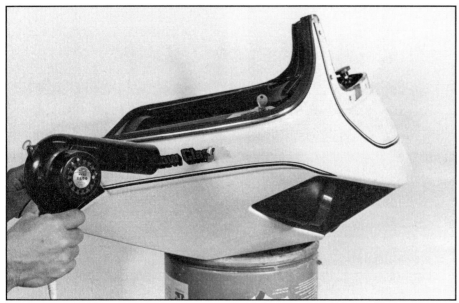

Carefully heat and peel as you go until decal is off.

Decals may be removed by first heating with heat gun. If you don't have a heat gun, a good hair dryer will work.

This is caused by the large flakes sticking through the clear-film surface. This brings up the main difference between metal flake and pearlescent: A different clear coat-application technique is required.

Start with catalyzed urethane mixed to specification. Spray two wet coats and allow sufficient curing time—or 6 to 24 hours, depending on the manufacturer. When completely cured, block-sand the entire surface with #400-grit wet-or-dry sandpaper. Be careful not to penetrate the clear-coat surface. This will damage the metal flakes and create black spots where the flakes were penetrated. When most of the orange peel, or surface peaks, have been sanded away, wipe the surface with clean towels, tack-off and spray two more full, wet coats. Color-sand with ultra-fine sandpaper and buff.

## DAY-GLO

Reflecting the upbeat mood of the 90's is a carryover from the late 40's: Day-Glo colors. In the 40's they were called fluorescent colors. The original designed color was a very dark pink. It was originally supposed to be used on aircraft to make them more visible. It fell from favor, however, around the mid-50's but continued in its orange color to help control highway traffic. Now Day-Glo is today's most modern color for motorcycle trim, bicycles, jet skis and hot boats. In Southern California we see it used on auto hub caps and bumpers!

**Application**—To get the best results begin with a white ground coat. Then, apply the Day-Glo color of your choice. Finish with a clear coat. You have two choices of clear coat: high gloss or flat. Both are acceptable; it's a matter of choice. Remember, you can add a flattening agent to achieve any degree of flatness you desire. If you use a gloss finish consider buffing it to achieve the highest gloss. A flat finish should not be buffed.

## POLYCHROME/CANDY- APPLE DERIVATIVES

The final specialty paint is a cross between polychrome and candy apple. Although referred to as a polychrome, these derivatives require a three-coat process. In the Ditzler paint lines, *Radiance* and *Sun-Gleam* use a silver-metallic base. Flake size is larger than that in candy-apple and conventional polychromatic paints, but smaller than the smallest used for metal-flake paint.

**Application**—These special polychromes are applied exactly like candy apples. A high-metallic, silver-based ground coat is applied using the high-pressure, mist-coat process. The color coat is followed next by a final clear coat.

## SPECIALTY PAINT SUMMARY

Like their production counterparts, specialty and custom paints are based on lacquer, acrylic, urethane and polyurethane systems, so handle them accordingly. Before determining

which to use, check several manufacturers' color charts. There are many different shades, tones, combinations and hues from which to choose. Besides those already prepared, there are many combinations you could try. We have a friend working on a candy-apple black! Consider what he's doing: a black base coat, medium-size metal flakes in a clear coat, topped with a candy-apple blue color coat and then a gloss, clear-coat. Interesting, huh?

## SPECIALTY ITEMS

There are many more specialty items, such as decals, plastic pin stripes and the old standby of hand-worked pin stripes.

**Decals**—Decals provide an easy, inexpensive way to add interest and color to a new paint job. They come in two styles. One is the old-style decal as used in model making. You must soak this type in water to remove the paper backing. Then you place the transparent decal over whatever you choose, and squeegee out bubbles and water. These decals generally are very ornate pin-striping figures of one to three colors. They are suitable for decorations under taillights, trunk centers, window treatments, hood centers and other areas requiring emphasis.

The other type of decal is made of durable vinyl or mylar. It has its own adhesive, protected by a paper backing. These decals cover a wide spectrum of colors, shapes and patterns. They are easy to install, wear well and generally can be removed without damaging the paint. Station-wagon wood graining is an example, as is the Firebird decal from the '70s.

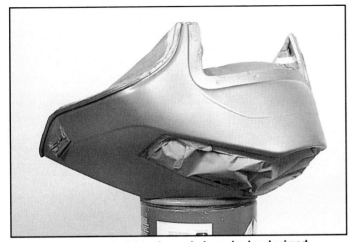

After removing decals, fairing is sanded, masked and primed.

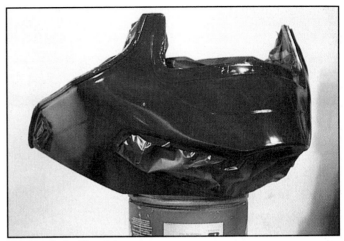

Fairing shot with paint

Tape pinstripe added

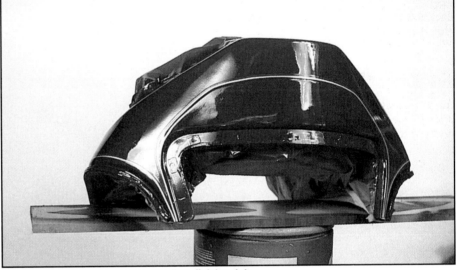

Clear coat, followed by color-sanding, finishes job.

To apply this type of decal, you must begin with an ultra-clean surface. Wash the area with soap and water, rinse and follow with a wax and silicone remover. The idea is to eliminate any foreign matter from the surface. Even the smallest bit of matter will stick out like a neon sign when trapped under a decal. Unlike its waterborne cousin, a vinyl decal cannot be adjusted once it contacts a dry surface. If the decal is large, you'd better enlist a friend to help.

Here's one method: If you're working with a simple graphic, strip the paper back, lay down one end and make sure the end is square with a door, belt, hood line or other reference line. You can even add your own reference marks with grease pencil or chalk. Just don't put these marks where they'll end up under the decal. Carefully wipe down the decal from the contact end to the end farthest away. This is why you need a friend.

He can hold up one end while you work the decal down, being careful not to trap air bubbles underneath.

Another, more satisfactory method is the one we call the *soap-and-water approach.* After cleaning the surface, spray the area to be covered with a solution of one part liquid dishwashing detergent to 20 parts water. Strip the paper back and gently lay the decal on the soap-covered surface. The soapy water will prevent the decal from adhering immediately, so you'll be able to reposition the decal.

Once you have the decal where you want it, use a 4- to 6-inch squeegee to work out all the bubbles and wrinkles. Work from the center of the decal to the edge. Allow about 24 hours for the water to evaporate. If you drive off while the underside is wet, the decal may blow off! If there are bubbles remaining after the soap solution

dries, prick them with a pin and push the area down with your finger tip.

**Removing Decals**—Once a mylar or vinyl decal has adhered to a painted surface, it cannot be removed by simply peeling it off. It can, however, be removed with heat. It's tricky though, to heat the decal enough to break the bond, but not lift or burn the paint. Use one of three pieces of equipment to remove a decal: a 750-watt heat gun, hair dryer or a 1000-watt heat lamp. Each will generate enough heat to soften the decal so it can be lifted from the paint. As soon as one end of the decal can be lifted, heat the next area and continue lifting.

**Pin Stripes**—One of the great boons to the amateur painter is the vinyl pin stripe. This thin, colorful trim is flexible enough to make tight inside or outside curves. Pin stripes are bright, decorative and come in hundreds of

Assembled bike with matching fairing, tank, bags and panels.

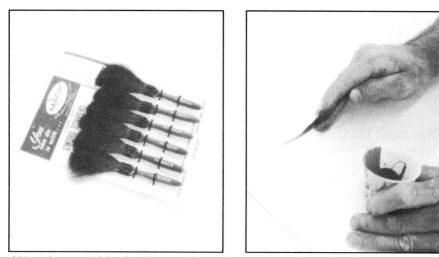
Although new striping brushes are fuzzy, they assume shape of a dagger or sword once bristles are saturated with paint. After using, clean brush in solvent and "grease" bristles with motor oil or petroleum jelly to keep bristles soft. Before reusing brush, remove oil or petroleum jelly with thinner. Practice striping on poster board or old body panels before you attempt your skills on a car. Photos by Tom Monroe.

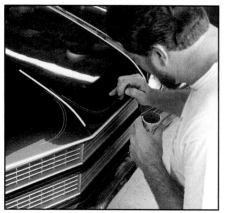
Bill Knight uses narrow masking tape as a striping guide. He uses a finger to guide and support brush rather than a *Mahl stick*—wooden dowel stuck in rubber ball. For striping, sign-lettering enamel is reduced slightly less than that required for spraying. Photo by Tom Monroe.

True sign of a pro; running pin stripe parallel to another. Two more colors will complete hood-striping job. Bill will finish job by signing his name. Signature must be readable and fit under a dime to be considered professional. Photo by Tom Monroe.

colors, widths and combinations of colors and widths.

To apply a pin stripe, peel a few inches off of its paper backing and *gently* "tack" down one end to a body line. Follow the body contour, gently pressing the stripe down as you go. You can lift the stripe back up and reposition it if necessary. When the stripe is completely placed, check its position closely. If you're satisfied, go back and press it down firmly. You won't be able to remove the stripe after this.

Here are a couple of tips: When you cross a hood, door, trunk or similar opening, wrap the stripe around the edge. Then cut it off. This gives a better appearance than if you cut off the stripe even with the edge. More importantly, the tape will have less tendency to detach at the end.

At the end of a stripe, do something fancy. If it's a double stripe, cut back the clear center and form a bullet end. If it's a single stripe, cut off an extra three inches and make a double-spear point. This gives a finishing touch.

To make a double stripe of two different colors, use 1/16- to 3/32-inch masking tape as a spacer. Lay the first stripe according to the body contour. Next, lay the masking tape directly along the side of the stripe. Follow this masking tape spacer with another color stripe. Finally, remove the masking tape and you'll have two evenly spaced pin stripes.

**Hand-painted pin stripes** present a completely different problem as compared to the vinyl stripe. Pin stripers were in great demand before the days of the plastic stripe. Like any art form, hand pin striping cannot be done satisfactorily without a lot of talent, practice and patience.

If you want to attempt hand striping, get a sable or camel's-hair *dagger brush*. Buy the best one available. Also purchase a 36-inch-long piece of 1/2-inch dowel. Sharpen one end and shove a small rubber ball over the point. This is your armrest. Hold the dowel in one hand with the ball resting on the surface you're striping. Rest your brush hand on the dowel and try to make smooth, even strokes with the dagger brush.

Practice is the only way to master the skill of hand pin striping. If you can find someone who knows how to pin stripe, watch him work so you can improve your technique.

# TROUBLESHOOTING

Courtesy of Ditzler Automotive Finishes.

## ACID & ALKALI SPOTTING

Appearance

Spotty discoloration of surface. (Various pigments react differently when in contact with acids of alkalies.)

Cause

Chemical change of pigments resulting from atmospheric contamination such as moisture or industrial emissions.

Remedy

a. Wash with detergent water and follow with vinegar bath.
b. Sand and refinish.
c. If contamination reached body material (metal, fiberglass or plastic) or subcoating, spot must be sanded down to body material before refinishing.

Prevention

a. Keep finish away from contaminated atmosphere.
b. Immediately following contamination, surface should be vigorously flushed with cool water and detergent.

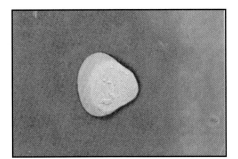

**Acid Spot**

## BLEEDING

Appearance

Discoloration refinish-color surface.

Cause

Solvent penetration from fresh color material dissolves old finish, usually reds and maroons, releasing dye that comes to the surface.

Remedy

a. Remove all color coats and recoat.
b. Or, allow surface to cure, then apply bleeder sealer and recoat.

Prevention

Apply bleeder sealer over suspected bleeder colors before spraying new color.

**Bleeding**

## BLISTERING

Appearance

a. Small swelled areas similar to water blister on human skin.
b. Lack of gloss if blisters are minute.
c. Broken edged craters if blisters have burst.

Cause

a. Rust under surface.
b. Painting over oil or grease.
c. Moisture in spray lines.
d. Trapped solvents.
e. Prolonged or repeated exposure of film to high humidity.

Remedy

Sand and refinish blistered areas.

Prevention

a. Thoroughly clean and treat body material.
b. Frequently drain water from air line.
c. Avoid use of overly fast thinners when temperature is high.
d. Allow proper drying time between coatings.

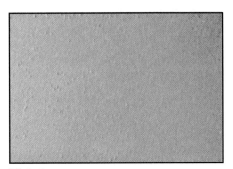

**Blistering**

## BLUSHING
## (Acrylic and Lacquer)

Appearance

Finish turns milky.

Cause

a. Fast thinners in high humidity.
b. Unbalanced thinners.
c. Condensation on old surface.

Remedy

a. Add retarder to thinner and respray.
b. Sand and refinish.

Prevention

a. Keep paint and surface to be painted at room temperature.
b. Select a high-quality thinner.
c. Use a retarder or reflow solvent when spraying in high humidity and warm temperatures.

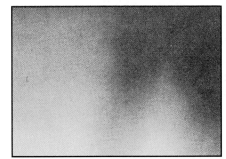

**Blushing**

## CHALKING

Appearance

a. Lack of gloss.
b. Powdery surface.

Cause

a. Natural weathering of paint films.
b. Lack of thorough agitation of paint.
c. Use of poorly balanced thinners create earlier failures.

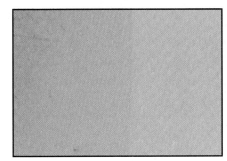

**Chalking**

Remedy

Sand to remove soft surface material, clean and refinish.

Prevention

a. Agitate color coats thoroughly.
b. Use a high-quality thinner for good balance.

## CHECKING-CRAZING-CRACKING

Appearance

a. Crowfoot separation (checking).
b. Formulation like shattered glass (crazing).
c. Irregular separation (cracking).

Cause

a. Insufficient drying of films prior to recoating.
b. Repeated extreme temperature changes.
c. Excessive heavy coats (cold checking).
d. Paint ingredients not thoroughly mixed.
e. Mixing materials not designed for each other (incompatibility).
f. Recoating a previously checked finish.
g. Thinner attacking strained surface of cured-acrylic lacquer (crazing).

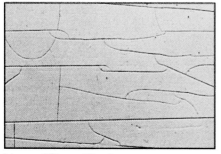

**Line and Figure Checks**

Remedy

Remove checked paint film and refinish.

Prevention

a. Follow proper drying times between coats.
b. Avoid extreme temperature changes.
c. Spray uniform coats, avoiding excess, particularly with lacquers.
d. Mix all ingredients thoroughly.
e. Use only recommended balanced materials, thinners, etc.

f. Remove previously checked finish before recoating.
g. Use DTL-151 DURACRYL or equivalent thinner to help prevent crazing of acrylic lacquer.
h. Use sealer.

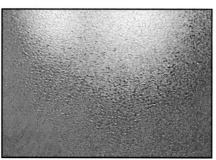

**Crazing**

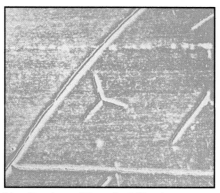

**Line Cracks and Crowfoot Checks**

## DIRT IN FINISH

Appearance

Foreign particles dried in paint films.

Cause

a. Improper cleaning of surface to be painted.
b. Defective air-regulator cleaning filter.
c. Dirty working area.
d. Defective or dirty air-inlet filters.
e. Dirty spray gun.

Remedy

a. Rub out finish with rubbing compound (Not for enamels).
b. If dirt is deep in finish, sand and compound to restore gloss. Metallic finishes may show mottling with this treatment and require additional color coats.

Prevention

a. Blow out all cracks and body joints.
b. Solvent clean and tack surface thoroughly.

c. Be sure equipment is clean.
d. Work in clean spray area.
e. Replace inset air filters if dirty or defective.
f. Strain paint to remove foreign matter.
g. Keep all containers closed when not in use to prevent contamination.

**Dirt in Finish**

## DULLED FINISH

Appearance

Gloss retards as film dries.

Cause

a. Compounding before thinner evaporates.
b. Using poorly balanced thinner or reducer.
c. Poorly cleaned surface.
d. Top coats put on wet subcoats.
e. Washing with caustic cleaners.
f. Inferior polishes.

Remedy

a. Allow finish to dry hard and rub with mild rubbing compound.

**Dulled Finish**

Prevention

a. Clean surface thoroughly.
b. Use recommended materials.
c. Allow all coatings sufficient drying time.

## FISHEYES & POOR WETTING

Appearance
- a. Separation of wet film.
- b. Previous finish can be seen in spots.

Cause
- a. Improper cleaning of old surface.
- b. Spraying over finishes that contain silicone.

Remedy

Wash off paint while still wet.

Prevention
- a. Clean surface with wax and grease remover.
- b. Use fisheye preventer in finish coats to be sprayed over old films containing silicone.

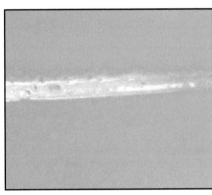

**Fisheyes and Poor Wetting**

## LIFTING

Appearance
- a. Raising and swelling of wet film.
- b. Peeling when surface is dry.

Cause
- a. Improper drying of previous coating.
- b. Sandwiching enamel between two lacquers or acrylics.
- c. Recoating improperly cured enamel.
- d. Spraying over unclean surfaces.

Remedy

Remove lifted surfaces and refinish.

Prevention
- a. Clean old surfaces thoroughly.
- b. Allow all subcoats full drying time.
- c. Seal old finishes.

**Lifting**

## MOTTLING

Appearance

Streaking of the color. Generally associated with metallic finishes.

Cause
- a. Excessive wetting of some areas.
- b. Heavier film thickness in some areas.

Remedy
- a. If color is freshly applied, increase gun distance and air pressure for final coat. Avoid over reduction.
- b. On a dried finish, scuff down and apply additional color.

Prevention
- a. Avoid excessive wetting or heavy film buildup in local areas.
- b. Be careful not to over-reduce color.

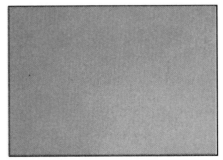

**Mottling**

## ORANGE PEEL

Appearance
- a. Resembles ballpeen-hammer dents in paint.
- b. Resembles skin of an orange.

Cause
- a. Under reduction.
- b. Improper thinning solvent.
- c. Lack of proper flow.
- d. Surface drying too fast.
- e. Improper air pressure.

Remedy
- a. (Enamel) Rub surface with a mild polishing compound.
  (Lacquer) Sand or use rubbing compound.
- b. Sand and refinish.

Prevention
- a. Proper air and gun adjustment.
- b. Proper thinning solvents.

**Orange Peel**

## PEELING

Appearance

Separation of a paint film from subsurface.

**Peeling**

Cause
- a. Improper surface preparation.
- b. Imcompatibility of one coat to another.

Remedy

Remove peeling paint completely, prepare body-surface material properly and refinish with compatible materials.

Prevention
- a. Thoroughly clean and treat old surface.
- b. Use recommended primers for special metals or other materials.

c. Follow acceptable refinish practices using compatible materials.

## PIN HOLES OR BLISTERING OVER PLASTIC FILLER

Appearance
- a. Pin-point holes in finish.
- b. Air bubbles raising film, causing craters when erupted.

Cause
- a. Excessive amounts of hardeners.
- b. Excessive vigorous stirring or beating in of hardener.

Remedy
Sand thoroughly and recoat with a glaze coat of body filler or spot putty.

Prevention
- a. Mix in recommended quantities of hardeners.
- b. Stir mildly; hardener goes in quickly.
- c. Work out possible air traps when applying filler.

## PITTING OR CRATERING

Appearance
- a. Small craters.
- b. Like dry spray or over spray.

Cause
Same as Blistering (except blisters have broken).

Remedy
Same as Blistering.

**Pitting or Cratering**

Prevention
Same as Blistering.

## PLASTIC BLEED-THROUGH

Appearance
Discoloration (normally yellowing) of top color coat.

Cause
- a. Excessive hardener.
- b. Applying top coat before plastic is cured.

Remedy
- a. Remove patch, or . . . .
- b. Cure top coat, sand and refinish.

Prevention
- a. Use correct amount of hardener.
- b. Allow adequate cure time before refinishing.

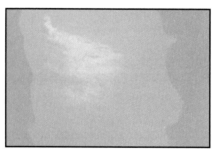
**Plastic Bleed-Through**

## PLASTIC FILLER NOT DRYING

Appearance
Stays soft after applying.

Cause
- a. Insufficient amount of hardener.
- b. Hardener exposed to sunlight.

Remedy
Scrape off plastic and reapply.

Prevention
- a. Add recommeded amount of hardener.
- b. Be sure hardener is fresh and avoid exposure to sunlight.

## RUST UNDER FINISH

Appearance
- a. Peeling or blistering.
- b. Raised surface spots.

Cause
- a. Improper metal preparation.
- b. Broken paint film allows moisture to creep under surrounding finish.
- c. Water in air lines.

Remedy
- a. Seal off entrance of moisture from inner part of panels.
- b. Sand down to body material, prepare bare surface and treat with phosphate before refinishing.

Prevention
- a. Locate source of moisture and seal off.
- b. When replacing ornaments or moulding, be careful not to break paint film and allow dissimilar metals to come in contact. Such contact can produce electrolysis that may cause a tearing away or loss of good bond with the film.

**Rust Under Finish**

## RUNS

Appearance
- a. Running of wet paint film in rivulets.
- b. Mass slippage of total film.

Cause
- a. Over reduction with low air pressure.
- b. Extra slow thinner.
- c. Painting on cold surface.
- d. Improperly cleaned surface.

Remedy
Wash off and refinish.

Prevention
- a. Use recommended thinner at specified reduction and air pressure.
- b. Do not paint over cold surface.
- c. Clean surface thoroughly.

## SAGS

Appearance
Partial slipping of paint in the form of curtains created by a film that is too heavy to support itself.

Cause
- a. Under reduction.
- b. Applying successive coats without allowing dry time between coats.

c. Low air pressure (lack of atomization).
d. Gun too close.
e. Gun out of adjustment.

**Runs and Sags**

Remedy
Sand or wash off and refinish.
Prevention
a. Use proper thinner at recommended reduction.
b. Adjust air pressure and gun for correct atomization.
c. Keep gun at correct distance from work.

## STONE BRUISES
Appearance
Small chips of paint missing from an otherwise firm finish.
Cause
a. Flying stones from tires or other vehicles.
b. Impact of other car doors in a parking lot.
Remedy
a. Thoroughly sand remaining paint film back several inches from damage point.
b. Properly treat metal and refinish.

**Stone Bruises**

## UNDERCOAT SHOW-THROUGH
Appearance
Variations in surface color.
Cause
a. Insufficient color coats.
b. Repeated compounding.
Remedy
Sand and refinish.
Prevention
a. Apply good coverage of color.
b. Avoid excessive compounding.

**Undercoat Show-Through**

## WATER SPOTTING
Appearance
a. Dulling of gloss in spots.
b. Mass of spots that appear as a large distortion of the film.
Cause
a. Spots of water drying on finish that is not thoroughly dry.
b. Washing finish in bright sunlight.
Remedy
Sand and refinish.
Prevention
a. Keep fresh paint job out of rain.
b. Do not allow water to dry on new finish.

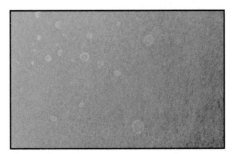
**Water Spotting**

## WET SPOTS
Appearance
Discolored and/or slow drying spots of various sizes.
Cause
a. Improper cleaning.
b. Excessively heavy undercoats not properly dried.
c. Sanding with gasoline or other chemically contaminated solvent.
Remedy
Sand or wash off thoroughly and refinish.
Prevention
a. Clean surface with wax and grease remover.
b. Allow undercoats to fully dry.
c. Use only water as a sanding lubricant.

## WRINKLING
Appearance
a. Puckering of enamel.
b. Prune-skin effect.
c. Loss of gloss as paint dries (minute wrinkling not visible to naked eye).

**Wrinkling**

Cause
a. Under reduction or air pressure too low causing excessive film thickness.
b. Excessive coats.
c. Fast reducers creating overloading.
d. Surface drying trapping solvents.
e. Fresh film subjected to heat too soon.
Remedy
Break open top surface by sanding and allow to dry thoroughly.
Prevention
a. Reduce enamels according to directions.
b. Apply as recommended.
c. Do not force dry until solvents have flashed off.

# GLOSSARY

**Abrasive**—Substance used for removing material through sanding or grinding. In automotive refinishing this includes sanding discs or sandpaper coated with aluminum oxide or silicon carbide.

**Abrasive Coating**—Manner in which abrasive grit is applied to the paper backing. In closed coating no backing is exposed; it is completely covered with abrasive material. In open coating the adhesive is exposed between the abrasive grain.

**Acrylic Resin**—Manufactured resin used in emulsion- and solvent-based paints, also available in both lacquer and enamel materials.

**Adhesion**—How well paint sticks to the surface to which it has been applied.

**Air Dry**—To dry paint at normal room temperature.

**Aluminum Oxide**—An abrasive grain used to make sandpaper and sanding discs.

**Atomization**—Extent to which the air at the spray-gun nozzle breaks up paint and solvent into small particles.

**Binder**—Non-volatile portion of paint which binds or cements the pigment particles together.

**Bleeder**—A color which tends to stain or "bleed" through succeeding coats of finishing materials.

**Blending**—Addition of one color to another so that they mix or blend gradually.

**Blistering**—Bubbles formed on the surface of paint, generally caused by moisture trapped in or behind the paint film.

**Bloom**—Cloudy appearance in the finish color.

**Blush**—Finish color becomes whitish during the drying period.

**Body**—Viscosity of a fluid.

**Cast**—Tendency of a color to take on the appearance of another color, such as for a blue to have a greenish cast.

**Caulking Compound**—A semi-drying material used to seal or fill crevices.

**Chalking**—Powdering of a paint surface due to aging.

**Checking**—Appearance of short, fine-line cracks in a paint film.

**Color Retention**—Ability of a color to retain its true shade over an extended period of time.

**Coverage**—Surface area that a given quantity of paint will cover; the ability of a given color to conceal a surface.

**Crazing**—Fine-line cracks on the surface of the paint finish.

**Die Back**—Loss of gloss in the color coat generally occurring in lacquer finishes after the color has been compounded. This is caused by continuing thinner evaporation.

**Dry Spray**—Paint-spray dust that does not dissolve (melt) into material being sprayed. Generally appears dull and rough. Usually caused by gun being held too far from the surface, too much air pressure or an excessively fast-evaporating solvent.

**Featheredge**—Sharp edge of a paint film that is caused by chips, bruises, or grinding must be sanded to a tapered edge. This tapered edge is known as the **featheredge.**

**Finish Coat**—Last coat of color applied.

**Fisheyes**—Small pits that appear in the color coats, caused by the failure to remove silicone polish or wax prior to painting.

**Flash Off**—Rapid evaporation of thinner.

**Fog Coat**—A final coat of properly reduced polychromatic acrylic enamel that is sprayed at a slightly increased air pressure and greater gun distance with the gun set for reduced fluid flow.

**Gloss**—Luster or sheen of the dry paint film.

**High Volume Low Pressure (HVLP)**—Spray equipment which delivers material at a low pressure of no more than 10 psi (at the cap), however, with greater volume of air.

**Low Volume Low Pressure (LVLP)**—Spray equipment which delivers material at low pressure (less than 10 psi at the cap) with a low volume of air.

**Mist Coat**—An extremely thin color coat sprayed wet as a final color coat for better flow of lacquer finishes.

**Orange Peel**—Textured appearance of the paint film that looks like an orange skin. May or may not have good gloss.

**Original Finish**—Paint applied by the car manufacturer.

**Overlap**—Portion of the spray pattern that laps over the previous swath of paint.

**Oxidation**—Oxygen from the air combining with the paint film. This process is how enamel cures over a period of several weeks. The chalking of a paint film during aging is another form of oxidation.

**Paint Film**—Thickness of the paint on the surface.

**Peeling**—Paint film coming off in relatively large pieces, generally caused by spraying over an unclean surface, or by moisture at back of the paint film.

**Pigment**—Fine powder used to impart color, opacity or other effects to paint.

**Polychrome**—Term used to describe the metallic effect in certain types of color coats, produced by adding aluminum powder to the paint.

**Sand Scratches**—Marks made in the old finish or metal by abrasive action. These same marks may show in the color coats due to improper filling or sealing.

**Solids**—Component of the paint that actually builds the paint film.

**Solvent**—A liquid capable of dissolving paint.

**Surface Dry**—Top film of a finish dries while underneath portion remains more or less soft.

**Tack Coat**—First coat of enamel. Usually permitted to dry until quite sticky, then followed by a final color coat.

**Tack Rag**—Cheesecloth impregnated with a non-drying varnish and used to remove dust, etc., from the surface just prior to application of the finish coats.

**Tooth**—Roughened surface that permits better adhesion of the coating to be applied. This is done either by using a metal-etching agent or by abrasive action.

**Viscosity**—Thickness of the material to be used.

**VOC**—Volatile Organic Compound. Any organic compound that participates in atmospheric photochemical reaction that is, any organic compound other than those that the administrator designates as having negligible photochemical reactivity.

**Weathering**—Aging or failure in paint caused by exposure.

*—Courtesy Martin Senour Paints*

# INDEX

**A**
A-pillar 26
abrasive 71, 51 - 52
  closed-coated 51, 52
  open-coated 51, 52
  types of 71
acetone 87
acetylene 28, 29
acrylic urethane 118
adhesion sealer 100
air compressor
  intercooled 93
  maintenance 105
  single-stage 103
  two-stage 93, 104
air filter 104
air hose 104
air-hose coupler 104
air-pressure regulator 104
Airco Welding Products 43
alloying elements 80
aluminum 3, 4
aluminum alloy 80
aluminum oxide 71
aluminum repair 80 - 84
aluminum
  annealing 81, 82, 83
  grades of 80
  quenching 83
  shrinking 83 - 84
  welding 84
aluminum-welding flux 35, 84
  Aladdin-73 35
  Alcoa-22 35
  Union Carbide 35
aluminum-welding lense 35
American Chain and Cable 43
American Welding Society 43
arc-welding 28, 38 - 42
arc-welding electrode 38, 39
arc-welding hood 39, 43
armrest 10
Au-ve-co 19
Autodata Manuals 43
automatic-transmission fluid (ATF) 72
aviation snips 60, 81

**B**
backtaping 126
bare-metal cleaner/etcher 75
barrier coat, see Sealer
base-coat/clear-coat systems 97
base metal 32
bastard file 49
beeswax 72, 74
Big Three Industries 43
blending 124 - 125, 127
block sander 71, 72
block sanding 72, 76, 124
blush 99
body file 50, 75
body filler 54, 68, 92
  heavy 69 - 70
  light 70
  plastic 75
body grinder 51, 52
body hammer 48
  long picking 48
  pick 44, 49, 73
  short picking 48
  shrinking 48
body jack 6, 45 - 46
body mount 24
body plug 8
body trim 19 - 21
body type 3 - 4
body-file holder 72
body-filler file 69
body-filler tools 72 - 73

bonding strip 89
Bondo 69
brazing 33 - 34, 55
buffing 71, 118 - 119
buffing compound 102, 119
bumper 20 - 21
butt weld 32, 41
butyl acetate 90
butyl seal 18
buzz box 38

**C**
C-pillar 7, 11, 14, 24, 25, 26
candy apple 123, 130
capillary action 33, 34
carburizing flame 31, 32, 38, back
  cover
carpet 14 - 15
casting resin 85
catalyst 69, 75, 76, 77
catalyzed resin 88
catalyzed-urethane clear-coat 98
chart, see Table
Chemetron Corp 43
Chilton Book Company 43
clear coat 98, 125, 130, 135
coach joint 24
coarseness 71
coated abrasive 71
  dry 71
  wet-or-dry 71
cold shrinking 52 - 53
cold working 5
color coat 97, 116, 130
color matching 123, 127 - 129
color perception 128
color
  adjust 128
  darken 127
  lighten 127
color sand 71, 95, 97, 118, 119, 125
  - 126
compressor, see *air compressor*
conditioner 102
crosshatching 77, 79
curing agent 69
curtain 97
custom finish 123, 129 - 136
cut-off saw 25
cutting torch 26, 31, 36, 37

**D**
damage
  accordion pleat 5
  oil-can dent 4, 5
  rolled and buckled 5
  simple bend 4
  stretch 4, 5
  upset 4 - 5
Day-Glo, 134
decal, remove 135
dermatologist 86
disassembly 7-27
disc sander 72, 73
Ditzler 91
dolly 48, 50
  general purpose 48
  heel 48
  toe 48
door beam 43
door glass 15 - 17
door handle 10, 20
door latch 15, 20
door lock 15, 20
door-lock knob 9, 10
door panel 9, 11
door removal 22
door-trim panel 9 - 11
door trim-panel clip 9, 10
  pliers 7

remover 9
double-action (D.A.) sander 51, 71,
  72, 109, 124, 125
draw filing 76
dual-purpose thinner 94
dust coat 79, 118
Dutchman's, see Aviation snips 60

**E**
elasticity 6
electrodes 39
electrode holder 38
enamel reducer 95, 99
enamel
  acrylic 91, 96, 97, 117, 118
  alkyd 93, 117
  alkyd melamine 94
  baked 96
  catalyzed 107
  catalyzed acrylic 96
  drying 117
  reflow 94
  synthetic 91, 95, 96, 116
ethyl acetate 90
ethyleneglycolmonoethyl ether 90
exothermic 85

**F**
fade out 125
featheredge 71, 124, 125
Featherfill 70
fender removal 23
fender trim 19
fiberglass 3, 4, 84, 87
  chopped 85
  cloth 84
  lay-up 85
  mat 85
  repair 84 - 89
  structural cracks 87 - 89
  surfacing mat 85
fiberglass-reinforced plastic (FRP)
  4, 80
file 50 - 51
file card 83
file holder 51
filler metal 39
filler rod 32, 33, 40
filler
  lead 50
  plastic 50
fillet weld 40, 41
finish metalwork 68 - 69
fire extinguisher 29
fire prevention 29
firebrick 29
fisheye eliminator 101, 102
flame cutting 37
flame suppressor, 30, 41
flash time 115
flash-off 77
flattening agent,101
flex-agent 100
flip-flop 126, 129
flow-out 95, 98, 99
flux 33, 35, 39, 40
  low-residue 34
flux-coated brazing rod 34
fog coat 97, 125
framing square 55
front clip 23
fumes 91
fusion welding 33

**G**
garnish molding 10, 12
garnish trim 11
gas metal-arc welding 42
gas-welding 28 - 37, 62
  pressure regulator 28 - 30
gas-welding aluminum 35 - 37

gas-welding cylinder 28
gas-welding flame 31
gas-welding pot metal 34 - 35
gas-welding safety 29
gas-welding torch 62
gel coat 87
gel-coat resin 86
glamour color 129
glazing putty 70, 78
gloss coat 97, 116
graphics 130
grille 20, 21
grinding disc 64
ground coat 130, 132
guide coat 78, 79, 118

**H**
H.C. Fastener Company 34
hammer
  ballpeen 50
  body 50, see also *body hammer*
  claw 50
  pick 51, 64, 75
  shrinking 84
  slide 54
hammer-and-dolly work 44, 48, 50,
  52, 61, 67, 69, 81, 82, 83
  hammer-off technique 49, 54, 56
  hammer-on technique 48
hammer-weld 59, 62, 63, 67
hammerforming 66
hand nibblers 60
hand-rubbing compound 102
hardening agent 69
headlight 20, 21
  eyebrow 21
  high beam 21
  low beam 21
  retaining ring 21
headliner 12 - 14
headliner tacking strip 13
health and safety tips 120 - 121
heat-shrinking 52, 64
heat-shrink aluminum 83
heating grid 19
heliarc welding, see TIG welding
hem flange 26, 27
high-strength steel 42
  repairing 42 - 43
  welding 42 - 43
hinge
  door 23
  hood 22
hood 21 - 22
hood bumper 23
hood support 22
Hopkins, Ed 131
HSLA-steel 60

**I**
isocyanates, 91

**J**
J-nut 24
jitter-bug sander 71

**K**
kick panel 11 - 12, 14
Kitty Hair 92
Knight, Bill 136

**L**
Lac bug 94
lacquer 91, 94
  acrylic 94, 116
  drying 117
  nitrocellulose 94
lacquer thinner
  acrylic 98
  bulk 94
  nitrocellulose 98
lap joint 24, 33

lead
  apply 74
  filler 73, 74
  poisoning 69
leading
  acid 75
  paddle 72
  tools 72
liquid sandpaper 109
long board 77, 78

**M**
Maaco Auto Painting and Bodyworks 111
MAPP gas 72
Mahl stick 136
martensitic steel 42
Masonite 9
McConnell, Mark 85
MEK 85, 87
*Metal Fabricator's Handbook* 41, 65, 80
MIG welding 41, 42, 43
Mitchell Manuals, Inc 43
Morgan-Nokker 47, 48, 54, 116
Motor Publication's 43
machine-rubbing compound 102
masking 111-112, 132
masking-paper/tape dispenser 112
masonry saw 25, 26
metal conditioner 75
metal flake 130, 131, 133
metal primer 100
metallics 127
methyl-ethyl-keytone, see MEK
metric conversions 122
moisture shield 11

**N**
naptha 90
National Standard Corp 43
neutral flame 31, 32, back cover
nibbler 81
nitrocellulose 3
non-aqueous dispersion (N.A.D.) 95

**O**
oil-can dent 54
open-coat 71
orange peel 95, 114
orbital sander 84
overspray 113
oxidation 99
oxidizing flame 31, 32, back cover
oxyacetylene 29
  cutting tip 28
  cutting torch 20
oxygen 28, 29

**P**
Pap's 94
paint
  mix 125
  remove 108
paint booth 107
  air washer 107
  dry 107
paint cast 128
paint code 127
paint cost 93 - 94
paint remover 108
paint system 90, 91
painting plastic 101
painting technique 113 - 116
paraffin 72
parking light 20
parts installation 8
pearlescent 123, 130, 132
pecking block 49
pecking hammer, see Hammer, pick
perfect panel 68
pick pull 56
picking block 64
pigmented dyes 94

pin stripe
  hand-painted 135 - 136
  tape 135 - 136
pin-striping brush 136
plastic deformation 5
plastic filler 69, 88
  applying 76
plasticity 5, 6
plug weld 65
pneumatic chisel 60, 81
pneumatic nibblers 60
pneumatic shears 81
Polaroid camera 7
polychromatic 96, 129, 132
polyester filler 70 - 71, 78
polymerization 85, 99
polyurethane 91, 117
Pop rivet 20
Porto-Power 45, 46, 47
pot metal 34, 35
power buffer 119
power window 16
PPG 91
primer 47, 91, 100
  for ABS 94
  for fiberglass 94
  for galvanized steel 94
  for nylon 94
primer/sealer 89, 100, 101, 115
primer/surfacer 70, 75, 77, 78, 79, 84, 100
primer/surfacer shrinkage 116
prybar 50
pull rod 55
PVC pipe 72, 76

**Q**
quarter panel, see Rear fender
quench 53

**R**
radiator support 23, 24
rear cowl 24
rear fender 24 - 25
rear-quarter trim 11
rear window 13, 19
reciprocating sander 72
recoat period 125
reducer 91, 95, 98, 99
  urethane enamel 99
regulator 15
Reid Avery Co. 43
resin 85 - 87
  air inhibited 85
  fiberglass 85
  finishing 85
  laminating 85
  non-air inhibited 85
resin catalyst 85
respirator 91
retarder 98
Rinshed-Mason (R-M) Paints 100
ripples 114
rod holder, see Electrode holder
roof 26
rosette tip 29
rubbing 71
rubbing compound 96
runs 97
rust removal 64 - 67

**S**
Sabre saw 66
safety 52, 91 - 93
  fiberglass 86
safety glasses 52
sag 97, 114
sandbag 65
sandblasting 108
sanding board 76
sandpaper 71, 109
  types of 70
  wet-or-dry 124

scissor assembly 15, 16
scissor mechanism 20
Scotch Brite pad 71, 109
scuff plate 14
sealer 100
  non-sanding 101
  sanding 101
seat removal 8
sectioning 58 - 64, 67
Seward, Dave 80
shellac 94
shotbag 65
shrinker 65
shrinking dolly 52, 84
side molding 19 - 20
skinning 26 - 27
slag 39, 40
slapper 65
soapstone 25, 37
spoon 49 - 50
  dinging 50
  medium crown 50
  surfacing 50
spot putty 35, 70, 78
spot repair 4, 123 - 127
spot weld 24, 25, 26, 59, 65
  drill 25
spot-welder 65
spray gun 105
  adjust 114
  bleeder 105
  DeVilbiss 105
  external-mix 105, 106
  gravity feed 105
  HVLP 106, 108
  internal mix 105
  LVLP 106
  non-bleeder 105, 106
  pressure feed 105
  Sharpe 105, 106
  siphon feed 105 - 106
spray-gun maintenance 106
spray-gun operation 106 - 107
spray-gun spray pattern 106 - 107
spray-gun type 105 - 106
spreaders 72
Steck Manufacturing 19
steel wool 74
stinger, see Electrode holder
stone deflector 23
stretcher 65
suction cup 54
suede base 101
sunburn agent, see flattening agent
surface preparation 109
Surform file 69, 73, 76, 89
swirl marks, see wheel mark
synthetic enamel 3, 93
system approach 70

**T**
T-bucket 130
T-joint 33
table
  hose size vs. air-pressure drop 104
  lighten/darken color 114, 127
  metallics tinting 129
  paint cast 128, 129
  paint color 128
  paint tinting 128
  paint-to-thinner proportioning 99
  painting plastic 101
  trouble-shooting 120 - 121
tack coat 116
tack rag 110
tack weld 33, 36, 60, 61, 62, 63, 67
Talamentes, Rick 111
Tempilstik 43
texturing agent 101
thermal conductivity 37
thermosetting paint 94
thermosetting plastic 85

thinner 91, 98 - 100
thixotropic 85
three-coat system 97, 126, 130
TIG welding 41
Tiger Hair 92
tinner's snips 60, 81
tinning 57, 74
tinning compound 74
tinting 128
tinting metallics (polychromes) 129
toluene 87
toluol 90
tools, finishing 50 - 52
trim stick 16
trim-clip remover 7
trouble-shooting guide 137
trunk lid 22

**U**
ultra-high-strength steel 42
undercoat 100
undercut 39
Uncle John's penny trick 56
Union Carbide Corp 43
urethane 107
  catalyst 94, 97

**V**
V-groove 33, 40
valance panel 23
vent window 10, 15
vinyl dye 102
vinyl spreader 73
vinyl-top repair 102
Vise-Grip pliers 17, 57, 60
Visqueen 11

**W**
wash thinner 100
water trap 104, 105
water-based paint 95
wax and silicone remover 90, 102, 109
weatherstrip 13, 16
weave bead 40, 41
weld penetration 32, 34, 35, 40
weld pot metal 34
weld puddle 32
welding 28 - 43
  backhand 32
  forehand 32
welding apparel 29
*Welding Handbook* 41
welding lense, tempered 29
welding rod, fluxless 34
welding-torch barrel 31
welding-torch body 30, 31
welting 24
wet coat 118
wet sanding 71
wheel-mark remover 122
wind wing, see Vent window
wind-lace 12, 13, 16
window crank 9, 10, 11
window regulator, power 17
windshield 7, 13, 17 - 19
windshield molding 18
windshield seal 18
windshield-wiper arm 17
wood paddle 74
work harden 5, 6, 46
woven roving 84

**X**
X-acto knife 13

**Y**
yield point 6

**Z**
zinc fumes 43
zinc primer 43